"No one has spent more time in the lab of high performance than Tommy Baker. He has an incredible pulse on what we're all after: pursuing our passions with purpose supported by a life filled with meaning and balance. This book shows you how to thread the needle on when to push and when to pause."

> —**Seth Mattison,** keynote speaker and Future of
> Work Advisor

"Finally, someone addresses the dichotomy that every single entrepreneur faces at some point in their career. Are we to forever play the role of the hustler as we race full speed down a path where we are not finding fulfillment? Or are we to slam on the brakes and own the role of the seeker as we journey inward to find answers without any real progress? The two ideologies could not be further apart, and yet Tommy beautifully illustrates how we can achieve self-actualization by bringing them together. This book is a must-read for anyone who has either felt burnt out from their drive or stuck in an endless loop of self-development with no results to show for it—so basically for every business owner."

> —**James Patrick,** author, photographer, and business coach

"In a culture that has normalized and celebrated force and stress as pathways to success, many have paid the price with health issues, chaotic relationships, and emotional bankruptcy. On the flipside, others are hopelessly stuck dreaming without the fortitude to manifest their soul's dreams into reality. In *Hustlers & Seekers*, Tommy Baker brilliantly decodes how to alchemize passion and discipline, stillness, and action—and faith with fierceness. If you're looking for a passionate, thriving and playful life . . . this book is a must read."

> —**Anahata Ananda,** Shamanic healer and soul guide

"*Hustlers & Seekers* hits home for me in so many ways. Somedays I would describe myself as a hustler, other days as a seeker, and oftentimes as both, which can create a lot of confusion. Since we live in a world where hustlers are celebrated, and seekers are considered lost, it's easy to miss the mark. Instead, Tommy combines both states and creates the bridge that allows you to truly have the best of both worlds. Inside these pages, you'll find the foundation you've been missing so you can have it all without making yourself insane."

—**Jay Nixon,** two-time author and owner of Thrive Forever Fit

"Tommy Baker's new book *Hustlers & Seekers* is a motivating read that gives clarity to anyone pursuing a goal. In his no-nonsense style, Tommy provides a self-ascribed and proven roadmap for helping the reader to avoid time-wasting thoughts and actions. The result is a book that helps end procrastination and gives readers a sense of confidence in how to move boldly forward in pursuit of their dreams!"

—**Howard Falco,** mental performance coach, spiritual teacher, and author of *I AM: The Power of Discovering Who You Really Are*

HUSTLERS

&
Seekers

HOW TO CRUSH IT AND FIND FULFILLMENT—
WITHOUT LOSING YOUR MIND

TOMMY BAKER

New York Chicago San Francisco Athens London Madrid
Mexico City Milan New Delhi Singapore Sydney Toronto

1 2 3 4 5 6 7 8 9   LCR   26 25 24 23 22 21

ISBN   978-1-264-26681-4
MHID   1-264-26681-2

e-ISBN 978-1-264-26682-1
e-MHID   1-264-26682-0

Library of Congress Cataloging-in-Publication Data

Names: Baker, Tommy, author.
Title: Hustlers and seekers : how to crush it and find fulfillment-without losing your mind / Tommy Baker.
Description: New York : McGraw Hill, [2022] | Includes bibliographical references and index.
Identifiers: LCCN 2021031357 (print) | LCCN 2021031358 (ebook) | ISBN 9781264266814 (hardback) | ISBN 9781264266821 (ebook)
Subjects: LCSH: Work-life balance. | Ambition. | Motivation (Psychology)
Classification: LCC HD4904.6 .B35 2022 (print) | LCC HD4904.6 (ebook) | DDC 306.3/6—dc23
LC record available at https://lccn.loc.gov/2021031357
LC ebook record available at https://lccn.loc.gov/2021031358

McGraw Hill books are available at special quantity discounts to use as premiums and sales promotions or for use in corporate training programs. To contact a representative, please visit the Contact Us pages at www.mhprofessional.com.

*To my parents, with whom I won the lottery and
who taught me how to both Hustle and Seek*

CONTENTS

INTRODUCTION

You're torn between two worlds.

In one world, there's the constant push toward doing more, tackling massive ambitions, and chasing your dreams at 100 mph. You need to be a grinder, a high performer, a go-getter. You must take relentless action.

Grind, baby, grind!

In this world, you're a ruthless achiever. You must wake up at 4:30 a.m., dominate your morning, and complete an 11-step ritual before sunrise. You can't ever take your foot off the gas. Otherwise, you're going to lose and succumb to a life of toil, averageness, and incessant mediocrity. That's the fear, right? You'll be left behind, forgotten. As good as dead.

A goner.

In the other world, detaching, creating space, and unplugging are crucial. This world is where you pause, meditate, align with your North Star. You must practice mindfulness and be aware. You must surrender and be here now, allowing the right doors to open through divine timing. Otherwise, you'll be left in the fetal position from burnout, spit into the abyss of ambition. That's what they say, right? You need to unplug, detach, breathe.

Ommmmm.

Some days, you feel a firehose of motivation flowing through your veins, blasting the latest Gary Vee video during your morning commute, dripping with the high-octane energy required to propel you through a 14-hour day. But on others, you want to retreat into the cave and triple down on self-care. You desire to spend your day in complete nothingness with an

Abraham Hicks monologue reverberating in the background contemplating the meaning of existence.

Namaste, bitches.

On the surface, these worlds seem entirely dissimilar. On one hand, you have the nose-to-the-grindstone, nitro-cold-brew-chugging lifestyle we'll call hustle—defined as the work ethic to fuel your boldest ambitions, or *doing*. On the other hand, you have the Eckhart Tolle be-here-now state of seeking—defined as the rituals and practices to create space, or *being*.

Like whiskey and kombucha, these two worlds couldn't be more different—right? The promises you're told, and often believe, go something like this:

▶ If you hustle hard and long enough, one day you'll have the full bank accounts and freedom to do the things you love, go on adventures you crave, have the experiences you've dreamed of—waking up in an oasis where your most painstaking decision is choosing between piña coladas and margaritas on a sun-soaked paradise, or . . .

▶ If you create enough space and seeking in your life, then one day you'll feel fulfilled inside, void of all attachments to the outer world, reaching a Zen-like state of nirvana that Buddha himself would be proud of, where life is a cascading flow of grace and ease as you rise above the "need" to create achievement, soaking in meditative, orgasmic bliss.

Pick one, but you *cannot* have both.

Because the moment you pick hustle, you're choosing to be obsessed. Anything less is sheer laziness; you're simply another talker who doesn't want it bad enough. Say good-bye to long weekends, self-care, and some much-needed "you" time. In the trenches of ambition, the price of admission is your every waking hour. Sleep when you're dead isn't a cliché; it's a life manifesto.

Hashtag committed.

When you pick seeking, you're opting out of the rat race, the material-obsessed hedonic treadmill to nowhere. You connect to universal truths, become a samurai of your emotions. You step away from the noise that tells you to work harder, turn your hobby into a side hustle, and quit your 9–5. You've got a one-way ticket to enlightenment.

Woke AF.

But you can't have both because kale and concrete don't go down easy with your morning smoothie. Because of this, you find yourself in a constant tug-of-war between:

▶ Doing and being
▶ Action and allowing
▶ Discipline and freedom
▶ Structure and surrender
▶ Intensity and nothingness
▶ Constraints and creativity
▶ Priorities and playfulness
▶ Rigidness and novelty
▶ "On" time and "off" time
▶ Hustling and seeking

To address this, you read a book on audacious goal-setting and then one on letting go. You listen to a podcast on focus and then one on surrender. You walk down the aisles of your actual (or virtual) bookstore and glance at one side of the shelves—crushing it, how to squeeze out every minute of the workday, and way too many books with expletives in their title. (Thank you, Mark Manson. Can we end this f*cking trend like, yesterday?)

But then you glance at the opposite shelf and notice a different array of titles—self-care, unplugging, how the universe has your back, why anything except the present moment is an illusion, and why *The Secret* is your path to the Porsche you so desire.

When you attempt to reconcile these worlds, you're left in a far-off, hazy land we'll refer to as the Messy Middle. In this place, clarity—knowing who you are, what you want, and what you're about—is a pipe dream as you slumber through your weeks, months, and years in a foglike haze.

Stuck between two worlds, you do *nothing*.

In the Messy Middle, indecision thrives. Overthinking becomes your modus operandi. Fear of missing out (FOMO) is the new baseline. Guilt starts to take up the prized real estate inside of your head . . . rent free. It brings overwhelm along for the ride; they're both freeloaders that suck up every ounce of your emotional energy. Sprinkle in an ample dose of distraction and you've got a recipe for plummeting fulfillment and performance. In the valley of the Messy Middle:

▶ There never seems to be enough time, energy, or money to achieve or enjoy your goals.

▶ Consistency is a pipe dream and momentum starts . . . stops . . . starts.

▶ Ideas, insights, and breakthroughs sound amazing but never become real.

▶ You know how to live an optimized life, but it seems to escape you.

▶ You yearn for progress and much more "you" time.

Ultimately, the Messy Middle is a void where emotional freedom—your ability to feel enduring states of peace—never lasts. Instead, you're simply trying to slog through the day.

But when did *this* become the standard?

If what I'm describing resonates on *any* level, don't fret. Understand you aren't at fault here. To desire and work toward a fuller life is courageous. But with clashing messages and an endless stream of content, tips, and hacks from both sides—this life can seem to escape you. I've been there. It is perfectly normal to feel overwhelmed. It's why you picked up this book; it is why I wrote it.

There is a better way.

In this place, you're able to tap into both ends of a life well lived. This includes achievement—making progress on your goals—and fulfillment—feeling engaged, alive, and present. You're able to extract the benefits of each side: momentum and results *plus* peace and clarity. In this place, you make a dent on what matters while having plenty of "you" time left over.

Before we get there, you may find yourself thinking: Who is this guy making these bold promises?

THIS BOOK WAS BORN OUT OF SELF-PRESERVATION

I've been torn between these worlds, I've been the sucker who was sold the faux promises of both—and had to immerse myself in each one to find out the capital-T truth.

In other words, I've done the dirty work for you.

I indoctrinated myself as a proud, fist-in-the-air hustler. I climbed the corporate ladder at a blistering pace and then took the hustler's classic plunge into starting my business. We built a staff of 12; I'd start the day at 4:30 a.m. and finish late into the night, fueled by ambition. I could not stop. I took zero days off.

"Uh, Tommy . . . people don't work on the Fourth of July or Christmas Eve" was a routine conversation with my staff. (Really? I found that hard to believe as I stared at a "crush your competition" quote on the wall.)

All of this technically worked, but not if that means, you know, having any semblance of a real life. My social life was relegated to Netflix and chill dates with my bulldog. He's a looker, but he snores and drools, too.

Worst of all, I didn't know *who* I was when I wasn't plugged in.

A hot date? Yeah, no . . . I didn't go on one for an entire year. Balance? That's . . . uh . . . not in my vocabulary. Disconnecting, fun, and play? Get the hell out of here!

Due to this, I barely recognized my successes. Every time I achieved a goal, I'd move the goalpost back. The high never lasted. It was never enough, which meant *I was never enough.* Dammit.

I searched for answers; there had to be a better way.

I found seeking; I unplugged into the void, embarking on a quest of epic proportions. I went to weeklong Buddhist retreats, became a yogi, started the day reading the Gita. I spent hundreds of hours in a sensory deprivation tank; I hung with gurus, monks, and sages.

This pursuit created obscene amounts of peace and allowed me to sit in the lotus position (oh hey, hips) for hours. But it also left me indifferent to goals and detached to the point of apathy. It led me to count every last penny and argue on the phone with Bank of America on why my account was overdrawn . . . for the seventh time. Those $35 charges really start to add up.

Clearly, this wasn't working either.

Stubborn to the bone, I dug my heels in deeper.

I found myself in nondescript shopping malls in Salt Lake City to train with those who built the Adonis-like bodies of the movie *300*. I spent a week on a vision quest searching for my life's purpose. I joined a men's transformation group resembling Fight Club—black eyes and torn ACLs included. I was dumped in the Pacific Ocean blindfolded; I stared into people's eyes for 40 minutes so far past the point of discomfort we both had crusted tears on our faces. I visited random cabins in the woods for emotional work; I spent time with mystics, healers, shamans.

If there was even a scant hope of transformation, I was all in.

As time passed, I became troubled. I noticed there was a prevailing disconnect. I'd meet uber-successful business owners who hated their home life. I met gifted creatives who lived a degenerate lifestyle, mirroring Bukowski. I'd notice the spiritual community shunned talking about money, progress, and results. I'd meet people who had achieved their dreams 10 times over but desperately needed more. I'd engage with those bursting at the seams with fulfillment, but knowing they weren't infusing their real lives with it.

Something was missing.

What I'd realized is these people were living as hustlers *or* seekers.

HUSTLERS *OR* SEEKERS

They'd planted a flag in one world that came with a prevailing narrative, a set of beliefs that may have been "working" to the outside world, but how are we defining *working*?

Conventional hustling and seeking both reach a point of diminishing return—when spending more time and energy in one world not only lessens the benefits one receives, but starts doing more harm than good:

▶ Hustlers add more work and intensity, shifting into overdrive, only to experience anxiety, stress, and a one-way ticket to Burnout, USA.

▶ Seekers add more space, self-care, and insight gathering, only to tip the scales of detachment and be bursting with wisdom but zero tangible results.

No, thanks.

Is this working?

A glance at our culture's busyness trap, plummeting engagement, and increased burnout makes it clear—it's not. Sixty-nine percent of workers are disengaged,[1] and two-thirds of employees have dealt with burnout.[2] Entrepreneurs are worse off: according to the National Institute of Mental Health, 72 percent are affected by mental health issues compared to 48 percent for non-entrepreneurs.[3]

On the flipside, Americans write a collective check to the tune of $14 billion for personal growth, mindfulness, and spiritual guidance every year.[4] Consciousness is now mainstream and a mainstay in people's budgets. And yet, we've never been more anxious, neurotic, and overwhelmed, as anxiety affects 40 million adults in America alone.[5]

There has to be a better way.

Instead of continuing to slam the accelerator in one direction or the other, these sides must coalesce. By coming together, they create a radical shift in perspective. They infuse each other with precisely what going past the point of diminishing returns cannot.

In other words, the right hustle can amplify seeking; the right seeking can amplify hustling. In this place, the Messy Middle is replaced with a sweet spot where you can extract the best of both worlds.

Hustling and Seeking

Once I removed the jargon, the "tells" from each world, it hit me like a splash of ice water to the face—both sides want the same things. The quest and application of high performance and mindfulness are the *same*. Stripped naked to their core, at their most essential, they're vying for what we all crave:

- ► Progress
- ► Meaning
- ► Peak states
- ► Performance
- ► Confidence
- ► Connection
- ► Freedom
- ► Emotional sanity
- ► Awe, wonder, bliss

Once the cute social media quotes, Sanskrit tattoos, and fist-bumping mannerisms are eliminated, we recognize the truth. Both sides are on the same highway with one clear destination: *growth*. Both desire the thrill of heart-thumping progress. Both have an endgame to feel alive. Both are trying to find themselves, create meaning, and connect to something palpable. Ultimately, both want freedom: from the past, their upbringing, the shackles of limitation.

These worlds aren't contradictory opposites at all; they're complementary. It is their approach, the *how*, that differs. At their most essential, they're equals. And what's missing in their quest isn't *more* of the same. They need something else. They need each other. They require contrast—the ability to gather insights and perspective—from an unfamiliar place.

Desperately.

Here's the rub: both sides miss out if they're unable to integrate each other. By having a compass in the future we're aiming for, we're able to be more present today—and by being more present—we're able to not miss *here* for *there* . . . which oddly enough increases our chances of getting there!

That was a mouthful, so I hope you're still with me. The mindsets and strategies from hustle expand your spiritual or "being" life. The right practices and commitment to seeking boost one's performance, creativity, and "doing" in professional life.

Not only can these two worlds coexist, but they must.

Each one fuels the other and increases critical markers of a life well lived: the fulfillment that comes with self-worth and the gratitude of doing what we're meant to, plus the freedom that arises with achievement. This includes more zeroes in your bank account and success in life, career, and business.

Isn't that what we're here for?

Whiplashed by this paradoxical sweet spot, I discovered everything had shifted.

I noticed others who'd merged these worlds. It was evident: They were incredibly high performers, yet grounded. They were living a life of a warrior and a sage. A do-er and a be-er. Driven, but soulful. Ambitious, yet humble. Obsessive at times, while having the *time of their lives*. They were able to show up and perform like no other, but then shut it off.

They weren't hustlers or seekers; they were hustlers *and* seekers.

With years of practice, integrating, and fine-tuning—I merged both. I could take action, and then allow the mystery of life to unfold. I could be disciplined in the pursuit, and then surrender to the moment. I could practice grit, and then experience a level of gratitude that brought me to my knees. I'd obsessively tackle my vision; then I'd unplug so as to be asked about it and say, "Uh, what vision?"

I was performing at an otherworldly rate, but instead of needing more, I never felt more at peace. This was the state I'd been longing for, yet it had felt so elusive, to the point of feeling impossible.

But this isn't about me, it's about you.

Like a mad scientist, I was the guinea pig to test these principles; those who followed me were on deck. I launched a platform with a successful podcast, the Resist Average Academy, coaching platform, and live events. I tested the principles and helped others who wanted to merge both worlds but, like the earlier version of myself, had no clue how.

I served clients from all over; they'd fly cross-country to learn how they could do the same. They too wanted the best of both worlds—to achieve their wildest dreams—but to do so feeling whole, complete, grounded. I spent nearly a thousand hours in the trenches having engaging conversations with the world's best on the Resist Average Academy podcast.

Millions of downloads, thousands of direct coaching hours, and several events later, I realized the wisdom had been screaming at all of us with the answers. But I'd been so caught up in the Messy Middle that I couldn't hear those answers. The reality is we all have an inner hustler, the part of ourselves that desires to bring an audacious dream to life. We also have an inner seeker, the part of us that yearns for a deeper, more meaningful existence.

When we deny either part of ourselves, we lose.

And so does everyone else.

When we honor both parts of ourselves, we show up like never before, grow at exponential rates, lift others up—and win. And by winning, I mean we're able to feel peace, freedom, and meaning plus bring goals to life with rewards, including access, options, bank deposits.

In other words, we *can* have the best of both worlds. To perform at the top of one's game, but not be defined by it. To bring together achievement and fulfillment. To feel whole, connected, and integrated. To feel a sense of progress, richness, and "aliveness" in our day-to-day. To merge doing and being.

Since you picked up this book, I'll take a wild guess this is what you want as well. But up to this point, you've been unable to bring it to life. And that's fine because you're where you need to be.

Let's dive into the road map of how we'll get you there.

HOW TO READ THIS BOOK

This book uses the principles, mindsets, and tactics that have helped countless transcend the Messy Middle that has become society's status quo. I get that your idea of a wild Saturday night has nothing to do with Google Scholar and a cold glass of kombucha, getting high off academia and mystical legends. I'm the nerd here, so let's get that out of the way.

With that in mind, I've written this to be digestible, engaging, and—*gasp!*—fun. Beyond the surface, there is a reservoir of research and ideologies. These include humanistic psychology, neuroscience, and studies on happiness. I coupled these with studies on performance, goal-setting, fulfillment, mysticism, flow states, mindfulness, and philosophy.

I borrow from pioneers who recognized the thread of performance and spirituality, athletic feats, and mysticism. These include psychologists William James, Abraham Maslow, Carl Rogers, and Viktor Frankl as well as current thought leaders such as Ken Wilbur, Mihaly Csikszentmihalyi, and Steven Kotler. I pair this with candid conversations with high performers and lifelong seekers who were honest about their struggles and academics who study this work for a living.

This book helps you coalesce both states of being and doing to arrive at a new sweet spot—to get you thinking, feeling, and acting in a way where you can reap the rewards. Ultimately, the goal is to help you integrate these two worlds from your life's macro big picture down to your day-to-day.

Let's examine how we're going to get you there.

In Part I, we'll dive headfirst into both hustling and seeking, sifting through why they are incredibly powerful . . . until they're not. We'll reveal the myths that keep people stuck and on the wrong side of diminishing returns. We'll strip away the noise that anything less than a 12-hour day means you're lazy and why seeking—despite its endless praise—has a dark side. We'll tackle the biggest myth of them all: that you must pick one or the other . . . or else. You'll recognize you can replace the "or" with "and." Part I sets the foundation.

In Part II, we'll showcase 16 chapters to put this into practice by merging one principle from each side. You'll learn hustle principles as a spiritual practice and spiritual practices as performance amplifiers. Each is deconstructed, stripped to its marrow, the best of what it has to offer. We'll explore the perils of too much of each and how to know when you've hit that point. While each chapter can be read independently, they are best digested whole.

A note of caution: this is not about equal balance.

In some periods of life and business, you may hustle 80 percent of the time and seek 20 percent of the time. In others, you may flip this entirely by seeking 70 percent of the time and hustling 30 percent. Part of the book's process is helping you identify what you need and dosing appropriately. What matters is you understand both are required at all times, to some degree, if you want to maximize growth, progress, results—and emotional freedom.

No matter who you are.

Armed with a new perspective, you're going to experience countless benefits from this potent blend.

Say hello to your new sweet spot.

Along the way, you'll be accessing what renowned psychologist Maslow called "peak states."[6] You'll tap into what Csikszentmihalyi (no, don't try to say it) deemed "flow"—those timeless, present moments in life that we never want to end.[7]

When both worlds come together, you self-actualize.

Contrary to popular belief, none of this is a selfish pursuit. When you and I live rich, meaningful lives with resources to match, we take the focus *off* ourselves. We are less self-absorbed, less neurotic. The pursuit of your best self is not selfish at all.

It's selflessness.

When we hit the sweet spot of performance and fulfillment, we enter a state of thriving. We lift others; we give more. We contribute to the tapestry of our communities. We are more compassionate, kind, and connected. As Maslow, who coined the term *self-actualization,* said, "It is empirical fact that self-actualizing people are altruistic."[8]

With this in mind, you're able to tap into the potential you've neglected. You'll experience a level of creativity you've dreamed of, and best of all—an inner, humble confidence of knowing you're where you need to be right now. Nothing is missing, and there is nothing to prove.

True freedom.

These are bold promises, I know. But you arrived at this material for a reason. It is my responsibility to follow through. To do so, you'll need to meet me halfway. You'll need to be open to a new path. Some of your deeply held beliefs about work, results, and fulfillment will be questioned.

Whether you've identified as a fist-pumping, defiant hustler; an unquenchable seeker; or a scrappy mix who flip-flops from one side to the other with inconsistent results—I'm asking you to consider a new approach. Don't worry, you will still get your fill from each side. And the work you'll do by tapping into the other world will only amplify the benefits you're receiving.

As a sidenote, I use a few words heavily through the text—which I'll define quickly so we're on the same page:

- ▶ **Ego** refers to the part of us that desperately wants to be approved and seen in the best light at all times . . . even when it doesn't make sense.
- ▶ **Clarity** refers to knowing who we are, what matters to us, and where we're going with our lives—from the big picture to a random Tuesday.
- ▶ **Alignment** is consistency among thoughts, words, actions, values, and the decisions we make.
- ▶ **Achievement** is our ability to perform, create results, and bring our goals to life consistently.
- ▶ **Fulfillment** is a deep state of peace that is accessed through meaning, purpose, and being excited about our lives.
- ▶ **Overwhelm** is that incessant feeling that we're doing the wrong things with our lives and are constantly falling behind.
- ▶ **Emotional freedom** refers to states where we are at peace with ourselves and free of the narrative that we're off course, flawed, or beholden to the past.

It's time to bring these two communities and ways of living, doing, and being together—to finally let your inner hustler out of the cage and onto the field of play and your inner seeker to roam free.

It's time to stop beating yourself up, free yourself from FOMO, and optimize these parts of who you are. It's time to escape the Messy Middle before it leaves you naked in the fetal position, tied to a cactus in Vegas, wondering how the hell you got there. (That's a story for another time.)

It's about time the hustlers and the seekers all threw a giant party and got along.

And I want you to be in the middle of it.

For a free audio masterclass and toolkit to help integrate this material as you read, visit www.ResistAverageAcademy.com/HustlersSeekers.

PART I

The Dilemma

It's time to dive into the specifics of both hustling and seeking—and their respective downsides—so you'll know when you're approaching the place where more is not more.

Here, you'll discover the mindsets, strategies, tactics, and language from hustling and seeking that work . . . until they start doing more harm than good. You'll recognize why both sides not only should coexist—but are meant to. Best of all, you'll release the myths that hold each side hostage with surprising consequences.

Armed with this crucial insight, you'll identify the places where you're doing it right . . . and where you have opportunities for rapid growth. Part I will set you up for success with Part II's principles, so you can develop a new sweet spot.

Let's get this show on the road, shall we?

Chapter

1

Hustle, Hustle, Burnout

Hustle, the unrelenting pursuit of achievement and win-at-all-costs ethos, is embedded into the American psyche so deep that it may as well drip red, white, and blue. In a world where we value external rewards above everything else, it's no surprise hustle is intoxicating. We must always have more, do more, achieve more.

But we also must ask ourselves, is it *working*?

When I use the word *working*, I'm asking if hustle *itself* leads to a fulfilling, thriving life from the inside out. One where we can be at peace, content, and proud of ourselves.

A life where we feel alive and emotionally free.

To answer this question, let's turn to the annals of high achievement, the National Football League. No country is more obsessed with competitive sports than America. We pedestal athletes. Kids plaster posters of their favorite stars on bedroom walls; parents pop a blood vessel as they shout from the sidelines of their child's travel games.

And that child is, uh, eight years old.

This obsession is defined by the NFL's soaring popularity and the cruel reality that for an athlete to even *make* a team sounds like a miracle. At any given time, there are about 2,000 active players. In a country with 327 million people—that represents 0.000610397 percent of the population.[1]

You can't get much closer to zero.

The coveted crown in this world is none other than the pinnacle of sport, the elusive Vince Lombardi trophy—granted to one champion every year who endures the torment of training camp, the 17-week season, and a winner-take-all playoff. Winning isn't elite; it's elite to the 34th square.

Naturally, you'd think for an athlete who has reached this pinnacle after hustling and enduring the agony of grueling practices, roster cuts, injuries, and a 24/7 obsession with performance since turning seven years old—this would indisputably be the greatest moment of that athlete's life. The apex of everything and anything they've ever wanted.

And then some.

But for Aaron Rodgers, the MVP-winning quarterback of the Green Bay Packers, it wasn't. Only hours after the clock struck double zeroes and the Packers were crowned 2010 Super Bowl champions, Rodgers sat on the team bus surrounded by the rousing energy of dozens of childhood dreams coming to life and enough champagne to kill a horse.

But something was missing.

As the alpha hustler, Rodgers has a rare combination of talent, skill, and lethal desire to prove the naysayers wrong. Driven by an underlying current that came from being a top 5 draft pick hopeful to an agonizing, public slide to the 25th pick in the 2005 draft, he kept a scoreboard.

Oh, did he ever.

As cameras panned at his dejected look on draft evening, an inner fire destined to last decades was brewing. All the people who'd wronged him, passed on him, or critiqued his play or attitude—general managers, journalists, his own coach, and even friends and family—drove him to sheer excellence. Rodgers expanded on this high-octane fuel in a 2017 interview with *ESPN Magazine,* saying, "That was what fueled me—to wake up at 5 o'clock and work out before school and stay after and do extra sets and do extra throwing. The root of that was to be great . . . to *prove a point* every single day."[2]

Winning would be his cure-all, the ultimate I-showed-you moment. Kiss the ring, baby! With the trophy in hand, he'd have his arrival moment—the one he'd dreamed of and wanted more than anything in the world.

He'd finally be *free* . . . right?

Sitting on the bus that evening with the cumulative energy from all those years, the reps, early mornings, hours of meticulous film study, public slights, the sports media talking heads—winning didn't offer him the respite he'd imagined. According to ESPN: "He didn't feel like he had risen to a higher plane. Rather, he realized he was still looking for something—for a sense of clarity, or purpose—that was beyond his current line of sight."[3]

"I hope I don't just do this," Rodgers thought to himself.

This is what came to mind as he reflected amidst the tears, partying, his teammates scooping up VIP tables at clubs reveling on the incredible win. Rodgers's sinking realization that hustle alone is *not* enough is common. Why? Because hustle alone does not give you peace. It doesn't provide lasting emotional freedom. It doesn't always deepen purpose or contribute to meaning. As Rodgers said months after his moment: "I've been to the bottom and been to the top, and peace will come from somewhere else."[4]

While winning had checked off every marker of hustler's golden child through boundless achievement, it hadn't filled the void of fulfillment—the confluence of meaning, peace, and emotional freedom we all crave. While hustle is oh so effective at filling up the bucket of achievement past the brim, it rarely pours over to the other bucket of a life well lived—the inner game of fulfillment.

And hence, the hustler's dilemma.

Relying on achievement alone is not a strategy for success unless one wants to "arrive" at the mountaintop and recognize, like Rodgers, that a void still exists. And because this pursuit typically entails years of sacrifice with the *expectation* that the arrival moment will be the ultimate cure-all, the results can be devastating.

But we've heard this before.

Rodgers's story is all too common; the rags-to-riches tale we hear on a podcast leading to an existential crisis, the celebrity who has a drug-induced breakdown, the author who sold millions of copies and became depressed after attaining everything he or she ever wanted.

We collectively yawn at these tales, muttering under our breath some variation of "must be nice" as we stubbornly believe we'll be the exception to the rule as long as we have our Jerry McGuire "show me the money" moment too.

I'm raising my hand. I've lit myself on fire with the jet fuel of ambition and with the staunch belief that when I got *there*, I'd be free too. All the fear, worry, and doubt would melt away. And if for some reason that wasn't the case—all I had to do was pull myself up by my bootstraps and conquer the *next* mountain.

Does this sound familiar?

But like Rodgers, I realized I wasn't the exception.

And neither are you.

To fully grasp the hustler's dilemma, we must first examine the oh-so-intoxicating energy that draws us into her world with a seductive allure.

WHY WE LOVE HUSTLE

Hustle is easy to love.

It's attractive, at times irresistible, and when taken too far, it can be deceptively addictive as the lines between a healthy pursuit and a full-blown obsession are blurred.

Why?

First, hustle is typically *yours*, and we all love autonomy in our lives and careers. Autonomy, simply defined, is the freedom needed to direct your own life, work, and growth.[5]

It is your hustle, your side hustle, your dream.

Hustle acts as an alluring bridge to our external desires, including cash in the bank, applause, letters after our name, and doors opening that otherwise are sealed shut. It allows us to prove others wrong, including our own inner critic. And it leads to winning.

Lots of winning.

Second, hustle satiates a core human motivator: progress. Research by Harvard professor Teresa Amabile and psychologist Steven Kramer studied what makes humans at work tick, why they stay motivated or fizzle out. In analyzing 12,000 diary entries of workers' emotions, they came to one conclusion. It's not money. It's not security. It's not approval. It's *progress.* Progress is more important than anything else.[6]

The world of hustle is soaking wet with progress. It allows you to cross off nine items from your to-do list and make a dent on your vision. It compels you to rise before sunrise and crush the high-intensity fitness session. It pushes you to polish up the résumé and make the bold pitch to the recruiter. Progress fuels our sense of self, builds self-esteem, and gives us an identity in the world.[7]

Check, check, check . . . pour me a double.

Third, we are engulfed in a culture of "getting shit done," or GSD. We obsess over productivity hacks; we squeeze every second of the workday. The modern world places immense value on accomplishment, achievement, and accolades. When we check off those boxes, we feel like we're part of the tribe.

We feel worthy.

Whether we're at the local cocktail mixer or our LinkedIn profiles are being perused, we feel a sense of pride when we're asked what we're working on or how snazzy our bio reads. The pull of hustle gets us from all angles.

On the surface, hustle seems to check all the boxes. It seems to give a healthy return on investment (ROI). When you input effort, you get back growth, self-esteem, progress, performance, pings of bank account deposits, and the brand-new apartment with that oh-so-perfect view.

What's not to like?

Well, for starters, a core part of hustle comes from an insatiable desire for external approval.[8] I'll refer to this as the dark side of hustle—and it's not necessarily bad; rather, it is hardwired into our DNA. It must be understood and acknowledged to be dealt with appropriately.

Otherwise, it can spit us out into an existential abyss where we question everything.

HOW HUSTLE (REALLY) DRIVES US

To grasp hustle's undeniable power, we first must understand one of its drivers of motivation—the desire to "make it."[9] Making it can be defined in myriad ways, and it acts as a palpable part of any endeavor, outcome, or goal.

Making it, of course, is entirely subjective. We tend to have a fuzzy image in our minds of what it *looks* and *feels* like. It's the six-figure salary or the corner office. It's the book deal, a star role, a check from the investor, meeting our soul mate, or a mishmash of all of these as we're fielding calls from media, fans, and followers.

It's the little blue checkmark after our name.

The desire to get *there* gets us up in the morning to do focused work. It keeps us awake to finish the paper. It gets us to do what marketing expert Seth Godin calls "shipping": hitting publish, sharing your work, displaying your art . . . even when no one cares, and few people (except Grandma—because she's awesome) are paying attention.[10]

This fire to make it burns deep inside, alchemized as high-octane fuel for you to execute. But this motivation doesn't always come from a wholesome place. It can lead us to achieve for the lone sake of external praise, awards, and accolades at the *expense* of our authentic desire.

Crazy, huh?

Take law school, an endeavor roughly 130,000 students experience at any moment.[11] This is a generalization, but many of these students have minimal desire to be attorneys. Many enroll simply because "they didn't know what else to do" and "everyone else seemed to be doing it."[12] They embark on the path for its superficial benefits—the freshly minted six-figure salary and the turning of heads at the summer BBQ when asked what they're doing after college. Parents vicariously live through their children, proudly displaying Yale Law bumper stickers as their kids fantasize passing the bar exam and having an "Esq" at the end of their name.

External, external, external.

But it doesn't come without a hefty cost. In fact, a study revealed that an estimated 30,000 to 60,000 law students struggle with depression at some point during their tenure, nearly *four times* above the general population.[13]

Let's face it, to enroll, endure, and finish law school requires hustle. To pass the bar exam requires hustle. To be recruited to a firm and slog away those years of "paying one's dues" requires hustle. To reach the promised land of partner, the oasis at the pinnacle of one's law career where the average age of such accomplishment is 52 years old[14] requires . . . well, you know the answer.

But to what end?

Now, if you're reading this and have a desire to be a real-life Atticus Finch, own it. The point can be made in any career, including mine. I was on a fast track on Wall Street, despite having moral aversion to the industry, being a joke with my own finances, and setting the all-time record for overdrafts in a day, according to Karl from Bank of America. (The record was 11, if you're wondering.)

Hustle, then, can become a trap of stoking our ambition through desperate, needy approval. It can lead to trading our mental sanity for years—no, decades—of hard work in order to be congratulated and looked up to at the *expense* of ourselves. While the endgame can be a trophy case of outer rewards, we feel empty. We get *there* only to realize we are hollow and apathetic. Sure, we ticked off the boxes and everyone's impressed—but so what?

Dr. Risa Stein, professor of psychology at Rockhurst University, expands on this point: "If our life plans or even just short-term goals are guided by external criteria . . . without a true understanding of what it is that we actually want or what fulfills and satisfies us, then we end up at minimum disconcerted and unhappy, and at worst, with a midlife crisis or severely depressed."[15]

Which leads us to the dark side of the hustle.

THE DARK SIDE OF HUSTLE

The dark side of hustle can lead us to pursue success from self-loathing and hatred, to prove others wrong, or to fill a void inside caused by past trauma. We all have some variation of these egoic needs; it's part of the human experience. But since hustle soothes this pain, it can become our identity. If we don't address it, our ambitions turn into a lifelong vendetta against faux haters, trolls, and critics.

To be clear, not *all* hustle comes from this dark place. Part of it comes from a healthy pursuit of a vision that fuels you from the inside, a clear purpose and desire to impact and serve. I'll explore this in each of the principles to extract the best of what it has to offer. The problem arises when we tip the scales and the attractive side of hustle turns sour.

This manifests in putting another hour in when you're tapped out as your mental sanity suffers. It's checking your email for the 88th time during your commute. It's being on date night with family and unconsciously checking business metrics, like a zombie who can't help but scroll. It can lead to frayed relationships, a rabbit hole of comparison, and becoming a workaholic to feel worthy.

What was once useful can turn into a full-blown, unstoppable addiction. Since achievement alone doesn't lead to fulfillment, the rabbit hole only gets deeper the farther we go. This is the inexplicable pull of external reward—the fact that it can lead us to create a life we never wanted in the first place *or* we obliterate our psyche, sanity, and relationships on the way to the mountaintop.

Or both.

Addictions, by definition, make us blind.

Consider the recent college admissions scandal in which parents were charged with bribing schools with buckets of cash to get their kids in. This is not normal behavior. It is an obsession gone haywire—where already privileged families took *illegal* action to fulfill the void. Or the infamous Fyre Festival, where belief turned into delusion, and delusion to negligence when a supposed luxury music festival became a scam destined for folklore, where "luxury" accommodations were disaster relief tents and a "uniquely authentic island cuisine experience" became a trending cheese sandwich.[16]

These are not random occurrences.

When we're drunk on external approval, we can't see clearly. Blitzed by ambition, we can't tell north from south or east from west. We make bad decisions. We lose ourselves . . . and sometimes the people we love. We wake up and wonder where it all went wrong.

To ensure you don't slide into the abyss of addictive hustle, you'll need to understand the Law of Diminishing Hustle.

In other words, you'll need to know when more is *not* more.

THE LAW OF DIMINISHING HUSTLE

You're doing work that matters, moving the needle, and reaping the benefits of forward progress. You're taking action and staying committed. All good things, right? However, move farther along this curve and you'll wind up hitting the point of diminishing returns—where more is *not* more. This breaking point is where your ability to add an input of time, energy, or effort no longer correlates with an output of growth, results, and progress.

And surely, no more fulfillment.

Stubbornly, our natural response is to pound the pavement harder, until we realize we're worse off. We've arrived at the Law of Diminishing Hustle—where every added input works *against* us. Every email, social media scroll, or sales call gets us *farther* away from our desired outcome.

And it costs us dearly.

Like some of life's universal pleasures, including summer nights, naps, caffeine, Netflix, and my guilty pleasure, Taylor Swift, things can work—until they don't. After days of slumber in bed, we become bored. Another dose of caffeine takes us from energized to paranoid, watching two hours of our favorite show is fun; binging for an entire week leaves us empty. (Okay, Taylor never gets old.)

Hustle is no exception. We know work ethic matters. We understand delaying gratification for a better future is a psychological trigger for success.[17] We get leaning into resistance instead of procrastinating pays off. But at this inflection point, more is not only less—performance falls off a cliff.

And it takes our sanity with it.

With the Law of Diminishing Hustle, the right hustle, at the right times, leads to an optimal level of results, until that very same hustle works against you.

But there's a problem. This inflection point happens *after* you've reached your peak state of hustle. You're firing on all cylinders, which makes it brutally hard to identify. Hopped up on hustle's addictive qualities, you burn the midnight oil for another three hours. But you know the extra time was essentially worthless because it was spent on the other side of the inflection point.

Consider research by professor John Pencavel of Stanford who aimed to find the sweet spot between hours worked and actual productivity, finding more is *not* more, saying, "productivity falls off a cliff after 55 hours [in one week]—someone who puts in 70 hours produces *nothing* more with those extra 15 hours."[18] Or a more extreme case from productivity expert Chris Bailey, who shared on the Resist Average Academy podcast that he accomplished *nearly* as much in 20-hour weeks as 90-hour weeks.[19]

Let that sink in.

Being drenched in hustle's dopamine is like having that fourth cocktail before dinner at happy hour. You're making grand declarations and hugging bartenders; you can't be trusted. Your friend has to concoct a random story about how you took the wrong medication as she hails you an Uber.

Even when it's obvious we're on the other side of the inflection point, we talk ourselves into more *doing.* Stopping is for quitters; taking breaks is for the entitled. Let's see how this law works.

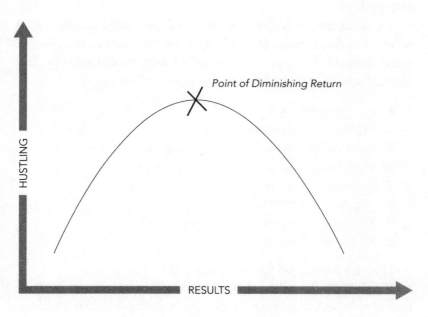

The Law of Diminishing Hustle

Think of your favorite food on the planet—the one you salivate simply thinking about, every last bite an orgasmic experience. I'm weird, but mine are Acai bowls from a particular place in the red rocks of Sedona, Arizona. I have dreams about these concoctions. They keep me up at night. They drive me wild. My fiancée is concerned. After I have one, I realize I can't just have one. That would be crazy talk.

The second one starts as amazing, and yet, halfway through, it starts to lose its potency. It's still incredible but wearing off. By the time I start the third bowl, I've got cramps, and this is no longer fun. If I keep going, my day is shot. Damn you, Acai, damn you. If it can happen with Acai, trust me, it can happen with *anything*.

Including hustle.

Like hustle, it has gone from mouthwatering to soul-crushing, from creative to destructive, from powerful to abysmal.

So, what happens *after* the point of diminishing returns? A series of consequences that suck the life force out of your peace, growth, and fulfillment, and oddly enough leads to *less* performance, specifically eight consequences, including:

1. It is never enough.
2. Fulfillment escapes you.
3. You think money will solve all your problems.
4. Work takes over your life.
5. Success feels unlike you.
6. You can't shut it off.
7. More success means less freedom.
8. You arrive at burnout.

Doesn't sound too fun now, does it?

It's time to dive into these consequences. Now you may be thinking—isn't it enough to call them out? Not quite. Because both hustling and seeking can take a stranglehold on our identity, you'll need to know the *exact* ways both work against you as they shapeshift in creative ways.

Being aware of these consequences will help you recognize them in real time and step away from the laptop, smartphone, and the incessant feeling that despite the progress you're creating—everyone on social media has it figured out. Except you.

Otherwise, the consequences are dire.

Chapter

2

The Dark Side of Hustle

Richard was like any struggling musician who'd worked his craft and tasted some success—but was struggling to make it work. At some point, the youthful exuberance of chasing one's creative dream fades when sleeping in random people's basements and scrounging loose cash loses its wonder.

It was time to move on.

He'd decided it was time to get serious by going home to Connecticut to teach philosophy at a community college.[1] Upon releasing his last album, an eclectic mash-up of electronic beats set to African music from the 1950s—he couldn't have been further from what was hot on radio—the likes of Britney Spears, Sugar Ray, and TLC.

Richard half-heartedly played a record release show in the basement of a Manhattan Virgin Records store to less than 50 people. Many of those folks paid little to no attention to the

balding man on the makeshift stage, another has-been disturb-
ing their shopping.[2]

And then the unexpected happened.

His record, *Play*, caught fire and would go on to sell more
than 10 million copies, transforming him into a bonafide
celebrity who dated models, hung with Bill Clinton, and went
on benders where raging hangovers became his de facto experience. Tours couldn't be booked fast enough. The demand was
insatiable.[3]

Hello, success.

Richard, known by his stage name, Moby, had caught the
tornado of fame and external reward. But he soon found out
that his humble beginnings didn't make him grateful for what
he had. As he attempted to grapple with the whiplash of unlimited options and going from being ignored to everyone wanting
a piece of him—he explains how it was never enough: "When
you have the four-bedroom apartment on Park and are dating
a supermodel, you want the six-bedroom apartment on Madi-
son and the younger model. It is truly miserable."[4]

Believing the myth of hustle, Moby nearly drove himself
into oblivion as he attempted suicide.[5] Along his destructive
path, he purchased castles, traveled to exotic lands, and dated
celebrities plastered on Page Six. But of course, it didn't work:
the further along he went—the emptier and *less* fulfilled he was.

Moby had experienced the first consequence of operating on
the other side of the Law of Diminishing Hustle.

1. IT IS NEVER ENOUGH

As Moby's story and countless others who have achieved world-
class success exemplify, achievement *alone* is not enough.

It never will be, thanks to comparison. There is *always*
someone creating more results. Someone who is better looking,
who has a more thriving relationship with bae, or who hangs
out with your guru.

This isn't anyone's fault; rather, comparison is hardwired into our DNA.[6] It is a survival tactic and can be healthy to a degree, letting us know we're on the right track in our lives. It acts as a reference point for operating in a functional society.

But taken too far and you're left with an unwinnable game.

Sure, you launched and doubled your business, but there's someone who quadrupled theirs. You left your 9–5 and had the courage to turn your passion of audio production into a profitable business, but others have done it for years. You got accepted into the program, but others are published.

Comparison has no endgame, except an existential, emotional crisis.

Think about it: For most of history, we compared ourselves to people in our communities. Because we saw them often, we could relate to them and see their eccentricities. Even in a diverse neighborhood, their lives were in the same universe as ours. This comparison, called downward or equal comparison, is psychologically healthy.[7]

But the harmful comparison is one we know too well.

Psychologists call this upward comparison, defined as "comparing ourselves to someone who is (perceived to be or performing) better than we are."[8] Thanks to social media, we no longer compare ourselves to our neighbors. With unlimited access, we compare ourselves to the 1 percent of the 1 percent . . . of the 1 percent.

We're fit, but we compare ourselves to 24-year-old fitness models in Bali. We're making career moves but look at Silicon Valley IPOs. We're connected in our relationship, but we're jealous of the influencer couple's New Zealand expedition. We're working our craft, but we're pissed our jawline doesn't look like Beyonce's.

And now we're *missing* something.

You'd think at some point we'd realize whatever successes we've had would be enough to hang back and enjoy the fruits of our effort. But that's not how it goes in the land of hustle.

Which means fulfillment is a pipe dream.

2. FULFILLMENT ESCAPES YOU

When you're always trying to exceed your own expectations or striving yourself to exhaustion, you never allow yourself to feel alive, present, and fulfilled right now.

Because you're driven to go *there* at the expense of *here*, it's easy to create an emotional thermostat based on results. This thermostat, which researchers call an emotional setpoint, acts as a constraint of how good (or bad) you allow yourself to feel at any moment.[9]

Since you haven't achieved everything on the vision board, you talk yourself out of appreciating where you are right now. You experience an incredible day but stop short of expressing it. You look into a loved one's eyes and feel deep connection but are thinking about a pending email. You feel confidence rise inside of you, but then look at your bank account and feel crappy.

In other words, you cap how good you allow yourself to feel.

This is no way to live. When you're constantly trying to accumulate more—success, accolades, money—everything in life becomes filtered through a lens of mediocrity and a feeling of not enough. You refuse feelings of freedom, peace, or unabashed joy for who you are and what you're about because you're not "there" yet.

If you only had enough cash, *then* you'd feel those . . . right?

3. YOU THINK MONEY WILL SOLVE ALL YOUR PROBLEMS

Hustlers believe, at a core level, that enough money, accolades, and external markers of success will fix all their problems.

But the reality is that once the halo of hustle fades away—a week, month, or year later—we're left with ourselves. We still have problems, emotional issues, quirks. Ultimately, the realization that arriving at our goal doesn't fundamentally change who we are is what *really* stings.

Nobel laureate Daniel Kahneman plotted happiness and life satisfaction with income and found a direct correlation . . . until $70,000.[10] But then, money's powers fade away and are replaced by internal needs—autonomy, mastery, purpose—that directly contribute to well-being.

Does that mean we should strive for $70,000 and call it a day? No, and let's be clear: money is amazing and there should be no shame around it. Writing a check solves problems in life, leads to access we wouldn't otherwise have—and if we spend it wisely—can increase happiness and fulfillment.[11]

Again, it is the *illusion* that money alone will change us from the inside out that is dangerous. Hustlers believe this, and it drives their ravenous desire to empty their tank in the pursuit of achievement.

And because they believe they're the exception to the rule, if they haven't "made it" yet, there's only one option—slam on the accelerator and work harder.

4. WORK TAKES OVER YOUR LIFE

If you're not where you want to be, there's one solution: white knuckle your efforts further. But because hustle and time are both finite, what happens when there's no time left and your capacity for effort is bone-dry?

Well then, you're screwed. At least in this model.

Because where are you going to find more time?

You're already guns blazing, so you look for it at the margins: cut off an hour of sleep, stop doing your favorite hobby, quit showering. These aren't advisable, and certainly not sustainable, and yet are often where we find ourselves. In the pursuit of more, *we* become an afterthought. Who the hell has time for self-care? Time with family will have to wait. We're building an empire.

Sleep when you're dead.

For Erin Callan, the former CEO of the now-defunct Lehman Brothers, her journey to personal burnout started with small concessions blurring the lines between work and home. She expands:

> I didn't start out with the goal of devoting all of myself to my job. It crept in over time. Each year that went by, slight modifications became the new normal. First, I spent a half-hour on Sunday organizing my e-mail, to-do list, and calendar to make Monday morning easier. Then I was working a few hours on Sunday, then all day. My boundaries slipped away until work was all that was left.[12]

The results of these small changes spoke volumes. A full-blown personal and professional crisis, a botched marriage, a lack of a life outside of work. When the work that consumed her was no longer there, she didn't know who she was because, in her own words, "What I did was who I was."[13]

Sound familiar? Many of us have been there.

This is a direct conseqence of hustle. We blur the lines between work and home life and pummel them into submission until there's nothing left. Eventually, hustle stops working altogether.

Which means we're not practicing emotional states of success.

5. SUCCESS FEELS UNLIKE YOU

Most of us are used to failure.

While disappointing, striking out is something we've all dealt with to some degree. Failure is, well, familiar.

But who among us is equipped to deal with success?

Success, for this reason, can be *more* emotionally disorienting than failure.

No, really.

If we've spent most of our lives chasing, striving, pushing—plus swinging and missing—what happens when we knock it out of the park? Whoosh, we can be hurled sideways; emotionally disoriented. Since we've trained ourselves to always pursue *more*, we've never practiced how to be at peace with *enough.* We've never learned to allow emotions above the set points we described earlier. Which means that success feels . . . *unlike* you.

There is nothing worse than winning the "championship" of your life, receiving the payoff for all that hustle, and then not knowing what to do with the foreign feelings of success. Because if you're not chasing a goalpost, if you're not relentlessly executing, if you're not dreaming of creating a start-up and making it rain when it launches its IPO, then you may not know who you are. And that's scary.

The question, then, becomes: Who are you when you're not hustling?

If you can't answer that, there's a problem.

Unfortunately, to avoid answering this question, many of us find it easier to just never shut the hustle off.

6. YOU CAN'T SHUT IT OFF

Hustlers live with a secret.

As they continue to rise above the next peak of their career, business, or craft, the secret gets quieter, yet holds a tighter grip on their lives.

They. Can't. Shut. It. Off.

The mindset of hustling with its drive for more is always *on*, even when it blatantly shouldn't be. This is the secret of the successful: what makes them great in many ways becomes their kryptonite. When you pour them a tequila on ice, get them to drop the ego and speak freely—they will tell you in a matter-of-fact, blunt way, they *want* to turn this part of themselves off.

But they can't.

Tom DeLong, a Harvard Business School professor, calls this the "hidden demons of high achievers," including what we've covered: addiction, operating out of guilt, never allowing themselves to fully relax for fear of losing their edge.[14]

An inability to "shut it off" isn't just a bummer, it hinders performance.

Writers who can't spend time away from their work miss out on their creative breakthrough. The filmmaker who can't take a few months off never taps into his or her passion project. The business owner who keeps going 24/7 never finds the new product that changes the game. The artist who is in a constant cycle of recording and touring never writes the magnus opus fans never saw coming—Radiohead's *Kid A,* U2's *Achtung Baby,* and Daft Punk's *Random Access Memories.*

Without being able to shut it down, you may find yourself in an all-too-common success trap: the more you experience success, the *less* freedom you actually have.

Weird, huh?

7. MORE SUCCESS MEANS LESS FREEDOM

Hustlers push, grind, and commit to audacious dreams with the expectation that if they do it right, today's sacrifice guarantees enough bank deposits to ride off into the sunset basking in freedom.

They fantasize of wide-open calendars; time is now on their terms. They dream of passive income and being a card-carrying member of those who also have "made it."

And yet one of the insidious traps of success under this model is the more you succeed, the *less* freedom you have.

WTF!?

You're making more money, but your calendar is crammed. You've expanded the business but added new roles to your plate. You've created something others love . . . then realize you're spending all your time promoting.

Because it's one thing to be driven by success without experiencing it—but once you taste it—now it's about holding on for dear life. You don't want to be a flash in the pan, a one-hit wonder, or the band who wrote the "you get knocked down, but you get up again" song (see, no one remembers them).

To counteract this fear, you fill your day with tasks and a blitz of action to soothe the ego's anxiousness. You say yes to an ungodly number of obligations and stale coffee meetings.

In other words, the main thing . . . is no longer the *main* thing.

Priorities, the essential needle-movers, what you're both best at and love doing, are given less time. Engagement plummets. You realize you're acquiring markers of success, and yet, at every checkpoint, you're adding ankle weights, strapping kettlebells to your legs, and adorning an 80-pound weight vest . . . until your run has become a dreadful crawl.

On a long enough timeline, there's only one endgame— physical, mental, or emotional burnout.

8. YOU ARRIVE AT BURNOUT

Hustlers emphasize and then re-emphasize the value of work ethic.

Thank you, Captain Obvious. Saying work ethic is essential is like my local Phoenix weatherman telling us we should expect 102 degrees in July. It's the desert, we get that.

We have oven mitts in our cars.

You see, work ethic for the *sake* of work ethic is pointless. Busyness, multitasking nine projects at once, and being the person who can't sit still for a moment and who scrolls while bumping into inanimate objects doesn't make sense. Working 80-hour weeks to show off on Twitter is useless. Because hustlers believe if you're not currently experiencing success, you're fooling yourself. You're simply not working hard enough.

Even if you definitely are.

This message reverberates through the life-coach-influencer world with one premise: with enough work, anything can happen. This underlying belief feeds into the big myth that by tackling your goals, *one day* you'll arrive at the promised land where you feel like you've made it too.

When we believe this, we never dare take our foot off the gas. The sheer thought of doing so means we slide back. Every moment not spent in pursuit is a moment lost, one where we can out-grit our competition, who doesn't have the same drive. While they nap, our eyeballs bleed.

But it's worth it, right?

Do this long enough and you don't simply arrive at burnout. It pummels you like a 30-foot swell, head over heels, staggering aimlessly in the water, praying for a split-second respite where you gasp for breath.

Here, it's already too late.

You're chewed up and spit out by hustle, disoriented and spiritually broke. The only respite is destruction, burning businesses to the ground, imploding marriages, and alcohol-fueled benders.

This belief is engulfed in guilt, shame, and a toxic obsession with work ethic, which looks at the world in binary ways—if you're not working your face off, you have no value. As a hustler who believes this, it means when you're not "doing," *you too* have no value. You feel guilty for taking time off; you become the checked-out parent during time with the kids. You don't like yourself when you're not in the grind.

Yeah, no thanks.

WHY WE MUST SEEK

"I hope I don't just do this."[15]

NFL quarterback Aaron Rodgers's feeling of something amiss after winning the Super Bowl is a familiar result of hustle's myths and consequences. We expect the grandiosity of the "arrival" moment to hurl us into a mythical oasis where any sign of lack and uncertainty are gone in a moment of ecstatic bliss.

When it doesn't happen, the reality can be crippling as you realize peace and fulfillment cannot *only* come from the world of star-studded triumphs.

If achievement alone isn't enough, then what?

Well, your outward drive, ambition, and desire must be paired with the world of seeking. You need space to let out all of your ambitious energy and drive so you can detach, unplug, and rest. You must do the inner work to know who you are . . . to align mind, body, spirit . . . and manufacture emotional states of success.

It's no wonder Rodgers went on a spiritual quest soon after the Super Bowl, explored his religious upbringing, went to India to meet the Dalai Lama, and hung out with former pastor Rob Bell.[16] Because while winning had checked off every box for hustler's golden child in the world of achievement—it hadn't filled the void of fulfillment.

Moby, too, barely survived the myth and now sees what he was lacking—acceptance of his chaotic childhood, a sense of purpose and meaning that can't be found in fame's excess. He has those now. He is at peace with his destructive past, has replaced alcoholism with environmentalism, and creates music . . . for the right reasons.[17]

If you're reading this book, it's because you don't want to become another worn-out cliché of those who arrive at their mountaintop only to recognize they've lost themselves.

Rather, you want to raise all boats, building a reservoir of fulfillment as you make a dent on what matters. But without desperation, neediness, or being beholden to a zero in a bank account or the letters on your business card.

To do so, you'll need to dose hustle and seeking appropriately.

However, much like hustle, seeking operates under its own myth, which comes with hefty consequences. This myth sounds compelling and brings people all over the world to commune at personal growth retreats, 10-day Vipassana meditations, barren deserts, and the self-transformation section of the bookstore.

While powerful when dosed wisely, seeking can turn a once-beautiful pursuit into bohemian excess, rabbit holes that never end, and becoming a bliss junkie full of insight . . . yet more confused than ever.

Weirdly enough, it can even rob you of the very peace it was designed to create.

Chapter

3

Seek, Seek, Go Down Rabbit Holes

She could be anybody's grandma, sweet with a heartwarming gaze, a kindheartedness that feels like your favorite wintertime blanket every time she says her trademark phrase, "oh, honey."

With an uncanny ability to gracefully face off with some of the darkest secrets anyone can have, Byron Katie's demeanor doesn't change whether the topic is a bad hair day or enduring the torment of sexual abuse. Her ability to hold judgment-free space in conversation is second to none.

She may just be the closest thing to enlightenment there is.

Katie is a legend in the self-help and healing space, achieving folklore status, known for a process she calls *The Work*—a startlingly simple method to observe one's thoughts and emotional triggers ranging from getting flipped the bird during rush hour to decades-old traumatic wounds. *The Work* encompasses a set of questions designed to create emotional freedom and release the baggage of the past.[1]

Watching her break someone's worldview down with unique gentleness betrays human logic. Her serenity seems to come in stark contrast with the topics at hand—intense grief, existential suffering, crippling divorce, midlife angst, or cancer ripping someone's life from underneath them.

But she does so every day, without flinching.

Oh, honey.

Katie lives in the world of seeking, where you go to unwind, disconnect, unplug, and work on yourself. Where you align your chakras, meditate, float naked in sensory deprivation tanks, head to the desert as a Burner, and take MDMA not to rave but to feel a swell of love inside of you.

Seeking encompasses self-care, journaling, reflecting, time unplugged, resolving past hurt, and ultimately, *being*. It is where you let go . . . where you detox and get away from the insanity of overwhelm, noise, and breaking news cycles. Seeking is the inner game in a world obsessed with the outer one. It is a long exhale after years of scattered inhales. It is *be-here-now* bumper stickers, the present moment.

It is not waking up, it is awakening.

And it's officially mainstream. Meditation apps proliferate, Fortune 500 companies allocate chunks of their budget to mindfulness. Pro teams, think tanks, and start-ups invest in personal growth seminars. The mission is to use seeking and space to produce a more balanced, engaged, connected, and, if done right, higher-performing team.

There are nap pods in offices. Companies hire experts on stillness and meditation. NFL players do yoga and engage in Zen Buddhism during training camp. Soccer moms do three-day fasts to cleanse mind and body. The word *quantum* is overheard in bustling L.A. coffee shops. Ayahuasca retreats appear in mainstream television shows like Showtime's *Billions*.[2]

But besides the undeniable gift of yoga pants, what makes seeking so captivating?

WHY WE LOVE SEEKING

Most seekers remember their first *hit*.

It is the undeniable moment where the seeker is initiated, flush with a labyrinth of feel-good chemicals arising from insight. Whether found in the middle of a heart-thumping ashtanga yoga session, the dingy basements of Landmark Forum, or reading the Bhagavad Gita—it's the moment truth becomes capitalized with a *big* "T."

Swoosh, the truth smacks us in the face and feels oh so good. These moments are biologically and emotionally stimulating. They leave an imprint.[3] Whether stripping away beliefs or having a vision of one's life go from barely visible to a high-definition movie with a tantalizing soundtrack, these states are potent. We become aware. We see ourselves clearly. We activate the inner hero or heroine. We finally give ourselves permission.

Flush with sublime possibility, we're on top of the world.

And hence, why it's easy to love seeking—we feel clear, alive, grounded. For the first time in months, years, or . . . ever, we go from aimlessly daydreaming to *fully awake*. We receive a life-altering insight. We release the baggage of the past. We allow ourselves to dream once again.

These peak states defined by psychologist Abraham Maslow hurl us into the present.[4] As he described, these states are "rare, exciting, oceanic, deeply moving, exhilarating, elevating experiences that generated an advanced form of perceiving reality and are even mystic and magical in their effects." Not only are they captivating, but it's a fire hose to experience a deep sense of meaning and purpose.[5]

Winner, winner, seaweed salad for dinner.

Besides the neurochemical firestorm, seeking is a direct path to the core ingredients of fulfillment: meaning, understanding who we are and our place in the world, and resolving pain, hurt, and trauma. It puts us back in the driver's seat of our emotions; it tells the inner critic to shut the hell up. We become aware and drop the petulant ego responsible for causing self-sabotage. We are more creative, peaceful, and connected. We see the human-ness in ourselves. We are more compassionate and operate with a little less fear of what other people think.

We are liberated; we are free.

Is it any wonder why we love this stuff?

HOW SEEKING REALLY DRIVES US

All of us are innately wired to search for truth, to seek answers to life's most daunting questions. To open our eyes, hearts, and minds to perspective and wisdom. We have what psychoanalyst Viktor Frankl called a "will to meaning,"[6] which is an insatia-ble desire to answer the following questions:

- ▶ Who am I?
- ▶ Why am I here?
- ▶ What is all of this about?
- ▶ What is the meaning of life?

Seeking, learning, and expanding our knowledge is part of the human condition, embedded in our DNA. Curiosity is rooted in who we are. One only needs to spend an afternoon with a five-year-old nephew and count the 37 times he asks *why* to get this. As Aristotle stated in his seminal work of *Meta-physics*, all humans come with a yearning to know.[7] To know oneself. To know the world we call home. To seek is as part of the human condition as gravity. The unexamined life, or in our terms, a life without seeking—is no life at all.

While we chase the answers to life's biggest questions, we're also all self-absorbed. It's what has kept us alive. Along with the existential questions, we dive inward and ask:

- ▶ What am I here to do?
- ▶ What are my strengths?
- ▶ What makes me happy?
- ▶ What is my purpose?
- ▶ How can I let go of the past?

The fact is seeking unlocks inner wonder, curiosity, and a desire to understand. By quenching this thirst, we experience the same highs from hustle—intense peaks with feelings of peace and freedom, the capture of breath during an aha moment. A synchronicity makes us throw our hands up in the air. A moment of awe leaves us stunned. We experience states of sheer bliss—the rapture of making sense of an insensible world. We transcend the ordinary. We self-actualize. We lose ourselves and then find ourselves like never before.

After experiencing these moments, we never want to let them go. It takes one take-your-breath-away sunrise or sunset. It takes one moment of clarity to make the mundane part of being human worth it for the next week.

Seeking is compelling, fleeting, irresistible.

In these moments our neurochemistry is producing absurd levels of norepinephrine, dopamine, serotonin, anandamide, and endorphins.[8] Alone, these chemicals shift our state; together they hurl us into cosmic bliss. In contrast with our day-to-day, this feeling is invigorating. Researchers of transcendent and religious experiences have found we all come with the "God gene"—identified as VMAT2 by geneticist Dean Hamer, who says it "acts by influencing the brain's capability for various types and forms of consciousness, which become the basis for spiritual experiences."[9]

In other words, we're hardwired to seek.

It's the rush of seeing Earth from space as the little blue marble, experiencing the vastness of the Grand Canyon for the first time, or gazing into a newborn's eyes and being reminded of the miracle of life. Here, all our so-called problems melt away into the ether.

Feeling this once is enough to carry us through the minutiae of our lives, our strung-out commutes and daily melancholy. This is what draws us back to the yoga mat, another go-around at Burning Man, or our daily meditation practice. These experiences give us the sheer hope that we can get back *there*—that state of flow where it *all* makes sense.

The anticipation is all the motivation we need.

But alas, much like hustle, seeking works . . . until it doesn't.

It can be as addictive as hustle. We can find ourselves in a never-ending quest for *more*. Our thirst never quenched—always needing one more hit, one more retreat, one more dose of novelty. We can become reliant on seeking to do *anything*, robbing ourselves of our agency—the psychological term for self-reliant decision-making.[10]

Paradoxically, when we take seeking too far, we can even experience *less* peace than when we started. We can become obese with insights yet have little to show for it. We can have one too many gurus' voices in our heads that confuse instead of inspire.

We can tip the scales of "letting go" to a state of avoidance.

Like all great things when we get seduced by them as a cure-all, we encounter unexpected consequences that do surprising harm. Like hustle, seeking also comes with diminishing returns, when more is not more.

More is less . . . no matter how good your favorite psychic makes you feel.

THE LAW OF DIMINISHING SEEKING

We know seeking is crucial. We recognize it increases our well-being, improves mental sanity, and allows us to take a much-needed time-out from the cult of speed our culture thrives on.

We know it creates the *gap*, that nanosecond between getting cut off in traffic where our primal self wants to oh-so-badly flip the bird, or hell, if you're on the East Coast, the double bird in a blaze of glory. But instead, you inhale, exhale, and choose an evolved response. You remind yourself that you just *never* know what someone is going through. Maybe the dude with the jacked-up Honda Civic needs to get to the hospital to see his ailing mother. *Maybe.*

While seeking is potent, at some point, going deeper into the rabbit hole begins to lose its payoff. Enter the Law of Diminishing Seeking.

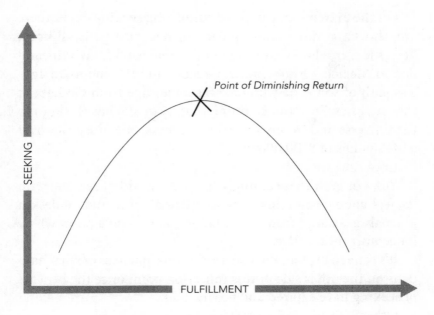

The Law of Diminishing Seeking

Here the right dosing leads to peace, clarity, calm, *and* increased performance, problem solving, and creativity.
Until it doesn't anymore, including:

- ▶ Spending more time analyzing your childhood means you never get full closure.
- ▶ An obsession with breakthrough means there's little integration in the real world.
- ▶ Tripling down on meditation can lead to apathy toward taking action outside of the comfy cushion.
- ▶ Going to another live-your-purpose retreat and hiring your fourth coach can lead to a loss of agency.
- ▶ Being obsessed with living in the present means never setting goals and robbing your creative potential.
- ▶ Getting past the point of diminishing returns can lead to spirituality becoming an avoidance mechanism for emotions crucial to growth.

On the extreme side of the diminishing seeking curve there are shocking downsides—gurus turned sex gods, Bikram Yoga's leader who faced numerous sexual assault lawsuits and fled to Mexico, Osho's cult in Oregon, and the supposed ego-less path of someone who receives a message from God about the end of civilization, claiming that he or she has the keys to the universe and in order to receive access, one must fork over a life savings of $300,000.[11]

Cool story, brah.

Yes, not even the seemingly innocent world of seeking with its feel-good wanderlust vibes, essential oils, and moleskin journals is exempt from being taken too far—to a point where it becomes destructive.

It's time to explore the real-world consequences of what happens on the other side of this inflection point once the benefits of seeking have expired and broken bad.

Otherwise . . .

Chapter

4

The Dark Side
of Seeking

James Arthur Ray was like many self-development gurus—tan, handsome, and charismatic. He'd spent a decade on stages gushing life, business, and spiritual advice to seekers all over the world. But his stages and audience were still small, and his business needed some serious *oomph*.

No one delivers that quite like Oprah—featuring Ray in 2007 to her raving fans.[1] After that, he made a brief appearance in *The Secret*, and shortly after, Ray was destined to be the next big thing in a litany of self-help and seeking gurus.

He was on top of the world.

Ray's business exploded to the point where he declared he'd become the first self-help billionaire. Along the way, he raised his prices as his cachet grew—climaxing in a yearly program called the Wealth Society for a cool $90,000.[2]

He hosted weeklong transformation events in the Red Rocks of Sedona, Arizona—a mecca for those seeking enlightenment—where psychics make an easy six figures and conversations with cashiers include phrases like "soul download" and "the vortex is strong today."

Ray's gatherings were not for the faint of heart, only for the most committed of seekers. As his notoriety grew, he dialed up the intensity: the quests now involved days of fasting, minimal water, and head-shaving climaxing in a makeshift sweat lodge—a form of heat-induced therapy—to cement the experience.

In 2015 and on the last day of one of these quests, his physically and emotionally drained followers drummed up the mental courage to enter the 200-degree hut as Ray coached them up: "It's going to feel like you're going to die; but you're not—a part of you will be let go of."[3]

Less than two hours later, his advice was spot-on: it felt like they were going to die, because, well . . . they did. Two attendees suffocated inside the tent with a third being airlifted to a local hospital, where she too would lose her life during the next nine days.[4]

When authorities came to question Ray, who fled the scene—they found a note on his hotel room door saying he was unavailable . . . and meditating. Finally, Ray was charged and convicted of manslaughter and sent to prison for two years; he is now pitching his comeback.

Say hello to seeking's dark side—where the pursuit of changing one's life or helping others do so becomes enmeshed with power, greed, and endless upsells with the promise of having all the answers.

Unfortunately, Ray's story is all too common.

Those who consume the material with good intent—the desire to improve their lives—can easily turn a healthy pursuit into a full-blown obsession. Slowly, they can become dependent on the material, the guru on stage, until they feel *less* peace, *less* clarity, and *less* agency.

The consequences of seeking include:

1. Seeking is used to bypass reality.
2. Everything is inside, so why bother?
3. Enlightenment solves all of life's problems.
4. Your ego is smaller than everyone else's.
5. One accumulates insights with no endgame.
6. You're out of alignment with yourself.
7. Seeking turns into taking spiritual selfies.

Let's examine and deconstruct these consequences once and for all.

1. SEEKING IS USED TO BYPASS REALITY

To grasp the core consequence of seeking, we'll tap into the greatest-selling, commercially available asset seekers have—a little documentary that changed it all.

The Secret came out in 1997 and became a blockbuster spawning millionaires and careers that reached various worlds,[5] including spirituality, performance, and celebrity—with stay-at-home mothers obsessing over every word and driven alpha males peering through the material (but ripping the cover off so as not to be seen holding a book with the words *law of attraction,* so help them, bro)—wondering what the craze was about.

This material had been shared before, so why the atomic success?

Even those involved were blindsided. Media outlets rushed to interview the stars; producer Rhonda Byrne grossed a cool $300 million.[6] And it's still going strong, with the latest iteration, released in 2020, becoming another *New York Times* bestseller.[7]

In retrospect, it's easy to understand its rousing success. This is what the masses want to hear: you don't need to work hard; you actually don't need to work at all. Making millions is easy. Building an empire is effortless, getting the fresh Lamborghini means I don't even have to take a shower.

It's *alllllllll* energetics, baby!

We live in a universe of energy and when we tap into it, anything is possible. I can get anything I want . . . in the same place I watch Netflix. Better yet, I can get everything I want *while* watching Netflix.

Of course, this didn't quite work out.

Because *The Secret* is the most plastic, digestible, and Westernized version of seeking available—which is precisely why the book has sold 30 million copies.[8] If there was a hint that making your vision come to life had any sense of messy effort, courageous action, rejection, getting doors slammed on you, clients ghosting invoices, social media trolls, taking out loans, or counting every last dollar to make rent, well, everyone would have run for the hills. And so, they chose not to include that part.

Ignorance is bliss, eh?

And therein lies this consequence—using spirituality to bypass reality. It can be a way to dodge squaring off with the messy emotions of being human under the guise of "everything is positive" and skipping key steps for emotional resilience to arrive at a faux reframe of "this is the best thing that ever happened to me." It can lead to an overly detached, aloof state where one is out of touch and dissociated. It can dishonor the very principles it boasts about.

It can lead to an even *bigger* ego than when one started.

Ultimately, it can lead to a term created by John Welwood, a clinical psychologist, who introduced "spiritual bypassing," defining it in an interview:

> Spiritual bypassing is a term I coined to describe a process I saw happening in the Buddhist community I was in, and also in myself. Although most of us were sincerely trying to work on ourselves, I noticed a widespread tendency to use spiritual ideas and practices to sidestep or avoid facing unresolved emotional issues, psychological wounds, and unfinished developmental tasks.[9]

Bypassing reality through seeking comes in all shapes and sizes and is more common than we tend to believe, including:

- ▶ Using spirituality as a distraction and avoidance
- ▶ Escaping under the guise of "inner growth" and space
- ▶ Avoiding "negative" emotions such as anger and sadness
- ▶ Exuding a form of toxic positivity to the point of delusion
- ▶ Blaming one's life on past lives, psychics, and horoscopes

Anyone who's tapped into seeking has seen this firsthand, and yet, we tend to gloss over it because seeking is supposed to be a pursuit chock-full of healthy virtues. But then intuition turns to delusion, pattern recognition to wild conspiracies, openness to gullibility.

It's hard to discern seeking's dark side, because, well, it's not as obvious as partnering with your cousin and cooking meth. And most people come into it with the *best* of intentions—to learn, grow, and heal. But those intentions can lead to the dark, often unexpressed corners of the seeking world that are meditated away.

Which leads us to the second consequence—the belief that everything we'll ever need is already inside of us.

2. EVERYTHING IS INSIDE, SO WHY BOTHER?

Seekers believe, to some degree, that at any given moment we have everything we'll ever need inside of us. We have the answers, cheat codes to life, and access to an unlimited buffet of experiences—so why bother going out into the "real" world?

Game over, finito, we've got it all!

We don't have to pursue goals. We don't need to advance our career. We don't need money. We don't need to imagine our future selves because, well, the future self is an illusion.

We sure as hell don't need to strive.

Although the premise can be sound and turn us inward in a world obsessed outwardly, its application can be abysmal. It can lead to apathy toward life. It can lead to avoiding the pursuit of a craft, acquiring skills, and making meaningful progress toward a vision or calling.

And yet humans are hardwired to be future-oriented, to imagine, to set goals.[10] Our brains are created for this very act—to believe what is inside is enough is to shut down a core driver of what makes us feel alive. As psychologist Robert Emmons found, putting effort toward striving boosts mood, happiness, joy, and life satisfaction, noting "goal-striving is vital to the good life."[11]

But if we already have everything inside of us—why the hell bother?

This belief can lead to a quiet resignation masked as inner work as we let ourselves off the hook. We don't integrate the principles we've learned. We become the holed-up yogi in the Himalayan ashram with no one else around.

We're enlightened, but to what end?

We don't start the business we dreamed of. We don't make the bold offer to an investor. We don't post the content on social media. Instead, when this belief goes haywire—we avoid putting ourselves out there under the guise of more seeking. We miss out on integration: the art of merging our internal and external worlds.

As psychologist Abraham Maslow repeated, and was frustrated by, self-actualization is hard-ass work. In fact, to get to that state of flow, those timeless moments of "effortless effort" require, well . . . a ton of effort. He said this about his students:

> They all seem to wait passively for it to happen without any effort on their part. It is hard work . . . it involves a calling to service from the external day-to-day world, not *only* a yearning from within.[12]

Sure, we may have the raw ingredients inside of us, but they're still raw. They need to be brought into the world and cooked, baked, or sautéed—take your pick. Otherwise, we never scratch our potential. Our raw material stays uncooked and waiting for the sucker who sits down to eat the dish only to have their head inside the porcelain bowl for the next eight hours, praying to the digestive gods for a lifeline.

(I've been that guy more times than I can count.)

And often, if this person does the work, it is done under the following incentive: there is a mythical place of enlightenment where all worries, problems, and human-ridden anxieties are gone for good.

We can put our feet up; our work is done here.

3. ENLIGHTENMENT SOLVES ALL OF LIFE'S PROBLEMS

Call it the oasis, enlightenment, oneness, or sheer nirvana. The belief of spiritual arrival, of permanent transcendence, comes with an undercurrent that one day we won't have to do the "work" of daily life. We won't need to square off with toil and lowly chores, the messiness and emotional tension of human existence.

We will be free.

Free from the shackles of the ordinary, perched on a spiritual penthouse sipping a kale cocktail with others who also have reached this blissful state. We relinquish the backbreaking work of being a human in the 21st century.

While Westernized seekers spit up their kombucha at the mention of discipline and rules, they're conveniently forgetting something—their Eastern colleagues in ashrams, yoga studios, and monasteries infuse *high* amounts of discipline into spiritual work. They wake before sunrise, do tedious chores, and have full days before they head back to their slumber. In other words, one could say, they . . . hustle.

Because they know better.

By avoiding, detaching, or meditating away from the work, seekers miss out on a core chunk of what makes us thrive, according to the pioneer of flow states, Mihaly

Csikszentmihalyi: "A person who has achieved control over psychic energy and has invested it in consciously chosen goals cannot help but grow into a more complex being. By stretching skills, by reaching toward higher challenges, such a person becomes an increasingly extraordinary individual."[13]

Even those who fundamentally know the work never ends can still be driven by the sheer hope that it *may* be true. But true enlightenment is not about avoiding the work, the chopping of wood and the carrying of water. As the old Zen Kōan adage goes: "Before enlightenment; chop wood, carry water. After enlightenment; chop wood, carry water."[14]

In other words, the oasis is a mythical fiction we construct in our minds as we read the Bhagavat Gita and see ourselves in Arjuna's naïveté. You recognize it doesn't exist; you won't be pounding tequila shots with Deepak anytime soon. Or rather, you might, but you'll still have to deal with a vile hangover. Tequila is *still* tequila even if one's chakras are on fleek.

Your problems and collective issues won't end.

Instead, so-called enlightenment is not the avoidance of reality; rather, it is a sheer and devout willingness to accept it fully, to find purpose in the mundane, thrill in the routine, and presence in the tedious.

Otherwise, this belief can hurl one into some spiritual upper class where the ego runs rampant by the very tools designed to quiet it.

4. YOUR EGO IS SMALLER THAN EVERYONE ELSE'S

One of the unspoken consequences of seeking is paradoxical: in the pursuit of minimizing your ego, it can take on a *stronger* grip. Sounds crazy, right? It's like that annoying birthday candle that gets stronger every time you blow on it. I hated those when I was seven. I've been waiting for cake all day, and now this?

Damn you, adults.

You've likely seen the person who has an awakening and lives on a soapbox of judgment toward anyone who hasn't "woken" up. Like James Arthur Ray, it produces gurus, cults, unethical leaders, and dangerous hierarchies of unlimited influence. It makes the yoga practice a place to compare oneself. My teacher studied in India with *this* guru. I have a *real* meditation practice . . . with an altar.

Instead of uniting, it separates, divides, and pushes away.

In minimizing the ego, it can take on a life of its own, turning what was a grounded practice into judging others who might not be on the same "level." This happens when seeking is taken too far, and the original principles (hey, what happened to, you know, compassion, empathy, and all that stuff you preach?) are forgotten on the side of the road.

Left unchecked, too much seeking can leave you with a general feeling that your ego is smaller than everyone else's. Because of that, it makes you *better* than them. What was originally designed to kill the ego, breathes life into it.

I told you the ego was sick.

And because the ego loves the status quo, it can lead to an addiction to break through with little to no integration.

In other words, playing spiritual video games.

5. ONE ACCUMULATES INSIGHTS WITH NO ENDGAME

I was full to the brim; punched in the face with knowledge and whiplashed by wisdom. If Eckhart Tolle and Gabrielle Bernstein had cocreated, I was their living embodiment.

We'd spent seven dawn-to-dusk days in Houston crammed into a conference room in the world of seeking. We solidified our life purpose and connected to universal truths. Fourteen-hour days with minimal breaks meant an influx of breakthrough.

During lunch the last day, a few of us left the hotel for a much-needed change of scenery. We engaged in small talk and reviewed takeaways. Then someone asked me, "What's *next* for you, Tommy?" I couldn't imagine a "what's next" besides taking the next six months to integrate the firehose of knowledge we'd been exposed to . . . and a nine-hour nap.

Then everyone shared.

I was stunned. They detailed flights to more retreats in Austin, Santa Monica, and Bali during the holidays. Their calendars were crammed with more seminars and vision quests. They'd see this teacher, that speaker, this famous leader. They traded itineraries, discount codes, and YouTube handles.

And that's when it hit me: seeking can be addictive.

It can have an escapist quality, like a socially accepted version of watching the Kardashians while on the couch crushing a pint of Rocky Road. Because clarity is oh so intoxicating, one bite *isn't* enough. The more one experiences possibility . . . the more one wants to get back into that state. And naturally, because this state is about potential and possibility (instead of what comes after, like *real* work), it can feel amazing. But, this cycle has no end in sight.

Often, seekers chase the next hit before they've integrated the material they just discovered into their lives, careers, and relationships.

What is integration? It's the daily work of taking your insight and turning it into something: a practice, a routine, a way to not simply achieve clarity, but you know, really live it, become it. To embody it.

Breakthrough, then, isn't the destination, it's the starting line. The aha moment isn't the end, it's when you roll up your sleeves. After that comes the work. The real work. The messy work. The uncomfortable work.

Ultimately, the work that will not only honor your clarity— but change who you are in your day-to-day. Otherwise, you'll talk a big game as you quote sages and mystics . . . yet have nothing to show for it.

6. YOU'RE OUT OF ALIGNMENT WITH YOURSELF

We've all met someone who has the advice on how to live an optimized life—regurgitating principles and one-liners—with whom we'd never trade places. They wax poetic about vision, but their words carry as much weight as papier-mâché.

Why? Because, well, they shower every other day, live in their parents' basement, and play Call of Duty nine hours a day.

And they're 39 years old.

Enter being out of alignment—a disconnect between who someone says they are and who they *really* are. Alignment is a consistent thread through a person's thoughts, words, actions, and choices.

We all know what alignment feels like. It's a palpable, attractive energy because it's rare in a world where people present a picturesque life in public yet are living an entirely different one in secret.

An overemphasis on seeking leads to an excess of insight with little action in the *real* world. It can give us the illusion that we're making progress when we swipe our credit card for the live-your-dharma digital course that remains unused. Because of this, we can find ourselves chock-full of insights, platitudes, and curated social media posts, but not *living* the principles.

Due to this, you don't change the habit and endure the messiness of change because you're flying on clouds of bliss. You don't take hard looks in the mirror at why nothing is changing. You're high on your own supply, that you know better, which makes you feel like you *are* better. And so, you don't, you know, actually do the work.

At the end of the day, it's simple hypocrisy: preaching one thing and then doing another—like the person who takes selfies while meditating, but then doesn't . . . *actually* meditate.

Ultimately, it can lead to unhealthy self-absorption.

7. SEEKING TURNS INTO TAKING SPIRITUAL SELFIES

The pursuit of seeking is an inward game.

As such, seekers tend to fixate on how they're feeling at any moment, their past and their emotions. We've covered the value of this in an external world, with immense benefit. The inner game is no doubt an asset for growth.

Until it's not.

We can invest *too much* attention in ourselves. We blur the lines between introspection and borderline neurotic self-examination. We enter an infinite loop of self-rumination—what researchers call overanalyzing—that makes us the center of the world.[15]

This can lead to justifying erratic, selfish behavior.

This is the seeker who shuts off the entire world so as to embark on a quest of self-discovery to the consequence of eroded relationships. It's the person who cuts everyone out of their life who isn't "aligned." It's those who lack empathy and compassion because their seeking has become about them . . . and *only* them.

This is the equivalent of taking spiritual selfies all day.

When this happens, one becomes consumed about a quest to actualization and sees everything as a pesky roadblock. It turns the once-beautiful pursuit of self-discovery into selfish, unbridled narcissism.

Yeah, no thanks.

THE CARDINAL MYTH: PICK ONE OR THE OTHER

Each side believes it has all the answers.

Hustlers gather in conference rooms and coworking spaces, making grand plans for world domination using their tools of choice: whiteboards, dry-erase markers, flip charts, and high-energy EDM to create a repetitive soundtrack acting as the pulse to fuel their relentless drive.

Seekers gather in similar rooms, but they've ditched the chairs to sit cross-legged in lotus position. The tools of choice are a meditation table, ambient music, Buddha ink, and obligatory bear hugs upon meeting strangers. They hold eye contact past the second it starts to get uncomfortable.

As they stay separated, they tune one another out.

What each group fails to realize is they're in neighboring rooms, next to one another, ultimately chasing the same things. They remain divided by context, but *not* desire.

Separated by aesthetic, but not objectives.

Worst of all, instead of learning from one another in a way that benefits all, they stay *disconnected*. Where the hustlers could use seeking to overcome stubborn plateaus, invite new perspective, or, you know, take a damn day off—the seekers could use hustle to turn insight into action, and ideas into tangible growth.

But they don't.

And the reason is simple: they're believing the cardinal myth—that they must pick one or the other.

Chapter

5

The Cardinal Myth:
You Must Pick
One or the Other

Will you be a hustler, or will you be a seeker?

(Drumroll.)

This moment of reckoning means you'll have to pick one side, one team, one way of acting, being, and doing—but you can't pick both. Binary. Black *or* white. Chocolate *or* peanut butter. Don't worry: only your life, future, performance, and fulfillment rest on the weight of this decision. And the clock's ticking . . . you better make your pick.

Now.

Since both sides give the illusion of separation, that they're fundamentally different from each other and are headed to unique destinations, it's easy to fall for this. Add in social dynamics where hustlers tend to hang with other hustlers, and seekers congregate with seekers, we can all believe it *has* to be one or the other.

This attitude permeates the conventions of performance and mindfulness. Pick a team. Once you have, there are rules, ways of operating, even a laundry list of cool lingo—subtle tells to let others know you're part of the tribe. You'll be initiated, see one another in the real world, and know what team you're on. It'll take only a head nod to know you are one of the same.

On one hand, you'll be referred to as someone who *gets* it, who crushes the game, a beast, a boss babe, a grinder, the CEO of You, Inc., committed AF. On the other, you'll be a free spirit, a sage, conscious, aligned, woke, connected, and oh so deep. But do you *really* have to pick? What if this was the cardinal myth, a fallacy stripping you of reaping the benefits of each?

It is.

This myth runs rampant while robbing both sides equally—the hustlers from tapping into their fullest creativity and emotional sanity as they pursue goals, and the seekers from using their internal quest to make the imagined real. Ultimately, it means you miss out on half of this experience of life.

Which isn't quite living at all.

PICKING ONE OR THE OTHER MEANS MISSING OUT

Picking one side or the other is like those personality tests we take on social media that frame us into a box—and we always fulfill who we believe ourselves to be and whom the world believes we are.[1] Even if you loosely put yourself on a particular side, the other world becomes largely inaccessible to you.

If you seek as a hustler, you're itching for the meditation to end so you can plug back in. Everything is about performance, a desperate need for your three-minute meditation to turn into a successful sales pitch.

If you hustle as a seeker, you can't wait to get back into a state of being with a three-hour recharge after a little work. It's all about your emotional state, vibes, and feels. Leaning into self-doubt and facing rejection can feel uncomfortable, so you return to the mat.

As you experiment, you skim the surface and wonder why it's not "working."

Because of this, you miss out on the power of contrast—plunged into new ways of thinking, doing, and being to create perspective that can't be found when everything is the same. Contrast is valuable: we need to feel pain to feel bliss; we need to *miss* someone to feel connected; we need a rainstorm in Phoenix to escape the 110-degree temperatures.

Missing out on half of life isn't quite living at all.

You're denying a part of yourself: the inner do-er *and* be-er. Believing the cardinal myth that you can't have both comes with dire consequences, including:

▶ **You miss out on half of your fulfillment.** Fulfillment comes from two places: doing meaningful work you care about as well as inner work from seeking.[2] By picking one side, you're barely able to scratch the surface of this duality.

▶ **You miss out on half of your results.** Progress in your business, career, and finances comes from the work. But seeking is a breeding ground for creativity, innovation, and new levels of performance. By picking one side, you stay rigid in one world and miss out on personal and professional progress.

▶ **You miss out on half of the emotional spectrum.** Peak states, as we've discussed, include presence, flow, clarity, and boundless joy. They make life worth living and create lasting meaning.[3] By picking one side, you have only one sandbox to play in—thus, missing out on a litany of powerful emotions from the other when these worlds come together.

▶ **You miss out on the power of novelty.** Contrast and novelty are crucial ingredients to create meaning, accelerate learning, and embody life lessons.[4] Without them, it's easy to feel stuck in the same feedback loop of life and feeling like nothing ever changes, and if it does . . . it doesn't last.

▶ **You miss out on life-altering perspective.** Perspective is seeing the familiar with new eyes, breaking rigid patterns. By picking a side, you stay *stuck* at the same level of thinking and hence, reduce the ability to see a problem through a new lens that encourages solutions, empathy, and compassion.

▶ **You miss out on unparalleled creativity.** Creativity knows no bounds; you can be creative as an artist or an accountant. Nothing we do comes without creativity and by picking one side, you rob yourself of your ability to bring new ideas and ways of thinking together.

▶ **You miss out on powerful relationships.** Hustlers hang with hustlers; seekers are surrounded by seekers. By staying compartmentalized, you miss out on powerful connections that allow for novelty, perspective, and not living in an echo chamber of the same ideas.

Let me be blunt: by seeking, you get better results in your performance, and by hustling, you can lead a deeper, more integrated spiritual life.

We need this contrast. We need the perspective that each side offers. We need to allow ourselves to miss a part of our lives, to come back reengaged. We need an ebb; we need a flow. The yin and the yang, the masculine and feminine, the sky and the dirt, the alpha and omega.

Otherwise, we turn rigid.

We close off, cementing our psyches with one way of operating; it becomes our crutch. On a long enough timeline, we find ourselves entrenched on either side, both stuck and blind:

▶ **Blind to ways of thinking.** Stuck in one world, we get trapped in what researchers call rumination, an endless pattern of the same thoughts.[5]

▶ **Blind to ways of operating.** If our thinking is stuck, our actions can turn into predictable patterns, leading to the same frustrating outcomes . . . even if we know better.

▶ **Blind to ways of responding.** We all deal with stress, challenge, and emotional triggers, yet can find ourselves responding on autopilot due to rigid neural patterns that lead to habitual actions.[6]

► **Blind to the ego.** A "quiet ego" is essential for a thriving life, according to social psychologist Heidi Wayment, who coined the term.[7] By picking one side, we are likely to let the ego's unhealthy mechanisms take over.

► **Blind to groupthink.** By picking one side, we become rooted in groupthink and miss out on putting ourselves in rooms with people who aren't exactly like us.

This endgame leaves us stuck reliving the past, anxious about a hazy future, or running into the same obstacles ad nauseam. Whether it's the exhaustion of endless striving or becoming codependent on seeking, picking a side leads to an emotional void. As we burden one side for *all* the answers and don't find what we're looking for, it leads us to think peace and clarity are ultimately unattainable.

And it's all *our* fault.

With this in mind, do you really want to pick one side—and what might you be costing yourself if you do so? Because the ultimate consequence is a one-way ticket to the frustrating, mind-bending land of self-sabotage.

HELLO, SELF-SABOTAGE

Tell hustlers to take a day off and do nothing: no agenda, email, or crushing content—and they'll freak. Sure, they may be able to tolerate a small dose, but as time passes, guilt consumes them. They haven't checked email in hours. Like an addict missing their hit, the tension builds until it becomes unbearable. They can't think straight, they're physically there but mentally checked out, consumed by the thought of—what could possibly be waiting inside their inbox!?!?

This gnawing feeling takes them into some fantasy land of worst- and best-case scenarios—either the business is tanking, or they missed an invitation to hang with Richard Branson at Necker Island.

In a bizarre twist, you recognize the reason they're striving to make money is the idea that money buys freedom and options, and more specifically—time freedom and lifestyle options. And yet, hustlers can't spend a few hours unplugged?

Sounds like they've got it twisted.

The seekers have the same problem flipped on its head: when they're not immersed in space, they feel off. They won't say it's guilt—*that's a low-frequency state, man!*—but when given a chance to step into the arena of their lives and careers to create something tangible, they feel lost. They create roadblocks that don't exist, referring to the "inner work" or "healing" the past. They blame their lethargy on horoscopes, psychics, bad juju. Every choice must be "tapped into" through meditation at best, or—robbed of their agency—they have to wait until their guru comes back from India to move forward.

And he's unreachable for three months.

Self-sabotage is self-sabotage no matter how many literary passes a Hallmark card writer gives it to make it sound palatable. Each side has its way of creating it—a natural consequence of the cardinal myth. By denying a side of you that is inherent to all of us, self-sabotage runs wild and becomes a pattern. For example:

- ▶ It's the accountant who worked his face off for the European vacation but can't enjoy it because he's dying to get back to the office.
- ▶ It's the entrepreneur who stops her meditation at the three-minute mark because she's worried about losing her "edge."
- ▶ It's the conscious free spirit who never finishes anything, and has a pile of half-done projects that never arrive at completion.
- ▶ It's the seeker who starts four businesses and who pivots into a new one every few weeks, in a constant quest for clarity.
- ▶ It's the grinder who feels agitated and stressed on Sunday mornings after being unplugged for two hours.

What each of these exaggerated, yet relatable examples reveal is self-sabotage in action. Neither the grinders nor seekers recognize what's on the *other* side waiting for them:

▶ By enjoying the moment, the accountant rekindles the passion and presence of the early years with his significant other.

▶ By staying with the meditation, the entrepreneur receives a creative insight to a challenge that'd been causing tension.

▶ By committing to finishing, the conscious free spirit sees manifestation in real time, from idea to tangible product.

▶ By making a decision and having the courage to pick *one* endeavor, the seeker feels enraptured by progress and results.

▶ By unplugging every Sunday, the grinder spends quality time with family and comes back to work excited and energized.

This is the power of not falling under the spell of the cardinal myth.

You release the rigidness of identity. Sure, at times, you'll need to double down and get focused as you embody your inner hustler. At others, you'll need to detach and fully let go to the present moment and "be" for a while. Furthermore, you break free from your current state, knowing that what got you *here* . . . will most certainly not get you *there*.

By doing so, you avoid the inherent consequences of staying imprisoned by one side; and you recognize the truth.

You are not a hustler and you are not a seeker.

You simply are.

YOU ARE NOT A HUSTLER OR A SEEKER—YOU ARE

You are multiple, limitless identities that can be chosen at any time.

Dependent on context, your identity is flexible.[8] We treat identity as an inelastic truth, like dried concrete that can no longer be shifted. We take personality tests and label ourselves introverts, extroverts, creative, logical.

We don't realize *we* created those labels. And often, those labels become prison cells with us locked inside not knowing the key was left hanging on the door, waiting to be opened. We can mix identities as needed and take on countless roles. Mothers, fathers, employees, leaders, business owners, creatives, those who seek adventure, and those who think gluten-free pizza on a Saturday night constitutes a cheat meal. (Yes, that's me.)

We need identities to move about the world, but we often get stuck on a prevailing identity that holds us hostage. We spend our time and energy there. We get lauded publicly as our ego holds on. Since identity drives the bus on our thoughts, words, and actions—we are in a constant state of reaffirmation.

As time passes, we become rooted into an identity that may have served us in the past but is now a roadblock. This mechanism, which I'll refer to as the Identity Loop, is shown below.

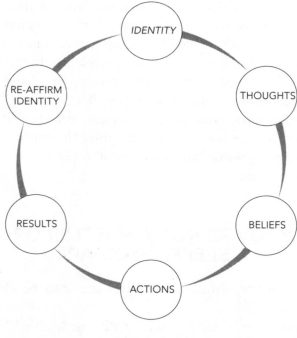

Identity Loop

To illustrate this, imagine two people stuck in their careers. They both want to expand, make more money, and grow . . . but they're on a plateau. Nothing is changing. One of them operates as a bona fide hustler (identity), which creates that person's thoughts while he or she is stuck. This person believes in grinding it out and *doing* more (thoughts), telling himself or herself "hard work is the answer" (belief), adding more time, energy, and effort. This person puts in a 76-hour workweek (action) to create a result, or lack thereof. This cycle repeats itself—even if the result doesn't come to life. He or she is caught in the same identity loop, with nothing changing and *still* repeating the same patterns.

Now, consider the second person who has the same problem, but who has a flexible identity. This person has different thoughts, including, "If what I'm doing isn't working, at least I have data" or "Nothing changes . . . if nothing changes." These thoughts create a belief—what got me here won't get me *there*. Because of this, this person is open to change. He or she sets strict boundaries at work and starts to tap into activities that increase fulfillment, insight, and creativity (action)—which end with a new result (an idea for a side hustle or career move).

With these two people, you see that unless the pattern is broken, the loop can become a self-contained prison of pounding one's head against the wall while nothing changes.

Because you cannot outrun, outgun, or outhustle identity.

This is why a lifelong seeker who chooses to make a dent on a dream must drop the cardinal myth—or face feeling uncomfortable with the sting of rejection. And someone who embodies the identity of a hustler will barely scratch the surface on seeking—unless that person is open to a new identity and drops the title of hustler alone. Why? Because identity will stay loyal to the golden rule: we will always revert back to who we *believe* ourselves to be.

However, who we believe ourselves to be is not rigid, it is a choice.

It can be changed on demand. You can shape shift your way in and out of various identities for varying contexts, at different times.

You can choose your own adventure.

CHOOSE YOUR OWN ADVENTURE

Selective identity is the ability to adopt an identity to serve you for a moment, an hour, a day, a week, or a season. When you do, you become that person *fully*, but as real as it is when you're in it, you can also eject.

It's like being nine years old and changing the cartridges of your video game to enter a brand-new world. Inside each game, you're a different person. The quest of Zelda, the charisma of Mario, the stealth of 007. Selective identity is the ability to embody an identity to serve you at any moment:

- ▶ In one moment, you may need to stop messing around and adopt the identity of a hustler, a do-er, someone who is disciplined and doesn't choose feelings over commitments. A person who follows through on one's word regardless of thoughts, feelings, circumstances, moods, the weather, or what Cardi B said on Twitter yesterday. *Action, action, action.*

- ▶ In another moment, you may need to take a break when you're riding high and adopt the identity of a seeker, a be-er, who knows any high brings a comedown. A person who understands one's emotions, who chooses to recover wisely so as to adapt faster, to unplug for a creative breakthrough, or to rekindle the energy of a first date in a marriage. *Space, space, space.*

Using selective identity is a skill.

This skill allows you to step into the right role, at the right time, for the right reasons. And, this skill is one we can learn how to use right now.

THE RUBBER BAND EFFECT

Consider your identity, right now, to be a rubber band at rest. It is relaxed and at ease and has minimal tension.

Imagine you are someone who values security and does not crave risk-taking. Out of the blue, your friend calls and asks if you want to go skydiving. For some reason, you agree. You recently went through a breakup and say *why the hell not*. You're in a season where you don't even know yourself, so you say f*ck it.

Every part of the skydiving process starts to stretch the rubber band of your identity:

You are *not* someone who says yes to danger.

You are *not* someone who skydives on a Wednesday.

You are *not* someone who jumps out of a moving plane.

You are *not* someone who straps themselves to Big Eddie who can't stop making parachute jokes with the pilot wearing a hand-me-down Metallica T-shirt.

As these behaviors, choices, and decisions stack up, the tension in the rubber band increases. It escalates so much that at some point, it gets to the place of overload. At this point, you're on the verge of breaking through to a new identity, but you're also most likely to *snap back* to your original state. (And sometimes, revert further back than when you started—see broke AF lottery winners; *Biggest Loser* winners who ballooned back to their original weight and then some; rags-to-riches stories who couldn't handle the riches, so they blew it all on Miami real estate Ponzi schemes.)

On the edge of a new identity, you're at the breeding ground for erratic behavior. You're most vulnerable and your old identity is fighting like hell. It'll make up false narratives to keep you where you are.

Knowing that this process happens every time you step outside of your current identity means you are equipped with the insight that the place of highest tension is the most emotionally challenging. You can either retreat to the safe harbor of your comfort zone or you can . . . jump.

By the time the plane is in the air, and your tandem skydiver is making jokes on packing the chute while scrolling social, it's too late. You've snapped the rubber band and are flying at 13,000 feet. The ego has no place to stand anymore.

Say hello to your new identity.

Selective identity is the freedom to embody varying identities as you traverse life. It's in this place that you're able to merge hustling and seeking—both mindsets, ways of looking at the world, and tactics—as needed. You can live in the present *and* be inspired by tomorrow's horizon. You can set goals *and* detach. You can knock 'em cold during a sales meeting, but not rely on the result to feel good.

By doing so, you develop insurance against the ego's pattern of clinging to one identity and staying stuck. Instead, you become more open to new experiences, harness the benefit of novelty, and surprise yourself. This "openness to experience" is a key psychological trait associated with well-being leading to less anxiety and overthinking.[9]

Ultimately, it allows you to eat your cake and have it too.

THE BEST OF BOTH WORLDS

With a random day off and nothing on your plate, do you dive into your passion project or take a three-hour hike with the dogs? Selective identify means dealer's choice—whether hustling or seeking, you know exactly what you need.

In other words, you can eat your cake and have it too.

All of it.

You can start your morning as a seeker, go deep into hustle mode, and then come back to the surface and be a seeker again. You can execute like hell and crush a deadline, but while others stay back at the office for another three hours, you eject. You understand both the Law of Diminishing Hustle and the Law of Diminishing Seeking. You leave your work at work, and your home life at home.

True freedom.

As you learned in the Introduction, some seasons of life will require varying degrees of both sides—a big career push may require 70 percent hustle and 30 percent seeking. A season of focusing on family or your inner world may mean you'll seek 80 percent of the time and then hustle with the leftover 20 percent.

The point is, at any given time, you will be dosing both to fuel each other.

Your time spent recovering and creating perspective during seeking is what gets you reinvigorated to tackle a new challenge at work. Your time spent taking action and completing your commitments helps you deepen the concept of cocreation and integrate your insights with seeking.

With the right intention, focus, and discipline to see both sides through—you reap the best of both worlds. You will step into places you'd never imagined, those that fuel your fulfillment and performance, including:

- ► Mastery
- ► Flow states
- ► Creativity
- ► Fulfillment
- ► Performance
- ► Connection
- ► Emotional freedom
- ► Autonomy
- ► Meaning

All of these represent a thriving life.

As you merge these worlds, you'll notice the barricades that once separated both dissolve. You'll have a seeking breakthrough and apply it to your career. You'll have a hustling breakthrough and apply it to your relationships.

Life becomes a 360-degree learning experience.

By merging these, you create transcendence—the ability to rise above the small-level thinking that separates these parts of yourself and ultimately, solve the paradox by understanding it through lived experience.

Instead, you are integrated, aligned, whole.

Ultimately, you become a hustler *and* a seeker.

PART II

The Principles

It's time to turn our attention to bridging the two seemingly separate worlds of hustling and seeking. This paradox, the dichotomy that each brings to the table, only intensifies their truth and application.

Each principle takes what was once a separate concept and merges it with this new realm of hustling *and* seeking. You'll discover how to extract the best of what each offers and its complementary opposite. By bringing them together, you create a benefit that would never come to life from only one side.

We'll flesh out the concept, mental framework, and tactical application for your life, career, or business. You'll understand why both matter and how to put them into practice.

HUSTLING	SWEET SPOT	SEEKING
Ambition	Thriving	Alignment
Declaration	Resilience	Tests
Relentless Action	Momentum	Celebration
Structure	Consistency	Novelty
Focus	Awareness	Perspective
Be Decisive	Clarity	Hone Intuition
Constraint	Innovation	Creativity
Compete	Confidence	Detach
Urgency	Faith	Divine Timing
Mentorship	Agency	Be Your Own Guru
Leave Comfort Zone	Adaptation	Recover Wisely
Priorities	Emotional Freedom	White Space
Grit	Appreciation	Gratitude
Show Up	Connection	Be Unavailable
Build Identity	Mastery	Slay Ego

The Sweet Spot of Hustling & Seeking

I've connected 16 complementary pairs for you, one from each side of the spectrum, to show how to go all in on hustle while also going all out in seeking. Then, I tell you what to leave behind with each side's conventional wisdom.

Each principle can stand on its own and can be read in any order, although it's best to read them as is. Consider this a blueprint, a primer, for you to bring to life as you move forward with a new way of doing and being.

When you do this right, you become a do-er *and* a be-er, a warrior *and* a sage, obsessive *and* detached, ambitious *and* aligned—you tap into the best of both worlds. Ultimately, it will become second nature.

Let's dive in.

Chapter

6

Ambition
&
Alignment

Elizabeth Holmes was Silicon Valley's rising star, the home-coming queen everyone wanted a piece of. Her fascination with being the next Steve Jobs ran so deep she even *dressed* like Jobs in a classic, black turtleneck. Adorning magazine covers as a revolutionary, she paraded across the event circuit hailed as the next iconic entrepreneur. She had a legion of fans hanging on her every word; a Rolodex of cultural titans anyone would foam at the mouth for.

In other words, she was on a rocket ship to success.

She couldn't—and would never—be stopped. Her company, Theranos, was a disruptive start-up destined to take over the world of pharmaceutical lab testing.[1]

The company had cracked the code on a breathtaking technology to allows any patient at any time to take hundreds of blood tests ... from a couch at home. Holmes poached the world's best in various fields, drumming up hundreds of millions of dollars in outside investment.

Except for one slight problem.

Her technology *didn't* work. It couldn't pull off the tests, and when it did, the accuracy was abysmal.[2] In fact, when she'd sign up real-life patients whose medical future depended on the tests—she used her competition's labs to provide results.[3] To be clear, that's like promising a Wagyu steak—and then storming off to the local drive-through and serving up a fast-food burger.

On stunning plates and utensils, of course.

In a classic case of cognitive dissonance—when beliefs and reality clash[4]—Holmes dug her heels in at every challenge. She'd berate her team as employees raised concerns about test validity. She stifled parts of the business meant to collaborate and had them work in silos. People were canned for asking basic questions. The company skirted regulation, journalists, and investors who brought up routine concerns, and evaded skeptics until there was all but one left.

And then it all came crashing down.

Holmes's unrestrained ambition plunged Theranos from being Silicon Valley's sweetheart with a $9 billion valuation to worthless and facing a litany of lawsuits.[5] The end result is a textbook case of ambition gone haywire. Belief turns into delusion. Confidence to narcissism. Sheltered by one's echo chamber, the only option is to double down. Because of this negligence, countless investors, employees, and family members paid a hefty price.

Sure, we need ambition. We must dream big. In fact, dreaming big is crucial to our psychological well-being.[6] A bigger goal, with all other things being equal, creates *more* motivation and productivity than a medium-sized one. We need to give ourselves permission to tap into our desire that so often gets lost by taking the safe path and being "realistic."

We need to unleash our inner dreamer.

And yet, without a foundation of alignment, the ego takes over and we talk ourselves into erratic decisions and the rabbit hole of delusion. Had Holmes filtered her ambition through alignment by being honest with herself and having a support system she sought *real* feedback and accountability from—we could be telling a completely different story here.

Welcome to harnessing ambition on the hustler's side—with the filter of alignment on the seeker's side. With both, you'll harness the creative energy of desire while checking yourself. You ensure you don't tip the scales of ambition gone bad and burn yourself into the ground while taking everyone else along for a joyride.

But first, allow yourself to tap into ambition like never before.

AMBITION IS JET FUEL

Ambition tends to get a bad rap, a negative connotation of the unrelenting pursuit of more, the Westernized constant of raising up one's lifestyle . . . and there never being enough. To always move the goalpost back so as to keep up with the throngs of social media influencers posting selfies from rented mansions and hashtagging #influencerlyfe behind leased vehicles.

There is no doubt ambition can be destructive.

It can tip the scales from rampant belief to delusion and create feelings of invincibility and dark obsessions. But we must separate context from content, because ambition itself is *not* inherently bad. Rather, it is the lens through which it is viewed that matters.

When one has no foundation, ambition can be used to avoid what's happening on the inside—a feeling of lack, not belonging, needing to prove people wrong. It can lead to workaholism as a bandage for past hurt, trauma, and wounds. It can easily break bad as it did with Elizabeth Holmes.

Ambition paired with alignment, however, moves mountains.

Alignment minimizes ambition for cheap egoic desires, to be accepted by the "in" crowd or to crush a competitor that used to be a trusted ally. It ensures we have a backbone for the work we're doing and a *why* that matters beyond fast cash.

It expands purpose, deepens mission, and accelerates service. It becomes a driving force for *good*, fostering levels of growth in mind, body, and spirit. It grows influence and touches lives.

Ambition done right starts with not apologizing for your desire. It's about letting yourself dream *big*. Because if you're going to bother going at all—you may as well go big. Why? Well, for starters—it takes nearly the same amount of energy to move the needle 10 percent as it does to shoot for 10 times that. Like a launch from Cape Canaveral, *most of the heavy lifting* happens at the start. You know, overcoming inertia. That resistance we feel when an idea is simply . . . an idea. When you suck at something, and you know it.

But let's be real: Is a 10 percent bump *really* going to get you out of bed in the morning with vigor? Big goals wake us up. They compel us in ways small goals can't. The pioneer of goal-setting, Gary Latham, says as much, noting if you want the highest level of motivation and productivity over a long period of time, then "big goals lead to the best outcomes."[7]

Ultimately, ambition is a force of creation to bring an idea, a spark, or a longing to life. It means not playing small when asked what you're up to by the stranger in the coffee shop. It is not letting the cultural zeitgeist of playing it safe stop you in New Zealand and Australia with tall poppy syndrome, a cultural fear of playing too big and being cut off.

And alignment is great and all, but to what end? Spend your time and energy aligned without a vehicle to express it—such as ambition and big goals—and your modus operandi becomes drifting through life under the guise of waiting for the "right" time. Consider ambition to be the kite in the sky, while alignment is holding it at the right angle so as to find the sweet spot of lift. If ambition takes over, it disappears into the ether. And if you focus only on alignment, it stays on the ground flaccid and unused.

To do this right, you'll combine ambition and alignment to create a palpable state of thriving.

THE QUESTIONS OF AMBITION AND ALIGNMENT

Ambition is stoking the fire to dream daringly, while alignment is curating the fire so as not to burn the house down. To do so, you'll need to allow yourself to dream bigger . . . while staying grounded.

If that sounds like a paradox to you, you're right.

In order to tap into these opposites, you'll filter them through a set of questions designed to rip the lid off belief and ensure it's what you want. These questions expand what's possible yet ground you in meaning.

These questions of ambition ensure you dream big, without hesitation, paralysis, or shame:

- ▶ What would you do if there was zero chance of failure?
- ▶ What would you do if you weren't afraid?
- ▶ What would you do if you had unlimited resources?
- ▶ What would you do if you fully trusted yourself?
- ▶ What would you love to do even if you failed?
- ▶ What would get you out of bed with excitement in the morning?
- ▶ What would you do if there was no need for external approval?
- ▶ What would you do if there were no limitations on your possibility?
- ▶ What would you do if someone wrote you a blank check to pursue what you really want?
- ▶ What would you do if money, time, and energy were wholly available?

We can answer half-heartedly or like our life depends on it. The questions of ambition are expansive, to help you sprint through the artificial brick walls of limitation we all have. By answering these, you'll notice themes emerge. Give yourself permission to answer without needing to figure out the "how" to get there. You'll know you did it right when:

▶ **You stop dreaming in secret.** The world is full of "secret" dreamers who never take a moment to take ownership. By doing so, you stop denying the part of yourself that is designed to bring a future reality to life.[8]

▶ **You give yourself permission.** These questions shift our need for permission from the outside to the inside. Instead of waiting for the educational degree, the parental approval, the venture capital firm, or the editor to say "yes," you choose yourself.

▶ **You use your unfiltered imagination.** As we age, we tend to lose our ambition as others tell us to "get realistic" and play it safe. And by doing so, we lose the imagination and wonder we all come with, which is a key to a thriving and fulfilling life.

Equipped with the raw energy of ambition, you'll pair this with the top-down congruence of who you are on the inside to match up to how you show up on the outside. We'll call this aligned ambition: the merging of honoring one's desire and living by principles and an internal check-in system that lets us put our head on the pillow at night and shut it down.

When you point the arrow of ambition through this lens, you create from a deeper place. You allow a grander vision to come to life. You recognize ambition through alignment is a thrilling test of your capacity to receive and allow grace into your life.

Most important, you don't find yourself chasing bigger goals to impress strangers on social media. You don't start something simply because your competition did. You escape the perils of hustle's consequences because you're playing a different game. When you're aligned and create success, it feels familiar . . . because you've done the work.

It feels *like* you.

If ambition is what you want to *do* and create in the world, then alignment is who you want to *be* and how you want to show up. Notice the difference, as it operates under a different model.

- ▶ The old model: In order to *be* more, you must *do* more.
- ▶ The second model: In order to *do* more, you must *be* more.
- ▶ The new model: By being *and* doing synergistically, you become whole.

Alignment can be felt from miles away. It's congruence between who you say you are and who you *really* are. It's being consistent across thoughts, words, and actions. And the moment you're not, you learn the lesson and, instead of beating yourself up, pivot back. Alignment is a super attractor of opportunities, connection, and resources designed to help you in your quest. In other words, alignment is sexy.

Consider these questions of alignment to ground one's ambition through purpose, meaning, and values:

- ▶ What would you do if you had three years to live?
- ▶ What would you do if you had zero concern of what others thought?
- ▶ What would you do if the marker of success was feeling alive every day?
- ▶ What would you do if you showed up as if nothing was missing?
- ▶ What would you do if you tapped into your heart's desire?
- ▶ What would you do if you didn't care if it made any "sense"?
- ▶ What would you do if you weren't trying to impress others?

By answering both sets of questions, you'll tap into a new framework: aligned ambition.

ALIGNED AMBITION

Aligned ambition is the best of both worlds; you let yourself dream without apology but stay grounded in who you are and what matters. You honor your original desire, the clarity of purpose, the dream inside—and make it real. You're unapologetic in the expression of your desire as long as it comes from a healthy place. It's the part of you that can sense the *truth* and alignment of your desire by the way it feels.

So, if you want the stunning three-bedroom house, own it. If you want to be able to take summer vacations with the family in Greece, own it. If you want to have enough assets to retire your parents, own it. If you want to quit the 9–5 and live the lifestyle of an entrepreneur, own it. If you want to be a *New York Times* bestseller, own it!

What matters is it matters to *you* and is done from a place of aligned ambition. This means:

> ► **Your intuition calls you toward it.** Beneath the surface of egoic desires, we tap into the part of ourselves that knows what is right. This is the internal compass we're all equipped with. By listening to it, you recognize what you truly want. We'll dive into intuition further in Chapter 11.
>
> ► **The sheer thought of your goal brings you life.** Being captivated emotionally by your desire means it breathes life into you today. It makes you feel freedom, excitement, and enthusiasm when you both imagine getting there *and* pursue it daily.
>
> ► **You desire it for the right internal reasons.** Our desires left unchecked are driven by what others want, or what we think the world wants us to be, do, and have. Instead, honor what you *really* want without the external world influencing you.

Because you embrace this dichotomy, you're able to transcend the neurotic attachment that is typically found in the ambitious. Rather, you strive because it makes you feel *alive*. You pursue because it deepens the understanding of yourself. You'll know you're doing it right when:

> ► You allow yourself to dream bigger than is comfortable while knowing fulfillment is an inside game.
>
> ► You strive for new goals not because of the myth that they will create an "arrival" moment, but because the pursuit makes you feel alive.
>
> ► You leave your comfort zone to get to know who you are when the stakes are high and when conditions are dicey.

- You view ambition through the right lens and then completely detach from need or desperation.
- You take the rigidness of ambition away and learn to love the process while having the time of your life.
- You don't white knuckle the process as some means to a future end; you recognize it is the end itself.
- You merge *doing* with *being,* your work with play, feeding each part of your life synergistically.
- You use tools, people, and feedback to check yourself against ambition and drop the ego as you experience success.
- You're able to look at tomorrow's horizon with excitement yet feel the rapture of gratitude now.

The end result is to enter a state of thriving.

We've all been there, the feeling that our lives are *working.* We're building toward something meaningful in the throngs of momentum while being content today. No matter how distant or unfamiliar that feels to you now, consider this state to be accessible to you as you integrate these principles.

WHAT TO LEAVE BEHIND WITH CONVENTIONAL AMBITION

Pouring ambition into your life requires self-awareness, or else the ego can get consumed in the pursuit of more and the can't-ever-win battle of comparison. Here's what to leave behind:

- **Doing more to *be* more.** You can never *be* more only by doing more—despite the tempting promise ambition covertly and, often, overtly shares.
- **Being ambitious for the sake of it.** The old model stems from not enough, a constant feeling of lack. There is never enough, and one cannot take their foot off the gas . . . or else.
- **Proving others wrong.** Ambition turns dark quick: the desire to prove others wrong, silence critics, or prove one's worth. Be aware of this, and use seeking principles to diffuse this energy.

WHAT TO LEAVE BEHIND WITH CONVENTIONAL ALIGNMENT

An aligned life is what we crave, often using words like "balance" that miss the mark. But chasing alignment and never stepping into the world also comes with consequences, including:

- ▶ **Not expressing alignment.** You're aligned, but to what end? There must be a vehicle for alignment; otherwise, it remains trapped as unexpressed potential.
- ▶ **Playing small with desires.** Those who seek alignment often say they don't *need* money or career growth. But that's beside the point: it's not about *need*, it's about desire. Need is desperate, desire isn't.
- ▶ **Labeling and judging.** Those who tap into alignment without ambition tend to judge and label others on the field of play—a reflection of what they're missing.

WHAT COULD HAVE BEEN

Elizabeth Holmes had the raw materials, skills, and connections to solve real problems in the world, create an undeniable impact, and accumulate all the resources she could have ever wanted . . . and then some. She was smart, talented, and ready to take on the world.

Destined to be a case study for future visionaries, she became a cautionary tale for those who can take ambition too far. She is one of countless, of course, because ambition is addictive—one hit is never enough—the ego always wants more.

But you know better, and it's why you're here.

There is no need to apologize for wanting a bigger life, to play a loftier game, to have a richer experience. When you merge this energy with alignment, you directly tap into both worlds that lead to a deep sense of fulfillment, at peace with who you are while performing your best to bring a desire to life without apology, shame, or guilt.

This is what we call a thriving life experience.

Life feels like it's constantly in momentum, in progress, even when there are challenges—*especially* when there are challenges. When these two worlds merge, you become whole.

You chase your goals with fury but love the process. You obsess over details but leave space for the mystery. You achieve like never before but aren't defined solely by achievement. You create success but stay humble. You show up like the best do but detach, too.

You are ambitiously aligned and aligned in your ambition.

Chapter

7

Declaration
&
Tests

Most of us live one of two lives.

There's the life we're currently living—the roads we pave daily that are safe, predictable, and "realistic." We are finance majors, accountants, or engineers, or if we find ourselves in the field we dream of—we do so in what writer Steven Pressfield calls a "shadow" career.[1]

It's the key grip on the movie set who dreams of being director, the MFA faculty member who desires to write novels, the manager at Patagonia who salivates at snowcapped mountains.

Close, but *oh so far.*

This all starts innocently; we tell ourselves we'll engage in these faux careers for a while as we figure out next steps. We'll work on our *real* dream on the side, at the margins of early mornings and late nights. Hell, maybe we'll even do it Gary Vee style and hustle from 7 p.m. to 2 a.m.—advice he dished out for years.[2]

But it never quite happens, does it?

We get anchored by bills, responsibilities, and little humans. We lose the spark of desire working for an egomaniac boss. We get promotions, titles, and cute email signatures laced with a dose of authority at our gig. We get societal applause, way too many LinkedIn requests (please, no more), and letters after our name.

In other words, we adapt to what we *don't* want.

Even though it's not what we want—it's working. When the person on the plane asks what we do, we have an answer. And when you have something to lose—a career, being on a team, direct deposits—it becomes that much harder to take a risk. Instead, we talk ourselves into staying where we are.

We should be grateful for what we have, right?

Now, if this gratitude is legit, do you. But what is common for many people is they've dreamed in secret and haven't owned what they *really* want. Gratitude, then, becomes a crutch to avoid the truth.

And since we're disturbingly susceptible to sunk cost fallacy—when we've put tons of time and effort into one path and stay *only* because of that—we can stay stuck forever.[3] As time passes, our enthusiasm fades until we wake up in an existential crisis and come to the sinking realization: we missed our shot.

So, what's a better way?

Consider declaration from the hustler's side—the unapologetic ownership of your dreams without qualifiers or rambling explanations. To honor the reason why you're being called forth, even if you don't know those reasons yet. As no action happens without consequence, consider the tests that will come your way and your ability to pass them with faith—to come from the seeker's side. These tests are designed to have you answer one question: Are you committed or are you simply another halfhearted talker?

Instead of seeing tests as convenient places to ditch or why your coworker was right about playing it safe—consider them opportunities to move toward your goals faster . . . and stand out from the pack.

Tests, then, are high-octane fuel for your growth.

By merging these, you tap into key ingredients of living a fulfilled life from the inside out—the self-trust that comes from declaring what you want and passing crucial tests along the way that demonstrate faith and resilience.

And it all starts with unapologetic declaration.

DECLARE, DECLARE, DECLARE

No one lacks clarity on what they really want to do.

It is a bold statement but hear me out—a lack of "clarity" is a convenient excuse the ego uses to avoid the vulnerability of owning our truth. This is what we're naturally pulled to, what we can't stop thinking about. It's how we'd choose to fill our time on a random Saturday morning with no chores. It's what we'd do if we got honest with ourselves.

It's what makes us feel alive.

And if we stripped away the noise and minimized the ego's chatter and put you in an environment with the right conditions—the clarity would ooze out like a freshly cracked egg at Sunday brunch.

This is not to say there is one be-all, end-all clarity you must excavate from within, but rather, clarity is a process, an evolution. It will transform as you move in the direction of what matters. As you evolve and expand, it follows suit. Ultimately, the goal is to live in harmony with this fluid clarity and integrate it into our lives.

To declare is to audaciously plant your flag.

This is what you want. It's what brings you a sense of aliveness, the rapture of doing what you're meant to—what no one has to motivate you for and what you don't need a double dose of caffeine to execute on. Rather, the sheer thought of it energizes you.

It doesn't wake us up; it awakens us.

Make no mistake; in a world of halfhearted dreamers, dabblers, and arm-chair visionaries—this energy moves mountains.

It gets you noticed. It builds a reservoir of faith. It makes you stand out. It gets you paid.

Say hello to declaring boldly, your time to get honest and unapologetic about what you want. To do this right, you'll:

- ▶ **Declare audaciously.** This is not about shouting from proverbial social media rooftops, but rather practicing radical honesty and declaring to yourself without justification or disclaimers.
- ▶ **Not think about the "how."** We tend to limit our desires as we get lost in the "how"—thinking we need to know every step. Now is not the time for this; allow yourself to release the monkey mind's obsession with the "how."
- ▶ **Let the world know.** Stake your claim, share openly. Put yourself out there when asked what you're about or what you "do" . . . *before* you're doing it.
- ▶ **Craft a statement and put it everywhere.** Move the vision out of your head and into your environment. Keep it simple yet choose your words wisely; make sure you can come back to them and feel what they mean.

Gone are the days of dreaming in secret. It's time to give yourself permission—before you feel "ready." (Hint: You will *never* feel ready.) Do it before you get the next degree or certification, before you climb the ladder of a shadow career. When you do this right, you'll reap the rewards of:

- ▶ **Having a compass.** Declaration means you now have an aim, a mountain in the distance you're walking toward, a guiding star—a lighthouse to point you in the right direction instead of aimlessly drifting.
- ▶ **Feeling alive in the pursuit.** We feel most alive while taking steps toward our declaration. Even if they are seemingly insignificant, we capture the feeling of progress from a place of autonomy, as we covered in Chapter 2.
- ▶ **Attracting opportunities.** Dreaming in secret means all the people, places, and opportunities to support you will never have a chance to help. Rather, they will help others who have the audacity to declare, those who are willing to be seen and heard.

▶ **Avoiding the pain of untapped potential.** When we don't declare and know we're meant for more—we resent ourselves and others who are doing what we want. We call them lucky and say it "must be nice." Yet we know the truth: this is the pain of untapped potential coming out.

By declaring, you'll harness the test-drive effect—the time you wanted your dream car and went to the dealer. You put both hands on the steering wheel, inhaled that new car smell, and went for a spin. Since it was specific: one brand and model of car and it gave you a precise feeling, you left the dealer . . . and saw it everywhere. Did half your city magically purchase it or was it there all along and what shifted was *your* awareness?

We know the answer; the same goes for our goals. When you declare, you notice doors open that were previously slammed shut as the right people show up at the right times as you experience "random" encounters that blow your mind.

But there's a reason most don't declare.

As we stated earlier, declaration comes with tests of varying degrees and sizes designed to filter you out and ensure you're not another talker. And these tests will come often.

Instead of seeing this as a bad thing, consider it a gift.

THE TESTS ARE THE VIP LINE

High-end dance clubs tend to look and feel the same with their obscenely overpriced drinks, blaring EDM tunes, way too many bros with heavy cologne—and a litany of social media influencers tending bar.

There are two lines: One is general admission, where the masses gather to be herded like cattle and dudes with plain cotton undershirts pray to be let in at the mercy of a guy whose shirt is at least one size too small and works biceps seven days a week.

Big Steve they call him. *Original.*

Off to the side, and much closer to the door, is where everyone wants to be: VIP. Blocked off with red carpets, the benefit of being treated like a human and for reasons unknown—piles of brown clipboards. Only the few, the chosen, those who are invited, connected, or pay to play get in.

If VIP is such a great experience, why can't the entire place be it?

The answer is obvious: it would lose its allure. It only exists because of its exclusivity. In essence, it is a filtering system built on supply and demand: there are only a certain number of tables. And even if they're not all sold out, there are still only a certain number of tables.

Right, Big Steve?

Much like the dance club, goals have their own filtering mechanism. Instead of relying on cash, gigantic bottles of vodka, and black AMEX cards, however, the currency of choice is the audacity to declare and overcome tests thrown your way.

On the regular.

Pay the currency, use your connections, and pass the tests and you'll find yourself in the middle of the dance floor with a cocktail in your hand going wild.

All because you passed the tests.

THE TESTS ARE FILTERS

Tests, then, are like Big Steve: he filters you out and either puts you in General Admission where you're going to freeze your face off in 21-degree weather for the next 87 minutes—or you'll make a beeline to VIP and have a cold cocktail in your hand . . . in about 4½ minutes.

An example may be helpful.

Imagine you've been working a job you can't stand and that has been making you white knuckle the 43-minute commute every day. You literally cannot take one more moment of this. But you told yourself this last week, last month, last year . . . and, uh, you're still here.

This time it feels different.

You muster up the courage to have the "talk" with your boss to put the cards on the table, knowing exactly what you're going to say—this is good-bye. You have dreams of your own. You feel urgency inside of you; it's now or never.

Do or die, baby.

You rehearse the talk in your car as the stakes rise. You're in that strange state where you're living your life, but it feels like a movie. You're actually doing it. You walk into your boss's office in defiance to deliver the news, yet something shocking happens—your boss reacts in a completely surprising manner.

Your boss "gets it," shows empathy, and showers you with praise. He or she confesses the work won't get done without you. Then you're reminded it's been five years and you have history. Starting over is hard. It's a risky time to be on your own. You had a plan but the unexpected happened . . . your boss offered you nearly double your salary to stay.

What . . . the . . . hell?

The money was decent, now it's *good*.

Like really good, in the sense that you won't be worrying about bills anymore . . . and have plenty left over. You imagine the possibilities: the fresh car, upgrading your place, the sun-soaked Tulum vacation. Your monthly take home has basically doubled!

Oh, the possibilities.

Disoriented by the haze of imagining new digits in your bank account, it hits you—what about your declaration? Oh, well . . . uh . . . about that.

Say hello to your test.

This is the ultimate filtering mechanism: a test of your desire, will, and commitment that determines everything.

What will you choose?

TESTS COME IN ALL SHAPES AND SIZES

Tests aren't a novel concept, except for the fact that most mention the blatantly obvious tests—moments of questioning, doubt, and fear. That's easy. Amateur hour. *Booooring.*

Then there are the agonizing tests that seem inconceivable, tend to come from unexpected places, and leave you disoriented. They dangle money, promotions, and status in front of your face, all in the pursuit to seek the answer to one question: Do you say you want it, or do you *really* want it?

In any test, no matter how insignificant or massive, there will be a fork in the road. And the fact is the dabblers see the tests as proof as why it *can't* happen for them. Why it's not the right time, why they picked the wrong market, and why their uncle was right about the economy even though he's worked at GE for 29 years and is riding the last wave of pension life.

Since we all come equipped with a hefty dose of self-doubt in regard to our desires anyway, the tests become a convenient out. Your excuses are now validated, justified, and rationalized.

You're officially off the hook.

But for the committed, those who are all in, the tests are proof as to why it's happening and why there's no turning back, specifically:

▶ **The tests are proof.** Every action causes a reaction, and tests show there's movement toward your dreams. You declared, you stepped into courage, and now there's some resistance: this is a good, no, a great thing.

▶ **The tests deepen resolve.** Every test becomes a way to double down on your belief, show more grit, have a little more faith, and stack a couple more bricks of whatever-it-takes energy into your life.

▶ **The tests are a filtering mechanism.** This mechanism is putting your words to the test to show yourself and others that you're serious this time—that you've gone from being a talker to a do-er.

▶ **The tests come in all shapes and sizes.** No test is the same. We all think we know what the tests will look like. But we don't, and often, the surprise of the test is enough to knock us back and make us retreat to our comfort zone.

Each time you pass a test, you leave the land of amateurs who talk a big game but fold like a house of cards at the first sign of challenge and digest their worn-out excuses.

So, what do you do when the tests come?

- ▶ **Zoom out.** When the test comes, don't rely on your automatic mechanisms—take a step back using the principles in this book. Detach from the movie set of your life and be an actor watching yourself on screen. Breathe.
- ▶ **Override the ego.** The ego gets triggered by tests, leading to erratic decision-making and odd behavior. Use the tools we'll cover to be aware of the ego and its petulant feedback mechanisms.
- ▶ **Counsel your future self.** When tested, we tend to run back to the warm blanket of our comfort zone. Instead, counsel your future self who has already accomplished the vision— what would your future self do? Listen.
- ▶ **Listen to your intuition.** This is the part of yourself that knows. Allow the answer to come up, even if it doesn't make logical sense, and especially if it doesn't.
- ▶ **Have someone in your corner.** Sometimes, we need someone else to believe in our dream as we pick ourselves up from the valley of a test. Ensure there's at least one person who has your back.
- ▶ **Release attachment.** We tend to be attached to whether or not something "worked" based on immediate results. Except we have no clue—and often what didn't "work" today ends up working six months later. Detach, detach, detach.

As you pass tests, you'll notice others fold up shop as you deepen your faith, self-trust, and resilience. Because passing a test here or there is easy, but those who do so long term are the ones who reach the mountaintop

ROOKIES LOVE POSSIBILITY

The starting line to any endeavor is flush with positive, enthusiastic energy and countless high-fives. Consider adventure races, long trail runs, Spartan experiences, or Ironmans.

At these events, you can spot the rookies from a mile away— they're chatting it up at the starting line, hopping up and down like Energizer Bunnies. They're saying they're going to "crush" it and how 12 miles doesn't seem "that bad" even though their longest training run was 3 miles.

They're caffeinated, confident, cheerful.

The rookies start on fire, burning up precious energy in the first miles, enjoying the few minutes of glory that come with being out front. They start to believe they can finish in the top tier. Despite their lack of training, maybe they can grit themselves into a podium finish. But they're rookies for a reason, and everyone knows it . . . including them.

The professionals, the committed, act different. They're subdued at the starting line, conserving energy. They've done this before. They start at a suboptimal pace to get the engines going—it's a long race. They let the rookies pass. They've put in the work. They know not to let hype interfere with the plan. They actually have a real plan, instead of shooting off like a rocket and holding on for dear life. As the tests come, the rookies fall off like social media influencers during a rainstorm.

They hit the brick wall of reality where minutes ago they were flying high off dopamine. Their legs torched, their lungs are hanging on by a dear thread. On mile 7, cramps take over and they're done—ready to go home as the allure of the comfy living room couch wins them over. It's Sunday, and football is on. Screw this, they tell themselves. They failed the tests.

They quit.

As the professionals pass them, they smile: it was a matter of time. They know tests make or break you; the starting line is full of fist-bumping energy. But as you pass the tests, the crowd thins out. People quit. They make excuses. They lie to themselves. They blame external factors. They justify their head trash. They sell out.

And they give up on their declaration.

At the top, there is a different energy—it's peaceful, serene almost.

There's no noise, hype, or hoopla. There is mutual respect for anyone who has made it this far. The experience at the top of the mountain, your mountain, will be the same.

You passed a series of tests along the way, each one making you stagger ever so slightly as you questioned yourself—acting as a filtering mechanism to test your grit, resilience, and faith.

As you passed tests, you noticed a shift.

You are more confident, yet humble. You are more committed, yet open. You are more disciplined, yet leave space for the unknown. You develop a level of faith that can't be found listening to high-octane motivational YouTube clips.

Best of all, you drop the ego because the tests make you do so.

WHAT TO LEAVE BEHIND WITH CONVENTIONAL DECLARING

Declaring is putting yourself on the line and not talking yourself out of it. However, not all declaration is worth keeping, including:

▶ **Declaring out of validation.** Your declaration is yours. It is worthless if one does it to sound cool, or to be approved at the Thanksgiving dinner table, or to get an engaging social media post.

▶ **Declaring to the wrong people.** While declaring is powerful, the wrong people talk you out of it. Not everyone deserves to know your biggest dream. Let them earn it.

▶ **Not taking immediate action.** A declaration that was once full can become empty without immediate action. No matter how small, use the principles we're covering to ensure you integrate ASAP.

WHAT TO LEAVE BEHIND WITH CONVENTIONAL TESTS

The tests will come in oh-so-creative ways, making you wonder who the hell has the time to mess with you. But we all know people who create tests for no reason. They're stranded at the airport. Their dog ran away. They lost their wallet, keys, and IDs ... for the third time this week. They got scammed by an IRS call from China.

Not all the tests are good, and here's what's not worth keeping:

- ▶ **Creating unnecessary tests.** Don't worry, when you dream big and bold enough, you'll have plenty of tests to deal with. Creating random tests for the sake of it is not worth keeping here. Save this energy for what matters.

- ▶ **Engaging in self-sabotage.** Self-sabotage is manufacturing a test when you're on the verge of a goal ... for no reason. Be alert when things are "too good." Pass the test and allow yourself to live in the thrill of overcoming a challenge. Then, move on.

NO TESTS . . . NO GROWTH

Actor Matthew McConaughey was as bankable as they come.

He'd replaced Hugh Grant as Hollywood's sure bet for the ever-popular romantic comedy genre—the category studios love due to the bargain budgets and easy sell to consumers who can't resist a cheap love story.

In other words, things were *easy*.

After McConaughey became a father, he noticed something—his work was missing challenge. He was going through the motions. He made killer cash and never wore a shirt ... and that was cool, but he didn't feel engaged or *alive* with his work. He was missing a spark.

And that's when he declared.

He rang his agent, counseled those closest to him, and declared he would no longer accept cookie-cutter roles—and would wait for a serious, dramatic one. There was one issue, however: those weren't on the table.

He'd been typecast into one role and decided he'd wait it out. To showcase his vow, McConaughey left the beaches of

California and its paparazzi behind, moving back to Texas. He unplugged with his family. He went off the radar.

And he waited as months passed with no word.

He received an offer in the genre with a unique tilt—does he turn his back on his declaration? The initial offer came in at $8 million, but he declined. The studio came back, $10 million. He stuck to his guns . . . until they came back with $12.5 million. No. And then, one last time, they came back with an irresistible offer—a $15 million offer.

For an *easy* gig.

In his own words, the very same script sounded captivating at $15 million—the rosy glow of plush bank accounts started to make the role stimulating. His ego started to lure him, but he resisted, speaking of this excruciating moment where his will was tested:

"For the next 12, 14 months . . . nothing came in. Nada, zilch, not an offer for anything. Now we're 20 months into this desert period. I didn't know what I was going to be, change my career . . . become a teacher, or a coach, go back to being a lawyer."[4] And then, all of the sudden, it happened.

He was sent scripts that were challenging, hard, serious.

In his own words, he had *unbranded* himself from his usual roles. He was a mystery, a clean slate yet again. The scripts were stimulating, compelling, unique. Among those was an offer for a dramatic, low-budget film named *Dallas Buyer's Club*. It won him the Oscar.

Following a lifelong dream he'd written down at the ripe age of 22—he'd pivoted back into the actor he wanted to be, with a litany of dream roles that woke him up from the slumber of complacency.

This is declaration and passing the tests so as to cultivate faith.

Now you may be thinking—that's cool for a Hollywood millionaire, but what about me?

You'll do the same. Merging declaration and passing tests is where you'll step into a place of alignment and where desire is matched with commitment. You'll see tests as a launchpad to your next success.

A dream without tests is not what you want.

Passing tests, then, will amplify all the principles as you expand your ambition, capacity, and grittiness to new heights—while you create the space and detachment from thinking something is wrong with you.

Ultimately, you develop a level of faith in yourself that is unshakable.

Chapter

8

Relentless Action
&
Celebration

Richard Branson's drive and creative action taking have thrust him to mythical status ever since he started Virgin Air on a whim. As the lore goes, with a backdrop of pissed-off passengers who'd also been bumped on a flight from Puerto Rico to the Virgin Islands, he dialed up Boeing and started selling tickets.

And the rest is history.[1]

Branson's rebellious nature and exponential success have turned him from mere mortal to entrepreneurial legend. However, for his crowd of fans, admirers, and coconspirators—that's *not* what makes him most special. What they value is his ability to match his relentless action with fun, play, and celebration.

Due to what we explored in Part I about the hustler's dilemma, Branson's unabashed enjoyment of his success is rarer than meets the eye. He could easily talk himself out of a monthlong sabbatical. He could force himself to live in a big city, accessible to investors. He could be chock-full of stress. He does have 70,000 employees and all.[2]

But he doesn't.

Instead, he's left the city life for his private island where he invites people from all over the world to unplug and revel. He creates more white space with success, not less. He has more time and freedom and radiates an authentic joy uncommon to many of his stature.

Because he *gets* it—celebrating the fruits of our effort is *as* important as creating them. And contrary to conventional wisdom, your ability to celebrate, play, and have fun increases your performance, not takes away from it. Make no mistake, this is why people fly all over the world to experience the magic of Necker Island. They can get business advice anywhere; it is the magical, zestful allure Branson operates with that they're *really* chasing.

And it is precisely what they're missing.

Branson's ability to create results through action—bold, courageous moves toward a vision—plus his unabashed enjoyment of success are rare. To bring forth your aligned ambition as we discussed in Chapter 6, you'll also need to harness the power of relentless action.

What is relentless action? It's leaving your comfort zone every day. It's making courageous decisions. It means staying committed to the vision after the high has faded. It means you don't take no at face value but rather, find unconventional solutions to problems most see as stone-faced obstacles. You'll no doubt feel the sting of rejection because it's part of any process—but you'll develop the resilience to understand a no leads to a better yes around the corner.

Now, let me be clear: relentless action is *not* random action. It is not taking action *for the sake* of action. One can take this too far and arrive at overwhelm, burnout, and hanging on by a thread as previously discussed.

As you pursue this relentless action, you're going to celebrate like there's no tomorrow.

You're going to practice what it feels like to be successful . . . before you reach the mountaintop. You're going to learn how to love the process and flip the script on the part of your psyche that loves to focus on what's not working.

Without this downtime, recovery, and ample celebration, you never adapt and you're always in fight-or-flight mode. It can lead to hitting checkpoints of success and always moving the goalpost back . . . without ever owning your wins.

On the flipside, spending too much time soaked in celebration with seeking can lead to lethargy. It can lead to complacency that robs you of momentum. It can even create "fake" gratitude—overusing this feel-good state to avoid the desire to grow.

When these principles merge, you make significant progress toward your goals, amplify your confidence, and build a reservoir of self-trust. The reality is most high achievers you admire have all the markers of success but are constantly feeling like it's not enough. Unlike Branson, they're not regularly tapping into joy, appreciation, and deep levels of gratitude.

All because they never take time to "be" with their successes.

DON'T MOVE THE GOALPOST BACK

"Every time I achieve a goal, something I've wanted to do for months, years, or even decades, I move the goalpost back. I don't let myself get complacent. And then, I put my head down and grind."[3]

I sat there in the middle of a podcast interview and those words from the person I was interviewing hit me hard. But not in the typical, rah-rah way. Instead of being motivated, I exhaled with fatigue—are you out of your mind!?

Let me be clear here: I *get* this mindset.

I've lived in the world of unhinged ambition. This conventional hustle mentality is pervasive, common, and encouraged. Moving the goalpost back can be found all over the world of hustle-porn content telling you to crush it and never take your foot off the gas.

The ambitious part of me didn't feel motivated, it felt sorry. Not for the person I was interviewing, because we all live with our own subjective realities, but for this narrative that what we create is *never* enough, especially when it's what we used to dream of.

Something felt off.

I couldn't help but think—this is *not* how I want to define success.

Pouring ourselves into our work, craft, or business and then receiving a reward but not celebrating seems asinine. And I don't simply mean knocking back a few cocktails; I mean celebrating in a way that allows us to "be" with our wins.

Hustlers love moving the goalpost back as if it's a subconscious tic as natural as breathing. Their constant push for more has conditioned them to focus on what's missing even *after* they achieved the result they dreamed of. Worst of all, they're quick to forget how much it mattered to them and discount their success by saying:

"Well, yeah, it's not that big of a deal."

"Yeah, but that person did it faster."

"I've still got a long ways to go."

No, no, and no—this is what you could only *dream* of 18 months ago. It's what you couldn't stop thinking about, but now you're discounting it? Achievement can be eccentric this way: as you capture it, the more elusive it seems to be. When we choose to not move the goalpost, we're going against our hardwiring of hedonic adaptation—the evolutionary mechanism rooted in survival to ensure we don't get so wrapped up in ecstatic bliss that we become someone's lunch.[4] We are reversing the notion that it is never enough, or that *we* are never enough. We are ceasing the habit of comparison. We are taking a stand. And maybe, for the first time, we're telling ourselves, "I'm proud of you."

When was the last time you spoke to yourself like that?

Probably a while ago, or maybe never.

The inner critic is ruthless. Even when we do get *there*, it finds a new problem or another way to have done it better. Or it goes straight to social media to see a total stranger who is miles ahead. And, just like that, you're behind again. A part of you had wanted to celebrate, but societal pressure and our inherent nature don't let you.

It's time to stop the insanity.

When you hit your goalpost, you're going to hang. Even if it's for a few hours, several days, or a week. You're going to own the work you put in. You're going to contemplate, reflect, and revel.

You're going to own that shit.

Otherwise, you'll be indoctrinated in a world where nothing is ever enough. And in turn, you will start to feel that *you're* never enough. The more you move toward your horizon, the farther it gets. Regardless of how high you crank the treadmill's speed, you realize that you're standing in the same place. Because you're the worst person on the planet to identify, own, and celebrate your own growth and progress.

And so am I.

YOU'RE THE WORST IN THE WORLD

You're the worst person on the planet to recognize your growth.

Let that sink in.

Now think about how much you have grown in the past 12, 24, and 48 months. Because we live in the trenches of our day-to-day lives, recognizing our growth can be an impossible task. Sure, we know we're better than before, but don't fully own it. We still feel behind. We're acutely aware of the daily mistakes we make. At the same time, others can be shocked at what we're doing while we brush it off as no big deal.

What the hell is happening here?

Consider those who have achieved transformation—physical changes to the tune of pounds melting off, big shifts in bank accounts, or career acceleration. To the outside world, they're obvious. Yet to the person living them, they have become the new normal, while *who* they became to create those changes becomes a distant memory.

This is why moving the goalpost back is, frankly, bullshit.

It stops you from appreciating what you've done. It doesn't let you own the self-doubt you conquered, how you stuck through adversity after the high wore off. It prevents you from deconstructing the lessons of your success, which often contain the same ingredients for future ones. Worst off, it sends a signal to the world that you're unwilling to unapologetically own your success.

And if you're not willing to own your success, who will?

It's time to not only let this mindset go, but torch it.

Recognize what you *have* done. You launched the business. You wrote the book. You asked them out. You stopped self-sabotaging and finished a Spartan race. One-third of Americans never read a book after high school . . . and here you are.[5]

Ownership fuels your ability to receive more of what you want.

When you celebrate your wins and hang out at your goalpost, you build from abundance. You build from wholeness. You shut off the inner critic. You see getting to the goalpost as proof you're capable of more, instead of using the past as proof as to why you're not.

In order to break the pattern, you're going to:

- ▶ **Practice success.** Instead of waiting to feel success for an external benchmark, make it a practice. Take yourself to the vision of your goal and what it feels like to live with it. The reality is Branson would never radiate his fun-loving energy if he hadn't *practiced* that state during the process of achievement. He'd be another rich mogul who desperately chases more.

- ▶ **Be with your wins.** When you achieve wins, park the car. Hang out and allow yourself to "be." This reconditions the goalpost mentality and amplifies self-worth and confidence. Celebrate however you'd like—a weekend getaway, a solo hike, or a shopping splurge.

► **Celebrate your growth.** Similar to the popular practice of writing down what you're grateful for on a daily basis, write down at least three wins every day. Then once a week look back at your daily list and curate a list of *10* weekly wins. With clients, we do this on Fridays as a way to celebrate and track progress. This practice also helps minimize the part of ourselves that tells us we're never doing enough.

► **Identify the ingredient of success for your win.** By doing so, you'll recognize you *already* have the ingredients of your future successes . . . now. Say one of your wins was waking up before the alarm and hitting your morning workout; the ingredient is discipline. Or you put the phone on airplane mode and did your creative work early; the ingredient could be focus.

► **Take time to integrate and incubate.** When you hit bigger goals, create enough space before tackling more so you can integrate and incubate. Integration is the process of deconstructing how you brought it to life—the mindsets, skills, tactics—to make it a part of you. Then, incubation is creating enough downtime to get creatively inspired again before immediately setting a new goal.

By following these steps to both practice and celebrate success, you'll relieve yourself of the consequences explored earlier. You'll recognize the emotional jet fuel of your smallest wins differs not by substance, only degree. Meaning: you are already equipped with the feelings of your biggest success, your mountaintop, your impossible vision. In fact, you are tapping into it daily, if you allow yourself to.

Naturally, this cultivates more belief and momentum. Across time, this begins to have a compounding effect.

BUT WHAT IF I CAN'T FIND WINS?

Now you may be asking: What if I truly have nothing to celebrate?

I hear this often and I always revert back to some much-needed real talk—this is the ego taking the wheel and talking you out of it. Because if you can't find at least three wins in any given day, you're addicted to self-sabotaging yourself.

(I warned you about the real talk.)

We can have the most chaotic, draining day of our lives and *still* find wins if we look closely. We find places where we did show up. And by doing so, we train ourselves to identify more wins regularly.

Mind you, this is not about delusion or living in a fantasy land. You can celebrate your wins and clearly identify challenges in life, too. It's about being willing to see past the ego's filter of not enough, the petulant joker who will do anything to bring you down and not celebrate yourself.

Here are a few crucial reminders to help you do so:

▶ **It's not the size of the win. It's what it feels like.** You're not going to have a colossal, life-shifting win every day. That's not what this is about; it's the feeling of the win. Whether that's being proud of yourself for not hitting snooze and showing up at the gym or getting the corner office—at their core, these wins feel the same. The feeling you get from making your first $97 online or from a $10,000 launch are more similar than you think.

▶ **For every win, train yourself to find a lesson.** Because hedonic adaptation wires us to focus on what's not working and how far the distance is between here and there, finding the win allows us to deconstruct *how* we did it. By doing so, we increase our awareness and recognize patterns in real time, leading to more wins in the future.

▶ **Celebrate in your unique style, and then move on.** With the bigger wins of your life, take extra time and space to celebrate. After being laughably broke for so many years, I remember having a huge profit day in my business. I went to the beach and celebrated by soaking in the view. When I got a book deal on my way back from an amazing trip in Spain, beers were on the celebration menu. Whatever feels right to you is what you should do.

WHAT TO LEAVE BEHIND WITH CONVENTIONAL RELENTLESS ACTION

Action is rewarded in our always-on culture, but we've all experienced the result of taking random action . . . that led nowhere. Here's what you'll be leaving behind:

▶ **Action for the sake of action.** There's a stark difference between *random* action . . . and deliberate action that moves the needle. Be willing to ask yourself: am I doing this to *feel* like I'm making progress, or does this genuinely create results?

▶ **Placing your self-worth around "doing."** If how you feel about yourself only comes from your actions, that's a problem. Be careful with tipping the scales of relentless action where *not doing* feels unfamiliar or induces feelings of guilt.

▶ **Using action as a soothing mechanism.** Make no mistake: hustlers can use action to avoid emotional challenges, feelings of inadequacy, or soothe a part of themselves they don't want to look at.

WHAT TO LEAVE BEHIND WITH CONVENTIONAL CELEBRATION

Celebration is rare when nothing is ever enough, and we have a built-in bias for focusing on what's not working, so here's what to be cautious of:

▶ **Sticking to one mode.** Change up how you celebrate and do so often: it's easy to get bored if our brains know precisely what the reward is. Be creative, playful, and engage others.

▶ **Staying surface level.** When you celebrate, make sure you're fully owning it and ensure you've tapped into the emotionality behind what you've created, as it'll stick with you.

▶ **Celebrating to the point of distraction.** Be intentional and have a blast with your celebration, but at some point, it's time to get back into a state of action. Otherwise, you may become the high school football star who's still celebrating . . . nineteen years later.

A RARE BREED FOR A REASON

Richard Branson is a rare breed—not because of his relentless, moonshot action-taking, or even his ability to bask in joy, fun, and play as he celebrates until the wee hours on Neckar Island.

It is the combination of both that makes him special.

Because the world is littered with "successful" people who achieve like their life depends on it but can't spend a moment *being* with their wins. This is admired in a meritocracy-based system, but to what end?

The pursuit of success is never a destination. Make $100,000 a year and now you're focused on making $150,000. Buy the house you love with three bedrooms; let time pass and now you want five and the bigger patio.

More achievement, less fulfillment.

Less fulfillment, more insanity.

It's time to break the pattern. Take action but also own your wins. Instead of setting a new goal the day you get there, bask in the moment. Think about the person you were when you set the goal and realize how far you've come.

Deconstruct your success by asking, How did you do it? What lessons did you learn? Why are you proud of yourself? Who helped you along the way? Reflect, ponder, and celebrate. Then, and only then, once your cup is full and you feel whole and reinspired, you can take the first steps toward your next mountain.

Eventually, you *will* be setting a new goal, but only after you have completed the process above. Instead of building from scarcity, you'll operate from a foundation of self-trust and radical ownership. You'll use your past as proof of possibility, instead of how the odds are stacked against you.

And how you choose to celebrate is up to you. It may be reflective, whipping out the journal and deconstructing how you brought it to life. Maybe you'll have a big old dance party. Whatever the case, don't move the goalpost back just yet.

You created this success. Now own it—because you deserve to.

Chapter

9

Structure
&
Novelty

Most people dream of wide-open calendars with zero obligations. In this world, their phone buzzes, signaling passive income deposits while they have nowhere to be and nothing to do—the day's sole assignment is to show up for the hot stone massage at noon with Sasha. In other words: pure, unabashed freedom.

But there's a problem: free time alone *doesn't* equal freedom.

After weeks of this world, we feel useless. After one too many days of 3 p.m. cocktails, we crave clarity. After a week of hitting the spa, we're ready *not* to have a stranger's hands on our neck. With nothing to chase, no incentive or desire to bring to life— we feel like something is missing.

And we're right.

While free time gives the illusion of freedom, it comes with a fatal flaw: humans are designed to set and chase goals.[1] We are hardwired to seek challenge, adapt, and recalibrate.[2] And without those, we *don't* feel alive.

Not only do we not feel alive, but we also barely scratch the limits of our potential and leave the thrill of our best performances tucked away in some back closet never to see the light of day.

Enter structure from the hustler's side—rules, boundaries, and guardrails against wandering aimlessly—creating progress, results, and growth. With these, we make a dent on what matters and satisfy our innate urge to set and accomplish goals; to have utility. To, you know, stop swiping right and leave the couch.

Then, on the seeker's side, we take structure and shatter it—to generate heart-thumping states of awe, wonder, and surprise. These flashes of novelty interrupt the prediction-making machine of our minds and invite those "aha" moments that make life worth living.

They wake us the hell up.

Ironically, structure delivers the freedom we craved all along . . . to a much greater degree. The freedom to show up and to perform, as well as a litany of elements that make life worth living. Merged with novelty, we unlock the intoxicating energy of larger-than-life moments.

Because sure, a day, week, or season of nothingness can be amazing, but a lack of structure in the long term leads to vicariously living through others at best and hopelessness at worst.

In other words, the opposite of freedom.

LACK OF STRUCTURE

Hustlers fantasize about the day they sell their business, make their seven-figure exit, and put their feet up in hedonic bliss. And yet, we know the truth—on a long enough timeline, doing nothing leaves us empty and buying red convertibles and Affliction tees at 57 years old.

Not a good look.

Seekers also dream of days with nothingness, to improvise their reality—tapping interstellar bliss at will and stretching a 30-minute meditation into three hours. And yet, they forget their Eastern counterparts are waking up at 4 a.m. to scrub the monastery and infuse discipline into seeking for a reason.

They *know* better.

A lack of structure on either side doesn't equal freedom. It's chaos, anxiety, and scrolling Reddit for conspiratorial fantasies. It creates pointless drama to fill space and leads to daydreaming about how we're far behind. Consider those who have cashed out at a young age, athletes and entrepreneurs who made it big during the early part of their careers.

They should be ecstatic, right?

Unfortunately, the frenzy is short-lived.

Early success out of the gates, while thrilling, comes with consequences: a fire hose of unfamiliar freedom, more options than the six-dollar Chinese buffet, a blitz of opportunities that create a disorienting feeling.

When author Mark Manson had stratospheric success with *The Subtle Art of Not Giving a F*ck*, which spent three years on the bestseller list, he was lost. His original stretch goal was to make it on the list, and so he had no idea what to do with himself once he was permanently glued to it, saying:

> You work your whole life with this idea of like, I'm going to accomplish my dream and that dream comes true, and you're like, okay, now what? This thing that provided a purpose for you is actually taken away. Now you don't have a purpose anymore. That really messed with me. Meanwhile, I'm sitting around in my underwear until four in the afternoon wondering what the hell to do with my life.[3]

Regardless of where it comes from—rousing success, debilitating failure, or ricocheting between both—the root cause of distress and malaise is a lack of structure.

Specifically, a lack of structure leads to:

▶ **Aimlessly drifting.** Without structure, we have no aim, no direction, no true north. With zero priorities, what do you do? Early on, this sounds amazing, but over time, it turns sour.

▶ **Comparison and overwhelm.** A life without priorities leads to filling our days and time with what's convenient— comparing ourselves through devices, scrolling under the guise of "market research," and arguing with BigRick287 on Reddit.

▶ **Inconsistent performance.** When you look under the hood of your favorite artists, filmmakers, creatives, or business moguls—you see high levels of structure that allow their performances to come to life.

▶ **A lack of meaning and identity.** There is an existential crisis among athletes who retire. They had highly structured, organized lives where they depended on someone telling them exactly where to be and at what time—and now that's gone.

▶ **The loss of a compelling horizon.** Our goal-seeking mechanisms must be satiated in some way, shape, or form or we lose meaning. We lose the connection with the part of ourselves that longs for a reason to wake up. We miss the spark of challenge.

▶ **Anxiousness, escapism, and addiction.** With a void inside, we turn to the easy outs—escapism, addiction, vicariously living. We crush cocktails, obsess over wild conspiracies on YouTube, or spend four hours analyzing fantasy football.

Now, let me be clear: you're supposed to enjoy the time and space you've created for yourself. You should pop the champagne, celebrate, and take as much time off as you'd like, as we covered in Chapter 8. You should take time off . . . albeit strategically.

But again, at some point—this void starts working against us. Because structure in our lives is the direct path to freedom.

EMBRACE STRUCTURE

We tend to get whiplashed by people's triumphs and ignore the structured process it took to get there. We see the finished product—the killer stand-up routine, the Super Bowl halftime show, the head-turning profits. We see arrival moments: the serene wedding day, the oh-so-perfect guitarist at open mic night who sounds like the second coming of John Mayer.

But how did they get there?

The answer is dosing structure, which acts as vital guardrails for performance, growth, and consistency.

For example:

▶ Haruki Murakami, the great Japanese novelist, structures intense writing time starting around 4:30 a.m. for four to five hours—followed by a 10K run or 1,500-meter swim in the afternoon to experience the freedom of art and physical vigor.

▶ Daniel Day Lewis may be the most obsessive method actor on the planet—harnessing intense structure as he disappears to study and stays in character even when he's not on set—to the tune of six Academy Award nominations and the freedom of craft mastery.

▶ Beyonce's legendary Coachella performance took eight months of grueling practice, rehearsals, and structure—as detailed in the documentary *Homecoming*—for the freedom of an iconic performance people *still* rave about today.

The list goes on, the point is simple: structure works.

With structure's limitations, you have a place to funnel mental, physical, and emotional energy. Without this constraint, energy scatters while you spend the day coming up with the wittiest Twitter one-liner no one ever reads. Enter the structure equation, which states:

More Front-End Structure = More Back-End Freedom

Let's examine why the structure equation works:

- ► **Structure gives us purpose.** Without purpose, we become a rudderless ship going nowhere. We need a reason to get up in the morning, to challenge ourselves, to have a destination that wakes us up from our daydream.
- ► **Structure acts as insurance.** Humans are complex with varying emotional states, random behaviors, and biases that keep us from showing up. Consider structure an insurance policy against erratic mood swings.
- ► **Structure elevates results.** Examine the greats or those at the top of your field and you'll recognize how their structure leads to the ability to "improvise" and make it look easy. It's *not* easy; mastery is making it look that way.
- ► **Structure leads to consistency.** Structure is the elixir of long-term consistency, showing up after the high has faded and making your success run on autopilot while others ask you for your "hack," "tip," or "secret."
- ► **Structure releases the need for motivation.** It doesn't care how motivated you are and whether or not the caffeine hit. Instead of needing to feel motivated to show up, one shows up . . . and feels motivated. And if you don't, well, you did the work anyway.

Let's dive into how to dose structure into your life.

HOW TO CREATE STRUCTURE

Infusing structure into our lives, then, is the ultimate source of freedom—progress, growth, and results, as well as having utility toward something bigger than ourselves. So, how do you create structure? We'll break it down into six main categories:

- ► **Personal habits.** The structure of *who* you want to be, including physical vitality, emotional headspace, consciousness practices, and relationships. The idea is to put as much of your success on autopilot as possible.

▶ **Professional habits.** The structure surrounding what you want to do in your career. These include what you consider your craft, your zone of genius, the skills you're acquiring, and your ability to produce results.

▶ **Morning and nightly routines.** Morning structure leads to peak emotional states of clarity to set the tone—leading to elevated performance and fulfillment. Nightly routines create transitions to wind down and recharge. Both are vital.

▶ **Systems and processes.** We all have systems for living, whether they're working or not. A system in our personal lives can be doing meal prep on Sunday—and having the freedom to not think about food. A system in our professional life could be sitting down on Monday morning to map out the three priorities for the week and having the freedom of not procrastinating.

▶ **Event-based goal-setting.** Having a date, time, and place to show up—whether that be a speech, a 10K race, or a revenue target—you need event-based goal-setting to create structure. Urgency is a meta-ingredient for success.

▶ **Owning your calendar.** Mention calendars to seekers and they'll spit out their spirulina smoothie—but here's the deal: your calendar is proof of your dreams coming true. Most of us are conditioned to hate our calendars because they're about someone else's vision.

All of this structure frees up mental real estate, minimizes the paradox of choice, and saves willpower. It compels you to show up, not leaving your growth to chance, how you feel, or what your horoscope said.

However, at some point, structure starts to work against us—which is precisely the moment we must torch it.

SHATTER YOUR STRUCTURE

Even the best routines, rituals, and habits can turn mundane, dull, and boring—what was once a gateway to clarity has become a rut. The morning ritual that used to blast us into space becomes normal, the killer workout turns lame, the date night loses its magic.

Enter novelty—the strategic dismantling of the very same habits that were once useful to change our day. Here we say yes to something we'd normally never do: listen to jazz when we prefer EDM, sign up for improv even though we're introverts, or take a random road trip on a Wednesday morning . . . just 'cause.

Novelty breaks the prediction-making machine our brains are masters at creating. As Michael Pollan wrote in *How to Change Your Mind*, our habit-forming mechanisms and pre-diction machine are a blessing and a curse, saying: "The good thing is I'm seldom surprised. The bad thing is I'm seldom surprised."[4]

And hence, why we *need* novelty.

So, what is novelty and how do you use it?

▶ **Shattering habits.** To harness novelty, we shatter habits and rituals that were "working" so as to provide some breathing room and perspective. For example, if you have a morning ritual you've done every day, turn it upside down and do something different.

▶ **Changing domains.** Are you obsessed with nonfiction books? Read a classic novel. Do you always watch the same comedy movies? Engage in a thriller. Change your domain and leave the comfort zone of the predictable to tap into novelty.

▶ **Saying yes.** The downside of structure is we tend to "predict" what we'll like in the future—and we're usually wrong. Novelty is saying yes to something you'd normally say no to—the random trip, the date, or the inconvenient adventure.

▶ **Dosing state-shifting experiences.** These experiences alter our emotional states and infuse curiosity, inspiration, and presence that can't be accessed in our structured lives. These are to be dosed monthly, weekly, and even daily—from a meditation to trekking up a mountain.

- ► **Tapping into improvisation.** Novelty is a complete lack of structure, to tap into unbridled improvisation and synchronicities based on being in the moment. Have parts of your day and week that are completely *unplanned*.
- ► **Undergoing cathartic experiences.** Catharsis is a therapeutic release of energy, to experience something so novel that it rejuvenates our mind, body, and spirit. For some, this may be losing their minds at a concert, going skydiving, diving with great white sharks, or watching a riveting sunrise.

By creating states of novelty, we tap into those elusive moments we can't get enough of—states of wonder, awe, and utter surprise—which are irresistible to the soul.

WONDER . . . AWE . . . AHA

When was the last time you experienced one of those aha moments where time stood still as you attempted to assemble the pieces of your psyche in childlike wonder? Hurled into the present, these moments of rapture remind us of what matters.

We are here, *here*.

For many, they can't remember the last time they felt this state.

And so, the endgame of novelty, besides its benefits of contrast and perspective, is to experience these states of wonder, surprise, and holy-shit insights that make life worth living. Even *one* moment of awe can shift us for weeks.

It's the purple sunrise that blows our minds. It's holding eye contact with a newborn. It's listening to that piece of music that moves our spirit as we try to reconcile how a mere mortal brought it to life. It's pushing ourselves physically and feeling that cocktail of endorphins, clarity, and heart-thumping aliveness.

Instead of waiting to experience these, we can nudge them along through the introduction of novelty on a yearly, quarterly, monthly, weekly, and even a daily basis.

Otherwise, we feel stuck and like nothing ever changes.

BEING STUCK

I'm *stuck*.

We've all muttered these words, complained that we feel like we're on a barren plateau with no end in sight—experiencing the same issues and banging our heads up against the wall as nothing changes.

Being stuck is both subjective and nebulous, making it brutally hard to fix.

And yet, if you've felt stuck, ask yourself:

- ▶ When was the last time you did something different?
- ▶ When was the last time you went against your normal operating procedure?
- ▶ When was the last time you listened to your intuition?
- ▶ When was the last time you did *anything* new—spoke to a stranger, tried salmon instead of chicken, read a novel instead of the paper?

Usually, the answers are predictable: life is busy, there's a lot on the plate, it's an intense season and there's a vacation next quarter.

Yawn.

Make no mistake: feeling stuck is a symptom of lacking novelty in our lives.

And while grand moments of novelty are amazing—you don't need to go on a weeklong European escapade or learn how to BASE jump to infuse your life with it.

In other words, start small.

Take a new route home from work. Change the three-mile run you've done a hundred times and hit CrossFit. If that's the norm, do a yin yoga class. Speak up in a meeting. Tell a joke when you'd normally be serious. Send a video message instead of a text. Look up at the night sky and put the phone in your pocket.

Just do something, *anything* . . . different.

Here's how:

▶ **Front-load structure, back-load novelty.** By front-loading structure, you set the tone for your day and week while creating the freedom of novelty. It's hard to be present when we're twitching from not checking our email.

▶ **Interrupt patterns.** Break a pattern once a day by going against your autopilot mechanisms. Find small ways to shift what you'd usually do and have a fun, playful, non-outcome-based approach.

▶ **Create novel experiences.** Put experiences on the calendar every single week and treat them as important as your career priorities—the lake trip, a creative date night, some much-needed "you" time at the bookstore.

▶ **Break the pattern before you need it.** Treat novelty with as much weight as structured work and make it preventive. Enroll others into what you're doing and be the leader by choosing the activity, place, and time.

These work both in the micro—our hour-by-hour and daily experiences—and in the macro, big-picture reality. For example, dose structured work "sprints" followed by strumming the guitar. Have an ironclad morning ritual, followed by a "flex" day. Finish a pending project with vigor; then tone it down for a couple weeks. By merging these two, you'll experience the freedom of progress and novelty.

WHAT TO LEAVE BEHIND WITH CONVENTIONAL STRUCTURE

We've all experienced too much structure—our days crammed with little breathing room that all but zaps our curiosity and passion. Here's what to leave behind:

▶ **Thinking more is better.** Like all else, a life that is on overdrive with structure leads to mental exhaustion. The key here is *strategic* structure. You are not artificial intelligence, you are a human and must dose appropriately.

▶ **Not balancing equally.** Structure is rigid by nature. This must be balanced by the same degree of a lack of structure to allow the mind, heart, and body to roam free, unencumbered, sans schedule.

WHAT TO LEAVE BEHIND WITH CONVENTIONAL NOVELTY

Novelty invites curiosity, wonder, and perspective but can also be taken too far—we have no ground to stand on and are flailing in the wind. Here's what to be careful of:

▶ **Endless novelty.** We all know the person with no backbone, drifting aimlessly: too much novelty means we never touch the ground. Routines are powerful, and without them, we become bohemian truth seekers addicted to another hit.

▶ **Making novelty complex.** You can create novelty as you read this book. Crank out five burpees. Put on your favorite song and dance your face off. Keep it simple; the feeling is what matters.

STRUCTURE BREEDS MAGIC

Keith Jarrett had driven five and a half backbreaking hours in a colossal rainstorm from Zurich to Cologne, Germany, to perform at the local opera house—and was packing his bags to go back home despite the 1,300 people expecting to see him play piano that evening.[5]

And he had every reason to.

Not only was he in terrible physical condition, but the piano on stage was a mistake—an abysmal rehearsal piano with jammed pedals and out-of-tune timbre—something you'd find in a crappy antique shop.

In other words, unusable.

Jarrett, ever the perfectionist, couldn't and wouldn't perform on such low-level equipment. Hell, it wasn't even a grand piano! As he got in the car to leave the venue that evening, the 17-year-old music student who'd scrappily arranged this concert came to his car window.

And that's when he knew he had to do it, at least for her.

That evening, Jarrett walked on stage in his trademark manner, using an instrument a high school player would balk at, and delivered a performance for the ages. His team recorded the concert as a cautionary tale of how messing up logistics can lead to a terrible experience.

When Jarrett played the first note, all bets were off.

He seemed to enter a trancelike state unlike any other—those in attendance instantly knew this would be special—delivering a career-defining performance as one of the greatest pianists of all time. It was mastery in action, genius in motion, creativity at its finest. And the live album that wasn't supposed to be, the *Köln Concert*, became the highest-selling live piano album of all time.[6]

And it was all improvised.

This is structure in action: the discipline of overpreparing, working on your craft, and practicing your skills—with novelty. It is the ability to shatter preparation, show up during chaos, and surprise yourself. Had Jarrett not been both obsessive about structure and willing to torch it, this magical night wouldn't have happened.

And you can do the same.

Chapter

10

Focus
&
Perspective

The rise of digital devices, 15-second soundbites, and clickbait news headlines, combined with an orchestra of zips, pings, and whistles emanating from our pocket, have turned us into Pavlov's dog. We're constantly salivating for the next hit of dopamine engineered by brilliant PhDs in Palo Alto with unlimited budgets to control one thing: our attention.

We're not losing this game, we're down 47–0 in the third quarter. And they keep launching Hail Marys and running up the score.

Because, well, they can.

Human attention spans are in the gutter. We no longer read long-form articles. We interrupt a book with scrolling. We go to dinner and check email the second the other person goes to the bathroom. We bump into strangers and inanimate objects. We have vaporized boredom, daydreaming, and thinking. We have faux conversations, time with our loved ones, and even sex.

We're there physically, but are we *really* there?

Our lack of focus isn't simply interrupting our days, it robs us of meaning, connection, and introspection. It destroys our ability to engage in work we love. It annihilates our performance. As author Cal Newport, PhD, told me during an interview: "We just feel better, and more satisfied, the more we find ourselves focusing on a small number of hard, but valuable things."[1]

Focus is a *life* amplifier.

The hustler's dilemma manifests in thinking that if hustlers had a 26-hour day, they'd be further along. Because in their eyes, if you're not where you want to be, then surely, it's about *more* time and effort.

Hustlers get focus wrong: focusing on the wrong things, too many things, or never stepping away to reap the benefit that comes from not being in the trenches. Think back to our law school example in Chapter 1. Hustlers can focus so intensely on achieving . . . without ever creating some much-needed space to maybe realize it's *not* what they want.

Until it's too late.

Furthermore, they tend to be the kings and queens of multitasking. The sad reality for most people grinding 13 hours a day is they're lacking clarity on priorities, filling their days with busywork, and laughably disorganized. To illustrate this point, consider the average American office worker is productive 1.8 to 2.5 hours out of a standard 8-hour workday.[2]

No, really.

Let that sink in as we examine the ways a company coerces employees: offices, mind-numbing meetings, performance reviews, and an obsession with email, BCCs, read receipts, and corporate leadership retreats that produce stunning binders that sit on the shelf and gather dust.

Oh, the insanity.

Enter training your focus while limiting how many balls you have in the air on the hustler's side. You'll create more by doing . . . *less*. You'll ditch multitasking and a flurry of action that feels great in the moment but leaves you wiped. You'll know when it's time to step away. Because while focus is vital, too much can all but kill creativity and develop the wrong kind of tunnel vision.

On the seeker's side, you'll practice the art of being the observer of life through detachment and perspective-seeking activities. You'll step away from the field of play to see the bigger picture. You'll stop short of being too detached, leading to an apathetic, aloof state.

The endgame of both of these worlds is awareness—the ultimate meta-skill for long-term results and transformation. Before we get there, let's dispel the chief myth of focus and productivity.

FOCUS MEANS DOING LESS, NOT MORE

The most pervasive myth inside the world of productivity and focus is that it's all about doing more . . . so you can, well, do more.

That's not how it works. Not at all.

For example, say you're working for a boss and you bring your "A" game, get laser-focused, and do a week's worth of work in one day. Then what?

Well, congrats, the next day, you'll get another stack of TPS reports.

Focus is not really about doing more or wearing the number of hours you hustled like a badge of honor to be shared on social; it's about:

▶ **Doing less.** With focus, you do less by doing more of the essential. You say good-bye to multitasking, browser tabs, being glued to email, and shoddy work that doesn't move the needle.

▶ **Valuing results.** Hustlers love talking about how much they're working. "Dude, I was at the coffee shop for six hours yesterday!" Uh, so what? Half of those were spent on social media and another third chatting with the nootropic bros; you did 64 minutes of *actual* work. Congrats, you're riding high on 15 percent efficiency and getting ripped off with sugar pills.

▶ **Increasing performance.** With focus, performance explodes. Speed and quality rise. You do better work . . . in less time. You do what used to take an entire day and finish it in 90 minutes. You tap into flowlike states.

The ethos of this principle requires focus.

There is no escaping this reality. Since we all have varying degrees of cyber addiction to stimulus, noise, and the fifth limb (no, not that one) that is our smartphone—training this skill is not negotiable.

Let's dive into the tactics to get you focused:

▶ **Focus is a skill.** This can't be overstated because any skill means you can improve (surprisingly quickly) to take back ownership of your focus.

▶ **Focus is trainable.** Skills are trainable; there are systematic ways to improve focus over time. Adopting a growth mindset of curiosity and practice will determine your success.

▶ **Focus rewards small wins.** Improving your focus isn't about a one-day blitz where you're going to be on fire for seven hours—rather, it's about small wins at the margins of life.

▶ **Focus compounds over time.** Like any practice, the compounding effect rewards consistency over intensity. It's better to do a 25-minute block of focused work daily than crush it on a random Saturday for hours.

▶ **Focus celebrates results.** Focus flips the script from time and effort to the actual result. If the same result took you 3.5 hours versus 49 minutes, which is better? The result in the least amount of time is what matters.

▶ **Focus creates flow.** Flow states of unbridled presence, performance, and total absorption are found on the other side of focus. Even if you think you're awful at focus, you currently spend about 5 percent of your time in flow, whether you know it or not.[3]

NO AIM MEANS NO FOCUS

One of the perils of focus is having no aim.

It's when you pop open the laptop for a 60-minute block of work but have no idea what to do—so you're doomed to scour social media under the guise of "market research."

We've all been there.

It's time to cultivate a practice around focus so you not only reclaim mental sanity—but perform at a level where you have plenty of time and space left over to recover. And, you know, live your life. If the average worker is productive two hours a day, imagine if you're able to hit four hours and shut it down.

To train, cultivate, and maximize your ability to focus, you'll:

1. **Be clear on your North Star.** Your North Star is the guiding light on the horizon, a compass to help guide you. You don't need to have it *all* figured out; a compass is not a map. A general idea is enough. Where do you want to be in three years? Start there.
2. **Be clear on your Big 3 priorities.** Covered in Chapter 17, these priorities are your North Star compressed for the next quarter, or 90-day period.
3. **Brain dump all actions for #2.** Once you're clear on your Big 3, make a list without overthinking of all the possible ways, steps, and ideas to bring those priorities to life—aim for at least 20 actions and don't focus on the how.
4. **Categorize as level 1, 2, or 3.** Take a break and come back with fresh eyes to review your list. Delete the obvious nonessentials, then categorize the steps in three levels, level 1 being most important down to level 3. Do this and

you should have three to six of the *most* important items left
to do.

5. **Start your day on airplane mode.** Level 1 priorities consist
   of the daily, important work that will move the needle. In
   order to bring these to life and retrain focus, you'll start your
   day *without* your phone. Aim for a minimum of 15 minutes at
   first and then work your way up to 30, 60, 90, and then, 120
   minutes.

6. **Batch themes.** Whether you work for someone else or for
   yourself, think of your day in themes. Podcaster James
   Altucher refers to the making, managing, marketing model.[4]
   The morning is for creative work, the middle of the day is
   for sales and marketing, and the end is for operations and
   administration. This is one example; create your own.

7. **Set hard rules.** Is your attention at someone else's beck and
   call? Open-door policies, endless pings on the phone, and
   browser tabs waiting to be read are recipes for disaster. Set
   boundaries. Say no. Set rules for how you operate. Respect
   your time and others will too.

8. **Set appointments with number one.** We treat time with
   others with respect, but when we have a time block for
   our dream, we slack. No more. Make an appointment with
   yourself to time block for a specific priority and treat it like
   you're meeting the most important person in your life . . .
   because you are.

9. **Be unavailable for distractions.** Put the phone away. Turn
   off the internet. Close the door. Pause the inbox. Set an
   autoresponder. Work from a place where you can think. As
   Steven Kotler, the Flow researcher, says: "If you can't put a
   sign up at your door that says fuck off, I'm flowing,you're a
   lost cause."[5]

10. **Celebrate progress, track your time, adapt.** Perfect isn't
    the goal, progress is. You may focus for 30 minutes a day
    for a week and think it's no big deal. It is. So, celebrate it.
    Then track your metrics, learn lessons, pivot, and course
    correct.

These tactics apply no matter who you are: someone growing a side hustle, a career professional, or a full-blown entrepreneur. Thanks to the rise of remote work, we have more freedom to design a results-based workflow. If you marched into your boss's office and proposed a setup that improved output by 40 percent, would they *really* say no? If they would, you may want to hatch your escape plan.

We've all had those days when we operated at a mile a minute, *feeling* like we were moving the needle, but if we're honest . . . we weren't. We cleared our inbox, watched other people's feeds, and consumed noise that left us empty at night. But we've also had the opposite: the days we leaned into the hardest, deepest work—and felt proud of ourselves and able to shut it down.

Which do you prefer? To master focus, time, and efficiency not only means you'll be awarded bigger opportunities, but it also means you'll have more *free* time.

But like everything else, too much focus works against us.

It zaps creative thinking, makes us miss the bigger picture, and diminishes our ability to see patterns. Why? Well, deep focus can be a hog on our mental, physical, and emotional resources.

To balance this out, you'll become the observer.

BE THE OBSERVER

I've spent 177 hours naked with the inability to see, touch, or hear, inside a sensory deprivation chamber. There is nothing to do. There is no stimulus. There is no light. Due to thousands of pounds of Epsom salt, it's as if I'm floating in a far-off galaxy, wandering through the fringes of consciousness.

This is complete nothingness.

For most, the thought of spending a minute inside their own head without distraction sounds abysmal. But the power of this practice is precisely that it is uncomfortable. In a stimulus-soaked world where an abundance of distractions are available all day, every day, there is power in unplugging.

There is power in *being*.

What makes floating powerful is the stripping of senses. Our senses are information-gathering hogs, scanning for data every waking moment, never satiated. Because they have no off switch, our senses are taking energy away from other things— insights, creativity, perspective.

When everything goes quiet, there is only one place to go: become the observer of life, instead of the operator. By doing so, you disconnect from the craziness and tap into rich clarity.

This is the opposite of maniacal focus.

For example, a quarterback who is *too focused* ends up tipping off the defense as he waits for one receiver to be open. But the quarterback who has developed awareness can see the game *within* the game and recognizes systematic patterns on the fly.

In business, think of Blockbuster's dramatic fall with CEO John Antioco being too focused on brick-and-mortar video stores. As technology shifted, the company was slow to adapt. Even when it did, creating serious momentum with its on-demand video service, it walked away. The company dug its heels in and went from 9,000 stores to *one* lone survivor in Bend, Oregon—acting as a nostalgic parlor trick.

The same applies to your life.

By balancing the intensity of focus, you'll become the observer and train a different part of focus: detached awareness. You'll see yourself in your day-to-day: at the dinner table, reacting to life, making decisions. This is perspective at a level we rarely get and gives us the answers we so often long for.

You notice patterns. You strip away the emotions that cloud our judgment when we're too focused. You create breathing room to see yourself from new angles, to invite life-shifting insights that will help you come back to focused work knowing what needs to be done . . . and what to let go of.

You'll sharpen intuition and see trends that were previously invisible. Not because they weren't there—but because you were too deep in your own life. Psychologists refer to this as the Overview Effect, the ability to see ourselves from different vantage points.[6]

When you become the observer, you transcend the minutiae of your day-to-day life and the smallness of the ego.

In other words, you create your own *Truman Show*.

CREATE YOUR OWN *TRUMAN SHOW*

Becoming the observer of your life lets you see how you're acting and moving around the world in real time. It's watching the *Truman Show* with the camera pointed at your own life.

Since we're hardwired to spend most of our lives on autopilot repeating the same behaviors (even when we know they're not working)—becoming the observer creates a gap between stimulus and response. Within this gap, you get your power back.

You become proactive, instead of reactive.

In the gap, you create a split-second moment to choose a deliberate response and not rely on the egoic part of yourself. Which means you're not only aware there is a gap—you expand it. This is awareness in action. By doing so, you're able to choose how to respond to a fact of daily life: emotional triggers.

What's an emotional trigger? It's those charged moments that hurl us into stress, anxiety, and sabotage. They come in all shapes and sizes: the look your partner gave you at the kitchen counter, a passive-aggressive email a coworker sent, the fact no one commented on your selfie, or the sinking feeling you should be further along in your life.

Emotional triggers are costly.

They've cost people fame, careers, and relationships. Even on a small scale, they're what separates a good day from a great one. And because days bleed into weeks, months, and years— this is the invisible part of growth that is oh so important.

We've all checked email during an emotionally heightened state. Our flight delayed, we were starving . . . and there it was.

The note from a colleague, boss, or client that sets us off. In that state, we became laser-focused: typing a mile a minute, and finally telling them the truth. No time for fluff talk.

Real talk, baby.

With the mouse hovering on send, the release of agitation was one click away. But at the last moment . . . you paused. You recognized how charged you were. You should come back to this, you told yourself.

A couple hours later, you're on your knees thanking the heavens for not sending the message. As the trigger wore off, you recognized how sending a scathing message was a terrible idea and could have gotten you *further away* from your goals. The person who wrote the message feels . . . unrecognizable.

This is the power of the gap—you create enough space between stimulus and response to ask:

- ▶ Is what I'm about to do and say in alignment with who I want to be?
- ▶ Is what I'm about to do and say going to stress me out more, or less?
- ▶ Is what I'm about to do and say going to get me closer to or further from my goals?

In most cases of responding to an emotional trigger, the answer is clear.

Sure, responding to the troll on social media feels good in the moment—it's the ego's version of a hot fudge sundae. But before you've finished the last bite, you realize you have irritable bowel syndrome. You're doomed. By interrupting your primal response, you get your power back.

You deliberately live your life.

And let's be clear: your primal response will never fade. Even the most aware on the planet have scathing thoughts at times. Emotional triggers are a part of life, and you're not training this out of your system. You are addressing the next step: do you take this at face value—or create perspective on the fly?

As you expand the gap, you'll:

- ▶ Take triggers that used to zap hours and get over them in minutes.
- ▶ Instantly pivot to clarity after a rejection, challenge, or "failure."
- ▶ Practice gratitude in the moment without waiting for hindsight.

As one-offs, none of these are monumental.

You'll be a little better, or a little less stressed. But compound it over weeks, months, and years and you have two different lives. In one, you're running on fumes, making strange decisions, and responding to emotional triggers galore. The other is a deliberate, intentional life. One where your restraint is attractive to others, instead of people avoiding you like the person on social media who posts political rants all day.

All because you created the gap.

HOW TO CREATE THE GAP

Creating the gap is being cut off in traffic and laughing it off.

Creating the gap is being told no and recognizing there is a benefit.

Creating the gap is being in a fight with your partner ... and inhaling deeply.

These won't only make you feel better, they elevate performance and create more progress, results, happiness, fulfillment, and cash. Here are some ways to create the gap:

▶ Meditation	▶ Massages	▶ Conversation
▶ Time in nature	▶ Daydreaming	▶ Energy work
▶ Physical fitness	▶ Creative work	▶ Cold therapy
▶ Yoga	▶ Walking	▶ Psychedelics
▶ Saunas	▶ Journaling	▶ Breathwork
▶ Solitude	▶ Therapy	▶ Retreats
▶ Float tanks	▶ Coaching	▶ Hypnosis

The end result of each of these is perspective.

With perspective, you go back into your day with awareness—the building block to long-term transformation. It's precisely why mindfulness has exploded across boardrooms, sports, creatives, and the everyday person. It trains awareness: the ability to see ourselves, recognize patterns in real time, and expand the gap on demand.

David Lynch, director of *Mulholland Drive*, *Eraserhead*, and *Twin Peaks*, swears by his twice-a-day meditation practice going on 40 years. He attributes it to not only saving his sanity from the cutthroat nature of filmmaking but also unleashing creativity, harboring ideas, crafting previously unavailable solutions, and having way more fun.

"The big ideas are found by going deep. The practice makes me more creative, allows me to tap into an ocean of solutions, and makes everything funner. Once I started meditating, the films became more creative and we had the best time on set."[7]

Small shifts in perspective pay off big. A 10 percent shift in creativity, performance, and resilience leads to a radically different day.

WHAT TO LEAVE BEHIND WITH CONVENTIONAL FOCUS

Not all focus is useful, and sometimes we need an off switch to take a step back. Here's what to avoid:

- ▶ **Not recovering wisely.** A focused life is rare, and concentration consumes bandwidth. You won't be able to do this for eight hours a day—don't bother. Recover from focused time using seeking principles.
- ▶ **Starting too big.** When people commit to focus, they start with a three-hour time block and ditch at minute 14. Start small. Do a 15-minute block and build from there. Celebrate wins. Build the skill.

WHAT TO LEAVE BEHIND WITH CONVENTIONAL PERSPECTIVE

Perspective is potent, until you find yourself equipped with endless insights that are competing for your time and attention. Here's what to be cautious of:

▶ **Living in the gap.** The gap is a tool, not a destination. Living there all day means you have nowhere to stand. All these tools of space can be powerful, but at some point, you must take the insights from the clouds and get your hands in the dirt.

▶ **Getting lost in insight.** Space creates insight, and yet, insight alone never changes behavior. We can analyze traumas and we can learn about our childhood wounds, but then what? Insight without utility can work against us.

BE FOCUSED . . .
BUT TAKE A STEP BACK

In 2007, Blackberry had amassed a market share of $70 billion and was seen as the unequivocal leader of an emerging industry—on a rocket ship to unthinkable success. A large part of what got Blackberry here was relentless focus by then CEO Mike Lazaridis. His ability to focus is a core ingredient of what started Blackberry's dizzying climb from obscurity to the knowledge worker's fifth limb . . . turning "Sent via Blackberry" into a status symbol and the infamous nickname, *crackberry*.

However . . .

The same ingredient that made Blackberry a market leader became the underpinning to its colossal downfall. In a sense, we could say the CEO was *too* focused . . . on the wrong things.

Especially as the market changed and new players arrived.

Ever obsessed with serving its core users—business and corporate executives—Blackberry failed to adapt. Mocking Apple's desire to ditch a traditional keyboard to appeal to everyday people who wanted a phone that could *do it all* . . . Blackberry dug its heels in. The company stayed focused on the business user, developing new encryption methods and touting its product as the most secure smartphone.

Except no one cared about security.

While Blackberry focused on its business users, Apple targeted consumers with a fresh look and a media-savvy piece of hardware that became a status symbol of ease, fun, and creativity. As journalist Vlad Savov at *The Verge* wrote, "focusing on the tens of millions of customers it already had, BlackBerry missed out on the billions that were to come."[8]

Because of a maniacal focus gone wrong, Blackberry went from $70 billion and 21 percent market share to $500 million and less than 1 percent market share.[9]

In just three years.

So, what does this mean for your life?

Focus, done right, is an undeniable force. By using it wisely, you'll drive meaningful results that spark the fire inside. You'll create the fulfillment we all crave while elevating performance—yesterday's task that took you two hours now takes 42 minutes. Three months later, it takes 19.

Which means, as you develop the skill of focus—you do *less*.

You'll create more progress before noon . . . than most do in a week. As an entrepreneur, you experience the freedom you craved all along. You do your best work and then hang with the kids at the park. As a career professional, you'll stand out from the pack. Your coworkers will ask for your "secret." You turn the 8-, 10-, or 12-hour workday into 5 focused hours of needle-moving work.

Oh, and because focus is an antidote to stress, comparison, and the gnawing feeling that we're drifting in our lives—you'll save yourself from hours of therapy or worthless rumination.

Then, you'll couple this focus with being the observer—seeing yourself in real time—to gather key insights. In doing so, you'll stay ahead of the curve . . . and see the bigger picture. You'll notice trends that can't be found in the trenches as you expand the *gap*. Because of this, you feel in control of life, *at cause* . . . not flailing in the wind. Best of all, you won't fall off a proverbial cliff because you were too rigid and full of yourself like Blackberry was.

Taking a step back, then, becomes your competitive advantage.

Through focus, you find freedom. And by being the observer, you create a level of perspective few have—allowing you to take this newfound wisdom and integrate it back into your focused work.

What else is there?

Chapter

11

Be Decisive
&
Hone Intuition

Indecision is a dream killer.

It halts your momentum, robs you of certainty, and leaves you in a land of analysis paralysis, going nowhere fast. High off possibility, the paradox of choice—the realization that more options create *less* freedom—takes over and starves your precious willpower.[1] In that place, you're no longer interested, as indecision leads to overthinking, hesitation, and apathy.

No, thanks.

The cult of busy and access to instantaneous, one-click-away comparisons make decisiveness a total nightmare. With a litany of inputs, it's no wonder we feel so out of tune with our inner voice. It can seem impossible to discern a real desire from one we feel pressured into. On top of this, you've got speakers lighting up stages and newsfeeds telling us we can *do* and *be* anything, leading to another dilemma: with unlimited options, what do we actually pick!?

Sigh.

We are all susceptible to being indecisive in a world where we have infinite choices and the fear of making the *wrong* one stops us. We tell ourselves we'll think about it and make a list of pros and cons—or meditate until we get the answer.

Yet, what we're really doing is avoiding.

On the hustler's side, decisiveness is a skill, a practice designed to collapse the time, energy, and mental bandwidth to make a choice. By doing so, we avoid fear of missing out (FOMO) as well as the tug-of-war between possibility and worst-case scenarios.

To value decisiveness means to value movement. That no matter what happens, it's better to be in momentum than stuck in the barren wasteland of indecision. I'll take it a step further: it's better to be going in the *wrong* direction learning valuable lessons than sitting on the couch vegetating on what could be.

On the seeker's side, you'll sharpen intuition—your gut feeling, what Ralph Waldo Emerson referred to as "blessed impulse"—using it as a compass for decisions. You'll minimize the signal-to-noise ratio between inner and outer worlds. You'll reduce the head trash that blocks your knowing. Ultimately, you'll tap into the part of you that knows what is *right*, even if it doesn't make sense.

Especially if it doesn't make sense.

Between these, you'll create the real-world clarity and progress that comes with decisiveness *and* intuition. You learn to trust yourself in a world that conditions us to ask for permission. You'll make decisions from the clarity you've harnessed in seeking.

By developing this skill, answers become second nature.

You know not to sign the contract because something feels off. You say no to a collaboration due to a gut feeling. You take a chance and bet on yourself because you know it's right. You hire the person who fits your culture over the one with a flawless résumé yet feels out of alignment.

You execute.

While doing so, you'll drop the illusion that more options is always better—more career paths, streaming movies, and tomato sauces at the grocery store when you're starving and can't possibly imagine *why* they have 17 flavors.

What happened to old reliable marinara?

Because on a long enough timeline, an abundance of options isn't freedom. It's complete and utter chaos.

THE DECISION CURVE

Options equal freedom, right?

There are few things our culture values more than freedom. All of us are spoiled with endless choices on what movie to watch on a Friday night, what person to date or marry, where to live, and what songs we're going to pick for our road trip out of the millions available. And let's face it: this freedom is incredible.

With choice, comes possibility.

But at some point, options aren't positive anymore; they become traps. We debate the career move aimlessly for weeks. We obsess over what side hustle to launch, losing precious momentum. We enter a constant state of comparison between the choice we made and *every* other alternative. Harvard researchers examined how having too many alternatives and the ability to turn our back on a decision both lead to plummeting happiness and fulfillment.[2]

With choice comes responsibility.

Equipped with the Decision Curve, you'll have a framework that shows options are valuable for a little while, but as time passes, they kill your energy, willpower, and clarity, leading to a state of questioning yourself. Or you don't make the move at all because you're stuck on best- and worst-case scenarios. Go on this path long enough, and freedom has the opposite effect.

Indecision. Paralysis. Avoidance.

Freedom without filtering becomes chaos.

THE STAGES OF THE DECISION CURVE

Consider the Decision Curve to help you recognize how the illusion can work against you in real time, be it as simple as what diet to go on before the summer getaway or bigger life choices involving your career, entrepreneurial ventures, or hiring an employee.

By using this framework, you'll be able to use options as leverage for opportunities but also recognize when more is *not* more.

Enter the Decision Curve, which operates as follows:

- ▶ **At Stage I**—freedom of choice is correlated with fulfillment, happiness, meaning.
  In this stage, having freedom has a positive correlation to well-being as we experience the power of agency. We feel autonomy and independence, the ability to choose.
- ▶ **At Stage II**—if we have not introduced a constraint by making a decision, we start to experience a dip.
  This is when we encounter a diminishing return. We haven't made a decision and are starting to experience the mental consequences of too many options, including fatigue, comparison, analyzing, and losing the clarity we had.
- ▶ **At Stage III**—freedom is correlated with anxiety, dissatisfaction, and major FOMO.
  Without making a decision, we enter a spiral of avoidance. We explore more options, creating more decision fatigue, a loss of willpower, and overthinking.

We all desire freedom, options, and agency, but the drop-off comes *much* sooner than we believe. Your ability to make a decision inside the sweet spot of the Decision Curve will determine how far along the curve you go. That sweet spot is found between Stage I and Stage II.

Understanding the practicality of the Decision Curve, your life becomes easier. Making choices and decisions becomes a skill. FOMO dissolves. If you pick a crappy restaurant, at least *you picked*. If you watched the worst movie of your life, at least you aren't sitting in the parking lot scrolling Rotten Tomatoes reviews from strangers you've never met who love avant-garde flicks. If you picked a path thinking it was your purpose and realize it's not—you're better off. Sometimes knowing what *doesn't* work is exactly what we need.

The Decision Curve isn't only a practical tool, it's a shift of values.

We tend to overvalue freedom and undervalue constraint, not realizing constraint *leads* to freedom. Stay with me: if you never pick a business idea, then you'll wind up where you are now . . . except more stuck after compiling 11 domain names with nothing to show for it.

It's time to value both freedom and constraint. To seek options, but then commit. To value possibility and choice. To recognize that making a decision creates clarity, even if it was the wrong decision. Especially if it was the wrong one! Here, you have *real* clarity and not the illusion of it.

Otherwise, progress becomes elusive at best, downright impossible at worst. Let's dive into some practices to help you stay on the right side of the Decision Curve:

- ▶ **Decide from abundance, not lack.** We tend to decide from a place of *not* wanting to lose what we already have instead of thinking of what we *could* have. In other words, we default to operating from lack.
- ▶ **Ask your future self.** We make decisions based on our past, or who we are today. The problem is this ensures we stay *exactly* the same or at best, improve incrementally. Instead, take yourself 2, 4, or 10 years down the line and ask: What would your future self choose?
- ▶ **Pick what you'd do if you weren't afraid.** This is another prompt designed to ensure you're acting and deciding courageously instead of seeking the cozy confines of the comfort zone or the tempting allure of societal approval.
- ▶ **Ask yourself if you'd still say yes if it was tomorrow at 9:00 a.m.** This releases the future time bias we have. In other words, we'll say yes to something we're not sure we want to do because it's six months away.

Pairing these decisiveness practices with your ability to tap into the inner signaling mechanism that knows exactly what must be done—also known as your intuition—you become unstoppable.

INTUITION AND SIGNAL TO NOISE

We often make decisions from the wrong framework—operating from lack, comparison, or fear of loss. We overthink and let our egos talk us into the *safe* choice even if we fundamentally know it is wrong.

We let the small part of ourselves run the show and wonder why we're not where we want to be in our lives, how we ended up in a dead-end career, ditched the hobby we used to love doing, or even chose the wrong mate.

Worst of all, we wonder why we can't trust ourselves.

All humans are intuitive by nature.[3] We are skilled at feeling before thinking. We have a sixth sense that is hard to describe, often overlooked. Think of a time when you met someone and felt something was *off* but were unable to articulate it. Going against this feeling, you gave that someone a shot and weeks later, his or her true colors showed, confirming your suspicions.

Research shows that it takes us only six seconds to have a solid understanding of a stranger's skills, personality, and level of introversion or extroversion.[4] To be clear, that's less than the time it took to read this sentence. This showcases the power of intuition; it knows *before* we can clearly explain why.

Our conscious minds are like a Greyhound bus on a rainy day: slow, plodding, and taking forever. Our intuition, because it operates from the language of the subconscious—which is *feeling*-based—is the F90 fighter jet traveling at supersonic speeds.

Which would you prefer to take cross-country?

Our intuition, then, is made to be sharpened, and if not used, it rusts over. With seeking, you'll step away from the noise, detach from expectations, and spend time in reflection to minimize the signal-to-noise ratio between your conscious mind and intuition.

When you make decisions from your intuition, you *cannot* lose.

You trust yourself, override the ego's mechanism of comfort and logic, attract the right opportunities at the right times, and live in a constant state of synchronicity.

But let's be real: most people's intuition resembles a 1998 dial-up connection on a clunky Compaq computer. The signal-to-noise ratio is an abysmal conflagration of stimulus and ALL CAPPED tweets from pseudo-leaders, a petulant ego that keeps us stuck in comparison to strangers.

To do this right, you'll need to make tapping into your intuition lightning fast, the 5G network that taps into this potent part of yourself that knows exactly what to do at any given time and trusts itself.

Even when it doesn't make sense.

Especially when it doesn't make sense.

HOW TO LEVEL UP INTUITION

Hustlers often can't hear themselves think due to the blaring noise booming through their headphones and thus miss out on clarity, creativity, and out-of-the-box thinking from intuition. What they fear is losing their edge, and they most certainly do, but not how they believe—they lose it by *not* seeking.

Seekers are drenched in practices that open the reservoir of intuition with key insights, messages, downloads. They practice rituals and routines, and spend ample time in solitude, nature, and space. But they miss out on acting on their intuition. They live for the anticipation of another slice of insight, but they're missing decisive action.

To sharpen your intuition and get the most out of your decision-making, you'll need to:

► **Minimize the signal-to-noise ratio.** The practices found in both hustling and seeking are designed to reduce residue that creates mental clutter, deleting the nonessential and allowing the clarity inside to come to the surface. For example, limit your inputs by setting boundaries around things like news, stimulus, and social media.

▶ **Stop trying to make "sense" of it.** The ego's attempt to make sense of our intuition is akin to trying to explain the big bang over cocktails. Often, your intuition will *not* make sense in the moment, but it will make all the sense in the world when you look back. For example, make one decision a day that *feels* right . . . but may not be logical.

▶ **Trust yourself to take action.** Self-trust is built when you take action based off the clarity from your intuition. Making it real is the breeding ground for not only incredible results, but also a thriving relationship with yourself. For example, take action at least once a day on the insights you've gathered.

▶ **Detach from immediate outcomes.** If you listened to your intuition and didn't get the result you imagined in two hours, did you make the wrong choice? Not at all—part of the process is detaching from timelines. For example, stop checking email and spend some much-needed "you" time to recharge.

▶ **Start small.** If you're new to this practice, start small. Listen to your intuition with the small stuff. Take a new route home from work. Stop at the park. Say yes to the thing you've been wanting to do, and build from there.

▶ **Embrace reflection and solitude.** By taking a step back from the daily chaos of our lives, we reflect and notice patterns. These patterns allow us to deepen our intuition and make better decisions from deconstructing our lives. As economist Daniel Kahneman said, "Intuition is defined as knowing without knowing how you know."[5]

▶ **Speed up access time.** As you practice, you'll develop a faster access time. If it takes you 20 minutes now to minimize the endless stream of thoughts and tap into deeper clarity, this is your starting point. With practice, you can turn this into nine minutes, three minutes, or instant access.

Consider your intuitive self fused with the power of decisiveness to be the optimal place to make decisions from. By harnessing this skill, you'll make decisions from the *right* place. You will step into the unknown with excitement instead of dread. You will understand sometimes saying no to something leads to a bigger yes you couldn't have imagined.

WHAT TO LEAVE BEHIND WITH CONVENTIONAL DECISIVENESS

Harnessing decisiveness means you're likely to be in a state of progress—from the seemingly insignificant decisions on what to eat and wear to life's bigger decisions. With this in mind, here's what to leave behind:

- ▶ **Getting caught up in more options.** Because freedom can be intoxicating, it's important to step back and assess when you have *enough* information to pair with intuition to minimize moving too far along the Decision Curve. This varies for everyone.
- ▶ **Being too "zoomed in."** When emotions are high, we tend to narrow our focus and time frames. Ensure you step back and zoom out enough to create perspective. Step away, literally and figuratively.
- ▶ **Not seeking for some decisions.** While speed is important, alignment with values is even more critical. While we value the ability to make quick decisions, sometimes you actually do need to "sleep on it" or seek feedback from trusted advisors—more on this in Chapter 14.

WHAT TO LEAVE BEHIND WITH CONVENTIONAL INTUITION

Building the skill of tapping into your intuition will serve every part of your life—but here's what to leave behind:

▶ **Gathering insight for the sake of it.** Once you have your insight, move. Bring it to life. Make a decision. Otherwise, the pursuit of more can lead to less clarity and leave you back at square one.

▶ **Starting big.** You did your first meditation, got the key codes to life's blueprint, and stepped into leaving your 10-year career and becoming a painter? I love the enthusiasm but start small and practice.

ONE DECISION SHIFTED A CAREER

At dusk on July 25, 1965, Robert Zimmerman took the stage at the Newport Folk Festival in characteristic style—donning a black jacket, black boots, and black denim—walking on stage to a crowd who'd seen him play his masterful acoustic guitar two years in a row.

Destined to be the face of American folk music for decades to come, nothing could stop this young man's ambition. Due to the chaos of the sixties, he was seen as a savior or, at the very least, the voice of hope for a generation during times of distress.

But then he did the completely unexpected.

Ever a folk singer, at a *folk* festival—he didn't walk on stage with his acoustic guitar. Sporting a Fender Stratocaster, he appeared on stage with other musicians; they all plugged into their amps.

And then let 'er rip.

Now referred to as "Dylan Goes Electric," the move is etched in the hall of fame of reinvention. It is characterized as *the* defining moment in music history. An act of radical defiance that would cement his legacy of always zigging when he was expected to zag.

It was punk rock before there was punk rock.

And let's be real: it's easy to make a move of reinvention when you're flailing as an unknown. But when you've worked your face off to build a tribe, a business, a set of raving fans, it takes balls to listen to this part of yourself.

What Dylan did that night was twofold: he made a decision and went all in despite the consequences. The *New York Times* reported that Dylan was ". . . booed by folk-song purists, who considered this innovation the worst sort of heresy."[6] His moment was completely unplanned until the night before—showcasing both decisiveness *and* the spontaneous manner of a gut feeling.

The only way to explain his decision was his willingness to listen to a part of himself that doesn't come from ego, but a deeper place. Artists call it the muse, spiritualists call it source, Einstein called it the "sacred gift"[7]—I'll call it intuition.

As you progress in your life, career, and goals, you'll harness decisiveness while tapping into your intuition to breed a rare level of self-trust. Using the Decision Curve, you'll follow through . . . valuing choice over wavering.

As you do, you'll release the biased timelines on whether or not something "worked"—knowing that sometimes what doesn't "work" today is exactly what was needed to open a door that was otherwise shut.

In hindsight, we're always able to connect the dots.

Making a choice, then, becomes the ultimate freedom by eliminating all other options. Instead of waffling back and forth for a week on a decision you need to make, you confidently make it in less than a day.

The end result of bridging these two worlds is unstoppable progress, clarity, and a level of self-trust that moves mountains . . . while releasing the noise of "what could have been."

Chapter

12

Constraint
&
Creativity

Creativity is elusive.

It taps the chosen few on the shoulder whisking them away from the confines of daily life to craft their masterpiece, right? The groundbreaking idea for the novel, screenplay, or business arrives at an odd hour and one is ushered to start. The creatives hit the studio and finish the work in a caffeine-laced, creatively inspired blitz—becoming the next genius, appearing on *Oprah*, and circling the globe drenched in fame.

Yeah, good luck with that.

Creativity is a loaded word, one we are either drawn to or repelled by—depending on context, beliefs, and experience. It acts either as a label or divider—you're creative or not. It is laced with assumptions on what creativity actually is: Writing a novel is creative, accounting is not. Painting is creative, but delivering a speech is not. Performing music is creative, but only if it doesn't go mainstream. You're a creative . . . as long as you don't sell out.

None of these are true because creativity, by its sheer essence, is boundless and unrestrained. Everyone is creative— even those who, like me for the first 27 years of my life—would never be caught dead using the word.

Like many, it took one slither of the creative realm: a drawing exercise at nine years old for me to label myself anything but creative. Because of this, I went down a societally accepted path of financial spreadsheets on Wall Street instead of what I really wanted: to write, create, and produce work.

It's time to reshape, reframe, and rebuild creativity.

We must drop the barriers between those in the creative upper class, sheltered by the seriousness of their work and the everyday person. It's time to recognize that both hustlers and seekers are creative, and by stepping into one another's world, creativity flourishes. It's time to release the myth of the starving, depressed artist.

By releasing the rigid, worn-out definitions of creativity, you'll recognize the places where you're already creative *and* where you can use this energy to put your unique spin on things, solve problems, and achieve the impossible.

You'll realize that constraints—rules, conventions, and guardrails—amplify creativity, not take away from it. And that creativity isn't some pie-in-the-sky energy we wait to be struck by from the heavens—we cultivate it. We show up and pour hefty doses of hustle into it.

When these worlds merge, you innovate on the regular, reinvent yourself to remain relevant, and avoid worn-out patterns that make you feel stuck. Along the way, you increase fulfillment and performance while realizing every problem has a creative solution.

Before we get there, let's get clear on the new rules of creativity.

THE NEW RULES OF CREATIVITY

How we define creativity determines if and how we'll think of, engage with, and use it. The new rules of creativity include:

▶ **We are all creative.** For many, creativity brings up imagery of painting canvasses, the Louvre in Paris, or their niece who studied art history and can't get a "real" job. It is none of those, and all of those, but the rule is simple: we are all creative. Everyone has *it*, whether they are engaging it as a parent, lawyer, line cook, or screenwriter.

▶ **Creativity does not fit in a box.** Creativity cannot be put into a box. The *arts* are a part of creativity, but they are not the whole. Creativity is vast. It's a shapeshifter that can be harnessed at any moment. We can be creative in a conversation, as we prepare a meal, or in how we draft an email.

▶ **Your creativity is not better.** Traditional creativity separates; the literary community scoffs at commercial success. Punk rock bands call those who sign with a label sellouts. Independent filmmakers snicker at Hollywood. Creativity is inclusive—no one's creativity is *better* than someone else's. It's a matter of taste, preference, and aesthetic.

▶ **Creativity is a life amplifier.** The world's biggest problems will be solved creatively. Your next level of growth will come from this realm, the unknown, the breeding ground for novel ideas that you couldn't think of inside the trenches.

▶ **Creativity requires constraint and discipline.** Creativity is not sitting on the couch waiting for brilliance. It takes a hefty dose of work ethic and showing up when one is riddled with impostor syndrome. When this drive to show up is coupled with time to think, breathe, play—you get the best of both worlds. Enough drive to get shit done, enough slack to call forth new ideas.

Hustlers rarely acknowledge their creativity since it can't be tracked, measured, or shown to have tangible ROI—return on investment. What they don't realize is they're already creative. By robbing themselves of more, they miss out. Why? Because often the most potent parts of life and business can't be measured. They are invisible, yet we all know them when we feel them.

Seekers engage this part of themselves more often, but also miss out. They believe if they simply "Make Good Art" as Neil Gaiman[1]—the bestselling author that has sold more than 45 million books said in a riveting commencement speech—they will be discovered on Pinterest. They scoff at promoting their work and miss out on putting themselves out there; they romanticize the starving, lonely artist.

Both of these worlds miss out.

In order to maximize these rules of creativity, you'll first have to own it without apology.

OWN YOUR CREATIVITY

Ask yourself—in the past 24 hours, how have you been creative?

If you can't think of something instantly, or several places where you harnessed creativity, you're operating under a worn-out model of creativity and not looking broadly enough.

To define creativity that aligns with these rules, we'll turn to a guest of the Academy podcast, a world-class action sports photographer turned entrepreneur, Chase Jarvis. When I asked Chase about creativity on the show, he defined it as "the practice of combining or rearranging two or more unlikely things in new and useful ways."[2]

Creativity is hardwired into our DNA; we create every day in countless cases including the way we draft an email, take the picture on our morning hike, present to our coworkers at the staff meeting, and hold a conversation with the eccentric yet hilarious Uber driver. Creativity, like gravity and your heart beating, is an inescapable part of life.

But are you owning your creativity, or have you put it in a box?

Even those who were creative for years have often had their moment of "getting serious" where they abandoned it. They stopped being a novelist and got real. They stopped recording music to become an accountant. They stopped exploring improv comedy in pursuit of an MBA.

And there is nothing wrong with pursuing these if they are meaningful. But to deny your inherent creativity is a travesty that not only costs you happiness and fulfillment but kills your performance. You can become robotic, complacent, and apathetic to the drudgery of life.

The first step in this process is to reclaim your creativity.

No matter where you land on the spectrum, take it back. Choose to start today. Be creative with a message to a loved one. Be creative with the headline for a blog post. Be creative with your social media biography. Be creative with your morning workout.

Then, introduce the power of constraint into your life so as to breed more creative output, not less.

CREATIVITY AND CONSTRAINT

Contrary to the glamorized image of the artist who creates a masterpiece out of thin air—creativity requires work. It requires discipline, intensity, grit. It demands we show up and engage it, and sometimes wrestle it to the ground in a no-holds-barred match of winner takes all. Often, that means getting our ass handed to us and feeling like a fraud, a fake, an impostor of the worst kind. And then waking up and doing it all over again.

In other words, creativity requires hustle . . . and constraint.

Toni Morrison, the legendary writer, was a notorious hustler. Working a full-time job and raising two boys as a single mother, she wrote at the margins of her life—waking up at 4:00 a.m. to write on limited time, with zero guarantee of success on the other side.[3]

Isaac Asimov wrote 500—yes, you read that right—books during his life. He had no secret hack except that he woke up and put "ass to chair" as Oliver Stone once said, starting at 9:30 every morning and wrapping up late in the evening. Seven days a week. He showed up regardless of how he felt.

David Fincher, the legendary filmmaker known for movies like *Fight Club, Seven,* and *Gone Girl,* is known to compulsively emphasize the details. The opening scene of *The Social Network* was shot 90 times and lasted a grand total of seven minutes. Without this intensity, he'd have stopped . . . around the ninth take.

Study the greats and you will notice their creative practice is messy, even chaotic at times. Like us, they experience unease. Their motivation comes . . . and it goes. This is precisely why they harness constraint. It allows them to show up long before anyone recognizes their work. To do the work in the dark when no one cares. We tend to mythologize prolific artists, when, to be frank, we'd be bored stiff if we followed them around.

Constraint, then, is the ability to funnel our creative energy through guardrails that keep us focused, deliberate, and engaged. By having rules, boundaries, and limits, we are *free* to create.

To fully embrace and enhance your creativity, you'll need to:

- ▶ **Introduce constraint.** Constraint could be a medium of choice (writing, filmmaking, cooking) or a physical environment where you sit down and do the work. It can mean the constraint of a deadline, event, or film festival.

- ▶ **Have a routine.** If creativity is hardwired into our DNA and a part of who we are, it must be a *daily* experience. This doesn't have to be complex; rather, it must be harnessed through routine. Protect your "making" time and treat it as valuably as anything else.

- ▶ **Embrace the suck.** Creativity is not immune from those backbreaking moments of frustration where you want to light your work on fire. It's being stuck on an angle for a marketing campaign. It's writing this book and torching 40,000 words. It's the middle of any creative work where you no longer see the light at the end of the tunnel . . . and *every other* idea sounds magical. And yet, you persist.

- ▶ **Harness discipline.** If you rely on being creative exclusively when you "feel" like it, mediocrity is guaranteed. This prerequisite means you'll rob yourself of skill, process, and craft. Motivation is unreliable. Instead, creativity requires discipline. Show up. Do the work. Ditch motivation for good.

▶ **Create deadlines.** Deadlines seem contradictory to the creative process, but they can fuel it. They make today matter. While there is a fine line, deadlines can be used to cultivate a sense of urgency and why today matters. We expand on this in Chapter 14 on urgency.

▶ **Ship and promote.** While creativity is often associated with making, it's also about sharing, promoting, and even *selling*. The world is littered with unshared novels and screenplays gathering dust in drawers that were never shared publicly.

▶ **Lower the bar.** By lowering the bar on your creative output, you set yourself up for success. Instead of a two-hour creative session, commit to 250 words. Commit to editing one scene. Do the smallest viable action, which tends to lead to more momentum and output. And even when it doesn't, you've still won.

Consider these constrictive practices to funnel your creative drive.

Like all principles, too much constraint can lead to losing our spark or dreading the thing that once made us feel alive. There is nothing worse than taking something we once loved—photography, podcasting, cooking—and losing it because we never unplugged.

Which is why on the other side of intense constraint, you'll embrace novelty and being unplugged.

CREATIVITY, OPEN SPACE, NOVELTY

We know discipline is essential to creativity.

But as important as sitting down and doing the work is—the other end of the spectrum requires a complete dissolution and letting go.

It requires stepping away.

It demands time to breathe, think, and forget about the work. It asks us to surrender and to reach the breaking point of a creative roadblock and experience new people, places, and ideas—even with a deadline looming. Research has shown introducing novelty into our lives induces awe, wonder, and aha moments of deep insight.[4] And it doesn't have to be complicated; the barrier for novelty is low.

This time away induces what creativity researchers call the "incubation phase"[5]—tapping into the part of the brain that is creating connections, putting new ideas together, and coalescing inputs . . . all while you're *not* working.

To hang back with our loved ones. To have a thrilling conversation. To hit the lake for the weekend. To spend time in a float tank or take a long nap. To read a work of fiction when we always read nonfiction, to listen to classical music when we're used to hip-hop, to pick up an old hobby we used to do before life got so busy.

In other words, to change something, *anything*.

The opposite of constraint includes:

1. **Letting go fully.** There comes a point in any endeavor where more is not more. We must leave the office if we need clarity. We must put the screenplay in the drawer if we've hit a roadblock. This is a conscious effort of faith and trust. It is not an excuse to be lazy; rather, it is a recognition that what got us *here* will not get us *there*.

2. **Shattering your routine.** While hustle embraces routine, seeking *shatters* it. It means going to a completely different place to create or writing in longhand instead of typing on a laptop. It means flipping the script on our daily habits.

3. **Stepping out of your arena.** We can become too constricted or fall prey to the expert's paradox, where we know too much and lose sight of the creative power of stepping into different arenas. Allow yourself to get inspired from a different world than the one you're operating in.

4. **Embracing play and adventure.** Play, fun, adventure—these are nonnegotiable practices to refuel, recharge, restore.

Oddly enough, the moment we loosen the grip on the project we're working on, the answers come in droves.

5. **Taking a specific amount of time off.** There will be times when none of the above will work in the sense of getting you unstuck. This is when you need to take deliberate time off—a few days, a week, a month, a quarter.

We've all been stuck on a problem to the point of frustration. Desperate, we had *no choice* but to step away from our work and engage the world. By tossing a Frisbee with our dog, going on a long walk, or watching an incredible film—insight hit us like a punch to the gut.

You came in with a question, you left with an answer. You came in with a creative block, you left with a fully scripted scene, or a solution to your graduate thesis.

And you weren't even trying!

It was there all along, yet you couldn't see it. This is the magic of stepping away: we receive answers we would have never found had we forced ourselves to stay in the grind.

But of course, this works both ways: sometimes, we have too much slack.

We have tipped the scales from novelty to wandering. We need to put our heads down. We need accountability and urgency.

By merging these, we find our creative sweet spot—the zone where we do our best work while harnessing the power of space, incubation, and some much-needed breathing room.

WHAT TO LEAVE BEHIND WITH CONVENTIONAL CONSTRAINT

While constraint creates guardrails that act as insurance policies for procrastination or wandering, here's what to watch out for:

▶ **Deploying constraint out of sheer force.** To do this right, you'll need to develop enough rules to do your work, but enough space to unplug. Sheer force zaps creativity and leaves you burned out.

▶ **Becoming too rigid with constraints.** Rigidness can become blinding and make you miss out on the lateral thinking and cross-fertilization that is crucial to bring novel ideas and projects into the world.

▶ **Never breaking rules.** To break the rules, we must first learn and abide by them. We must understand genre, tone, and how to fit into a box. Then, we must break free and create our own rules.

WHAT TO LEAVE BEHIND WITH CONVENTIONAL CREATIVITY

While creativity is a performance and fulfillment amplifier, there are worn-down ways of thinking about creativity that do more harm than good, including:

▶ **Believing the myth of the starving artist.** You don't need to be broke to be creative and do great work. In fact, the ability to step out into the world and share your work with it allows for more resources to foster your creative potential.

▶ **Believing the myth of being "discovered."** The days of gatekeepers who hold the keys to distribution are all but gone. While beneficial to all of us, it means *everyone* has access. Being randomly found on YouTube and getting a prime-time TV series is likely not happening. So, discover what you're capable of for yourself instead.

▶ **Waiting for inspiration.** Waiting to feel motivated and on fire with a creative idea means you'll not only be waiting forever but you'll soothe the pain by consuming everyone else's ideas. So, instead of waiting for inspiration . . . create it.

CONSTRAINTS EQUAL FREEDOM

Jack White is best known for making up half of The White Stripes—whose heart-thumping guitar riff from *Seven Nation*

Army may be the most well-known of all time. In the span of eight years, the duo released six records and nabbed 19 major music awards. He's also a producer, label owner, filmmaker, and obsessive furniture upholsterer.

In other words, a creative phenom.

You'd think for someone with this level of innate genius, talent, and artistic know-how, creativity would flow unencumbered like red wine from Napa Valley, right?

Well, not quite.

Because White gets it . . . creativity is *wild*. It's a fickle force that needs a place to go, to be corralled. Otherwise, it spews out in all directions. It goes from a high-octane fire hose designed to put out raging flames . . . to the dented garden hose that drips, drips, drips in our basement.

So, what's the secret to his success?

Intense constraints, rules, and limitations . . . with *everything*. Ditching the typical three-, four-, or five-piece band, he chose two. No bass? No problem. Instead of fancy equipment, his trademark bright red guitar retailed for $99. Even the band's aesthetic came with rules: only red, white, and black. He doses aggressive deadlines and tight recording schedules and removes the friction of too many options.

The result? A creative output unmatched in this world. According to White: "Our idea was to strip away everything unnecessary, to put ourselves in a box, to make rules for ourselves . . . the whole point of the White Stripes is the *liberation* of limiting yourself."[6]

And you can do the same.

While you may not be crafting epic guitar riffs, you've got an even *bigger* gig—creating your life. To do so, have rules. Set guardrails and constraints. Harness the power of choice, and recognize constriction equals *freedom*. And then, unplug into the void. Let your creative energy rest, incubate, and come to life yet again. Be willing to step away.

Along the way, you'll notice your best work comes from the *combination* of structure, constraint, and white space. By the time you look up again, you'll have crafted your masterpiece, too.

Chapter 13

Compete & Detach

Competition is part of life, hardwired in the strands of DNA that make us. It is as natural as gravity, as biological as reproduction, and as physiological as desire.[1] When you're told not to compete, you're asked to deny a part of yourself. You're asked to ignore what makes you human . . . and ultimately, what determines your ability to perform on demand and generate one of the most potent energies on the planet—momentum.

Give yourself permission to compete. In this place, the magic happens as you step out of the safe havens of your comfort zone. You brush up against self-inflicted boundaries you took as real and obliterate them. You endure instead of quitting as you unlock a level of performance you hardly knew existed.

You bring out your inner badass.

By competing, you'll work on your craft, perform with vigor, and actually *care* about the scoreboard. Mind you, this is not the conventional hustler's ego-based competition to win at all costs. Rather, it is competition from a place of inner and outer respect while using seeking to strip away unhealthy residue.

Think back to a time in your life where you did what you had considered impossible. Maybe it was an athletic or academic feat, a creative endeavor, or the scholarship you wanted. If you did it right, when all was said and done, whether you "won" or "lost" was irrelevant because the process got you reacquainted with that part of yourself that had been lying dormant. And if others were involved, you thanked them.

Why? Because they brought out the best in you.

On the seeker's side, you'll counter competitive energy by embracing detachment. You'll forget the scoreboard and embrace others on the field of play with respect. You'll use this energy to eject into the void.

Competitive energy is part of who we are.

Which means we can either use it for good . . . or it will use *us* for bad. If we don't use this energy wisely, it bleeds into the margins of our lives. It comes out as random anger, disappointment, frustration. It leads to comparison, procrastination, or feeling sorry for ourselves. It leads to looking at someone who is living the life we desire and saying, "Must be nice."

Competitive energy, left dormant, becomes destructive.

Competitive energy, used intelligently, becomes creative.

The question is will you use it to create—or destroy?

CREATE OR DESTROY

Competitive energy has to go somewhere.[2]

Conventional seekers proclaim they're above this energy, thinking they can override 10,000 years of human development. The reality is they're avoiding a part of who they are under the façade of "oneness." Don't get it twisted. Many seekers strive for spirituality *as much* as their hustling counterparts. They've traded the scoreboards of bank digits for the most aligned of chakras, or who can quote Rumi faster.

Since competition is innate to humans,[3] it is not something you can opt out of. You can't run away from it or head to the hilltop to meditate. Ashley Merryman, who studies the neuroscience of competition, says there is no such thing as a person who isn't competitive, including orthodox gender biases, saying: "There is no evidence that women in competition are any less committed, determined, or competitive."[4] She argues that competition fuels motivation, creativity, and fulfillment in ways that build a complete psyche.

Which means this energy can be used as a catalyst to create, including:

- ▶ Create your life.
- ▶ Create your business.
- ▶ Create your mental state.
- ▶ Create your mind, body, and spirit.
- ▶ Create your routines, habits, and rituals.

By summoning this competitive energy from a place of alignment as we covered in Chapter 6—you'll not only move toward your goals but transform into the person capable of those goals . . . and then some. This spirit gets you up in the morning, fuels your action-taking, and activates the part of yourself that endures when excuses are begging you to stop.

But the opposite is also true.

Left abandoned on the side of the road, this energy has nowhere to go. Instead of creating and and being funneled into places that matter, it gets locked down, pressurized. As time passes, it can only go one place: destruction.

Destruction may seem obscure, but it's not:

- ▶ Destructive habits
- ▶ Destructive mindsets
- ▶ Destructive actions
- ▶ Destructive choices
- ▶ Destructive relationships

This can range from having one too many cocktails to creating random drama because you're bored . . . for no reason. It's being in denial about finances and putting it all on Red 27 at the roulette table. It's the social media troll we've all seen who is always bringing others down.

Creation and destruction use the same energy source. The difference is *how* this energy is used, where it goes, and whether it is alchemized toward an intentional end.

Without one, it dissipates into the ether.

Imagine a scenario where you've been in the running for a promotion all year, patiently waiting. On a random Friday, you're told you didn't get the gig but your coworker with two years of *less* experience did. You're ticked off, you experience a fight-or-flight reaction, and you feel competitive energy rise inside. You now have a choice.

Do you use this to propel you to where you want to go and the person you want to become? Great, use this energy to hit your nighttime workout or focus for another 30 minutes. Use it to start your side hustle. Harness it to send that email that's been in the drafts folder to the recruiter. Use it to remind yourself that most companies or bosses aren't loyal to *you*. Maybe give yourself permission to stop waiting. In other words, use it to serve.

Or, do you use this energy to call the girlfriends and hit happy hour? Have a martini, complain about the boss, chug another. Start letting the feeling fester, while also becoming numb. You feel in control, and out of control, all at once. Here, competitive energy is owning you. It's still there and it leads to an argument with your significant other. Exhausted, the next morning you're in a cycle of negativity and reminded of the promotion you didn't get. The cycle repeats itself; destruction breeds destruction, creation breeds creation. Sure, this is a simple example, but the point is simple: if competitive energy is part of who we are, why not use it for *good*?

No marketplace is immune to this energy—including poets, scientists, those who show dogs, and spelling bee contestants—because it's natural. The seekers will aim to deny it, but they have it too as they post pictures with their celebrity gurus to impress others.

Ultimately, competition is designed to bring out the best of what you have to offer.

If you do it right, of course.

COMPETITION BRINGS OUT THE BEST IN YOU

Ask anyone who's competed in any endeavor where they learned their biggest lessons. Ask them where they cultivated a deeper belief in themselves. Ask them when they recommitted to their dream. It rarely happens basking in the glory of winning, especially if it wasn't earned through an 11th place ribbon.

Rather, it happens by tasting the bitter pill of losing.

It happens when they don't get the prize. It happens when there's one scholarship awarded, and it's not to them. It happens when a gatekeeper says, "We'll pass." To harness this energy means to acknowledge:

- ▶ **Competition is part of life.** We are hardwired to compete, to adapt among the fittest, to extract our potential. To deny this isn't only useless, it comes out in unproductive ways (see: scrolling Instagram all day and taking jabs at other people's results).
- ▶ **Competition is naturally healthy.** When defined the *right* way, it can be one of the healthiest endeavors to recognize who we are—which both creates meaning and leads to results. Win-win.
- ▶ **Competition is a tool.** Competition isn't inherently good or bad, it's a tool. Tools can be used all different types of ways; it is the intent of the person who is using them that determines their effect.

Of course, hustlers have no problem competing for the wrong reasons. They compete with made-up social media critics; they create false narratives in their heads of people from high school who are still slighting them. They can't shut it off, and they have a me-against-the-world mentality that borders on senile.

Seekers, on the other hand, balk at the concept of competition. They believe it is based on a worn-out, merit-based paradigm that creates a divide from the haves or have-nots, an incessant desire for the ambitious to fill a dark cloud that was created when they were nine years old and their parents divorced.

Who's right?

Well, like most things—the truth is both can be.

For this principle, we'll first have to define "competition."

Then you'll know how to apply this competitive energy, understand the ways you think about and act on it, and, finally, recognize how to eject and detach at the right times.

By redefining competition, using it to *serve* and then ejecting—you tap into the insatiable feeling of momentum.

THE NEW COMPETITION

In 2006, when Pixar was purchased by Disney, it was ending a near-perfect run of films—akin to a batter crushing home runs on every pitch. One out-of-the-park film can happen haphazardly. Two is an anomaly. But five, six, or seven? That's unmistakable.

There was something in the water.

Initially, the idea was to merge both animation studios, the obvious choice with tremendous benefit: cost savings, efficiency, and collaboration. But Ed Catmull, Pixar's cofounder, had an intuitive hunch—keep them separate. He envisioned Disney and Pixar as competitors, albeit under one roof.

This meant each studio would use its own resources, even if the other was in a pinch. One team wouldn't have veto power over another team's movie. Each was a separate entity—and would build their own culture, ethos, and narratives into their films. Pixar would keep its branding at the office.

In other words, they'd compete.

Fast-forward a decade, and this uncommon strategy worked: Disney turned its slogging animation department into a category leader and nabbed Oscars—while Pixar continued to do the unthinkable and expand on its rousing success. A former Pixar employee likened it to a sibling rivalry, saying: "If a brother or sister goes out and does something awesome, you then want to go out and do something awesome."[5]

Would they have done the same had they coalesced and *not* had anyone to compete with next door? It's doubtful.

You may wonder—can't that create negative energy in my life? No, as long as you leverage it and put it in the right places. Here's how to redefine competition and use it for good:

- ▸ **Compete against yourself.** This isn't from a place of lack. Rather, it's from a place of owning the potential you've been blessed with out of respect and appreciation for life.

- ▸ **Compete against the ego.** The ego wants you to play small and stay stuck in the comfortable past. Even if it causes you pain, and sometimes especially if it causes you pain. More on this in Chapter 20.

- ▸ **Compete against your standards**. We all have standards, what some call values, that drive our behaviors. When we compete, we tend to raise those standards and identify *new* ones in alignment with who we are today.

- ▸ **Compete against your potential.** Ignoring potential is a lack of appreciation for the human spirit. Compete against this threshold and meet a prior unrecognizable version of yourself.

- ▸ **Compete against the status quo.** Society wants you to fit in convenient boxes. It wants you to follow a straight, linear, and predictable path. Many cultures don't want you to dream big, or else you'll be exposed.

- ▸ **Compete against those who want you to lose.** Yes, some people are waiting for your downfall. Not everyone will support you. When you put yourself out there, others will want you to lose, even if they fake applaud you from the sidelines. Use this as fuel to serve.

This type of competitive energy wakes you up.

It gets the work done. It doesn't allow you the time to over-think or to question your motivation based on how you feel. It brings out a level of performance you didn't know you had, from the depths of your being. And then, you learn to release this energy into the ether, to not bring it home with you, to exhale and let it go.

COMPETE LIKE HELL AND THEN DETACH

Competition isn't simply a performance amplifier; it gets you reacquainted with a part of yourself that lies dormant. By revealing this inner hero or heroine, you activate the spark to do what you once deemed impossible. Upon reflection, you almost can't describe *how* you did it. This breeds confidence, meaning, humility, self-trust, and awareness.[6]

Once you've tapped into your competitive fuel, you'll let go and detach. You won't be taking this home with you. You won't be waking up at 4 a.m. thinking about crushing your competition. You won't scour YouTube comments searching for trolls. To detach fully, you will:

- ▶ **Let go of competitive energy with as much fervor as you pursued it.** This is a conscious choice; to shut it down, to recognize competition is about utility. You exhale and celebrate that full effort is full victory. For example, developing a "wind-down" routine that signals to your brain that your work is done.
- ▶ **Create buffers.** A buffer is a block of time that allows you to go from being on the field of play to the podium or from the office to the dinner table with the family. Allow 15 minutes to let the energy simmer and create a new intention for what's next.
- ▶ **Have respect.** The best competitors have a healthy respect for others; they know what it takes. Detach enough to see others with respect and celebrate when they win. Rid yourself of the standard conventions that say when they *win*, you lose. Send someone on the same path an appreciation note.

Letting go, using buffers, and having transitions can be simple.

Close the laptop, slide the phone to airplane mode, and set an intention as you prepare for family time. Go for a walk around the block and send a signal to your brain that competitive energy is no longer needed.

Ultimately, competition tests our capacity, challenging us and revealing a force within. Through this process of competing and detaching, you'll:

▶ **Develop confidence.** Not the look-at-me, instant gratification confidence that comes with showing off. Instead, this is a deep and humble confidence that you can handle anything thrown your way.

▶ **Increase self-awareness.** Self-awareness is the meta-skill that makes everything else easier: by pushing your limits, you'll develop it faster, equipping yourself with a skill that will pay off time and time again.

▶ **Stop being a talker.** Those who compete at the highest levels don't talk about what they do, they simply do it. Meaning: there is no need to talk a big game, they simply are felt when they walk into a room. Navy SEALS and elite martial artists don't need to talk, their work is felt in their presence.

▶ **Expand your skill sets.** By stepping into the arena to compete, you'll develop valuable skills that can't be found when one is drifting. These skills become your competitive advantage to grow both personally and professionally, including emotional resilience, discipline, and consistency.

When these ingredients come together, you tap into that feeling we all crave—momentum. We all know what momentum *feels* like; our lives have gone from a stagnant low tide to tidal waves of progress, forward motion, results . . . and consistency.

And contrary to what most people do—wait for an external reward or cue to feel momentum—you'll generate it. Momentum begets momentum and only grows as we produce more of it every day.

WHAT TO LEAVE BEHIND WITH CONVENTIONAL COMPETITION

We all know the dark side of competition: a gnawing feeling that everyone has to be *crushed*, leading to petty disagreements or full-blown crises over little things. Here's what to leave behind with competing:

- ▶ **Competing 24/7.** Sure, this will be part of your identity, but your ability to switch on and switch off is crucial. Being able to eject through seeking is nonnegotiable.
- ▶ **Allowing competition to bleed over.** You don't take this energy home with you. What propels you in your craft is what will bring you down in other areas of your life—family, social, and community.
- ▶ **Competing to the point of breakdown.** There's a reason the Olympics happen every four years, and why there's one championship in a sport on a yearly basis followed by a long off-season: competition takes energy.

WHAT TO LEAVE BEHIND WITH CONVENTIONAL DETACHMENT

Releasing competitive energy is crucial to your emotional sanity, but it can also be taken too far and start to work against you, including:

- ▶ **Letting complacency take over.** The more you've grown, expanded, and experienced results, the easier it is to get complacent. Being complacent means you lose this part we all have and feel a lack of being challenged and stimulated.
- ▶ **Being "above" the need to compete.** This is a common trap to let ourselves off the hook from tapping into deeper potential. We're led to believe we can "rise above" this energy, when that's not the point.

▶ **Missing the new definition.** Too many seekers look at
competition through a lens of morality and miss the point.
It is not about being *better* than anyone; rather, it is about
accelerating a universal principle of growth.

COMPETITION EQUALS RESPECT

Combined, the two sisters have spent more than 330 weeks
ranked as number one in the world, 30 Grand Slam titles, nine
Olympic gold medals, and sport a litany of trophies, awards,
and honors. They've also become household names.

Venus and Serena Williams have played each other head-on
31 times.

Known as lethal competitors, driven obsessively with a
laser-focus on winning bordering maniacal—they compete.
Hard. But they're also sisters, and the closest of them.

So, what gives?

We all know sibling rivalries are precarious to begin with—
add in fame, success, and championships and the conditions
are ripe for a not-so-pretty ending full of backhanded slights
and gnawing resentment.

Not here.

Instead, competitive energy acts as the elixir to fuel their
relationship out of deep love, respect, and appreciation. It
brings them closer, not farther away. As Serena says, "I know
when I play her, I have to play my best tennis . . . she does too.
We have pushed each other to be the best that we can be."[7] And
Venus counters, saying, "The best part is that we bring out the
best in each other."[8]

This is competition done right: using it to become the best
version of yourself, to access a level of potential, performance,
and fulfillment that was previously absent. Use it to not let
yourself off the hook. Instead, override the part of yourself that
wants to stay the same—to hit snooze, skip the workout, and
do nothing.

Use this as fuel.

But also, be able to let go of this energy as fast as it came. This energy is addictive, fun, and a blend of neurochemicals you can't get away from. Used wisely, they create a strong mindset, an aligned set of behaviors. A mind, body, and spirit all working in tandem.

When mixed with detachment, you become the warrior: the humble, grounded, yet lethal version of yourself no one messes with. You are felt when you walk into rooms. This energy attracts people and opportunities your way. Because everyone wants to be around someone who strives for, and embodies, alignment.

Compete, and then applaud when others win.

You'll find respect with those on the field of play who don't talk a big game but embody it. And as the warrior, you become those who are the most lethal, yet eerily humble and grounded . . . the last ones to pick up the sword.

Full of momentum, you can't be stopped.

Chapter

14

Urgency
&
Divine Timing

You're already a world-class performer.

No, really. You are.

You show up like nobody's business, take daring action before you have the answers—and put yourself on the line. You execute, move the needle, and stave off procrastination like a Jedi master. You do the work regardless of emotions, moods, or tweeting politicians, and you harness a level of self-discipline that is stunning to others.

If.

And it's a big if—*if* there's enough urgency, *if* your back is up against the wall, *if* there are real consequences, and *if* there's a real-world deadline staring you in the face.

Think back to a time you squared off with a deadline and waited until the last moment. Here, you had no option. This urgency acted as an IV drip of high-octane fuel in your veins that pummeled fear, doubt, and laziness in one fell swoop. There was literally no time to overthink, overanalyze, or scroll social media.

It was do or die.

Say hello to urgency from the hustler's side—a do-it-now attitude that compels action. To make the bold pitch, to stop waiting and ensure the pain of not doing it . . . is greater than leaning in. And contrary to what it sounds like, urgency is *not* stressful.

Rather, urgency becomes an antidote to stress.

With urgency, you counteract your hardwired desire to hit snooze and put it off until tomorrow. You experience the freedom, peace, and clarity that come with doing needle-moving work.

You send the world a signal you're not messing around.

On the seeker's side, you'll pair urgency with trust in divine timing—recognizing that while you can influence and nudge your goals, they're not *exclusively* on your timeline. You can't out-hustle, out-grit, out-Gary Vee your outcomes. You concede there are greater forces at play. You can't see the whole chessboard . . . and you're not supposed to.

And even if you could—would you *want* to?

Think back to life's best moments, the rapture of the unknown, a "random" synchronicity. These are the electrifying moments that can't be planned. Did you know *all* the answers ahead of time?

Of course not.

While divine timing may send a shudder up hustlers' spines as they file it under some New Age scam found in Encinitas among gurus and crystal shops—divine timing requires *more* emotional grit than ruthless action. (For, uh, my less spiritually inclined, feel free to replace "divine timing" with "patience.")

For someone who is used to being in control—which is no doubt the hustler's ethos—I feel your pain. But stay with me. By releasing the kung fu grip on your goals, you may find yourself getting there *faster* . . . or in unexpected, exciting ways.

Ultimately, you'll have the audacity to take messy action while letting go. You make decisions but listen to your gut. You play full tilt but leave space for the mystery. Best of all, you cocreate your future in real time while being open to a completely *new* way of arriving at your goals. Which means you're adaptable and ready when opportunity strikes.

But we're getting ahead of ourselves.

First, it's time to manufacture a level of urgency that moves mountains.

THE URGENCY EQUATION

We've established how you're a badass when there's something on the line. But let's face it—this energy is rare. Most of us operate with the same level of urgency toward our goals as booking a routine colonoscopy.

The thesis is due in six months, so we hang back today. We have a year to hit the sales target, so we scroll social media and avoid picking up the phone. Our client deadline is weeks way, so we pretend to work at the coffee shop.

The Pareto Principle states that work expands given the time on hand, so without urgency we wait until the consequences are so dire that we have no other choice but to stay up in a multi-night bender.

Not exactly a formula for life success.

The urgency equation goes as follows:

Urgency = Consequences + Deadline + Focus

Let's break these components of urgency down:

- ► **Consequences.** Get clear about the consequences of not following through—which must be *greater* than the discomfort of overcoming inertia.
- ► **Deadline.** There must be a real-world deadline: a date and time you have to show up, execute, finish, be tested, hand in the paper, or perform.

▶ **Focus.** Once we have the first two, we have *no other option* but to focus. We eliminate distractions, set boundaries, and say no.

The urgency equation is universal in its application.

Whether you're completing your first half marathon, writing a book, launching the business, planning the wedding . . . it works. Unless of course, you do what most people do: drift aimlessly and wait for urgency to strike you over the head.

WAITING FOR URGENCY

Most people wait for a rock-bottom moment to harness the power of urgency. And sure, urgency is at an all-time high as our world dissolves into a few glaring essentials. Action is the obvious—no, only choice. But waiting for a part of our lives to crumble to finally wake up is not a strategy. It's debilitating, soul-crushing, and painful.

Its consequences are felt, sometimes, for life.

Instead, we must recognize *now* matters. We have to make waiting more painful than today's discomfort. We have to operate from two places that drive human behavior—running from pain and seeking pleasure[1]—by:

▶ **Amplifying future consequences.** Our ability to visualize our future makes us human. To create urgency, we must feel the future consequence of not taking action.

▶ **Amplifying future benefits.** We must tap into the benefit of what we're doing above solely running from pain so as to be pulled by tomorrow's compelling horizon.

Urgency lives between these two, the feeling that now is the time.

Many mistakenly associate urgency with stress, but it relieves stress. By eliminating options, we minimize overwhelm. By setting deadlines, we take action on what matters. Otherwise, "someday" takes over our vocabulary as we put it off for another day—slowly killing our belief—until it's all but gone.

AMPLIFY FUTURE PAIN AND PARADISE

We've all run from pain; we're dealt a financial blow and now we've rid ourselves of the trepidation with sales calls. We've had *the* fight in relationships and now we're reinvesting in date nights. We have a health scare and the next day we sign up for the gym and consult with a naturopath.

Pain leads to clarity, clarity breeds action.

But at this point, change becomes a colossal effort. The energetic toll of being so far on the other side of where we want to be is draining at best and downright crushing at worst. Instead, we must amplify future pain based on today's not-so-painful circumstance to get *moving*, including:

1. **Get clear about today's facts.** Even if they hurt, stare reality in the face without the haze of emotions.
2. **Imagine the future cost.** Future pace. Take yourself 12, 24, 48 months down the line and imagine *not* changing anything.
3. **Reverse visualization.** See yourself living with the fact you're not only experiencing pain in the future but the emotional toll of knowing you wanted to change something—but didn't.
4. **Write down five reasons why it's time.** Allow yourself to get honest and vulnerable, ensuring these are important to you.
5. **Start now.** Take the smallest possible action that creates a feeling of progress, that you *did* something: a choice, decision, taking it out of your head and into the real world.

We start with pain, because it is the elixir to compel change. Once you've done this, we now turn our attention to the compelling horizon:

1. **Step into your future self.** Visualize the self that has accomplished your goal, dream, target . . . embody it.
2. **Imagine the future benefit.** Imagine what your day-to-day looks and *feels* like; be specific and vivid.
3. **Allow yourself to go deep.** Look at how your horizon changed your inner chatter, your relationships, and how you show up.

4. **Feel your target in the body.** Close your eyes and focus on where in your body you feel the emotions that compel you to act. Tap into that sense of aliveness in your chest, the flutter in your belly, the pulse in your arms.

5. **Start now.** Do the smallest possible action that creates a feeling of progress, that you *did* something: take a choice or decision out of your head and put it into the real world.

You'll notice the last step is the same: without doing something *real*, urgency is lost. When you make a real-world dent, your brain will start tuning its fork of awareness toward that goal. It will search for *anything* to help get you there faster. What matters is not the size of the action but that you got started. In fact, you want to start laughably small.

Now you're going to take your deadlines and compress them by at least half.

COMPRESS DEADLINES
BY 50 PERCENT

If you want to run a triathlon this year, sign up for the race happening in the next few months. If you want to write a novel, commit to a first draft in half the time. If you want to have the finances to turn your side hustle full-time and quit your 9–5, compress your timeline by half.

Deadlines work.

They compel us to get uncomfortable today, turn off Netflix and say no to crushing happy hour because today matters. Deadlines create healthy pressure: if the rough draft is due in 90 days, well, today's writing session *really* matters. If the trail run is in eight weeks, then skipping a Sunday run has consequences.

Most deadlines give us so much runway that urgency is clouded as we buy into the illusion of doing it *mañana*. Since we're hardwired to survive, our brain wants to save all the energy it can. Which means when facing whether to move toward your target or vegetate on the couch, the couch is undefeated.

To harness the power of deadlines, make sure to:

- ▶ Compress all deadlines by 50 percent—this is the cardinal rule.
- ▶ Have a clear, specific, and committed date and time for completion.
- ▶ Be obsessive about putting this date where you can see it daily.
- ▶ Enroll someone else within this deadline; make sure they're invested.
- ▶ Pay real money, as in deposit actual cash, toward your deadline.
- ▶ Ensure your deadline creates enough anxiety to compel action, but not so much as to overwhelm you.

The last part of deadlines is counterintuitive: you may not hit them every time, especially if you're challenging yourself.

It also doesn't matter.

By setting aggressive deadlines, you'll be further along than you could have imagined. You'll stop using "how you feel" as an excuse. You'll progress and gain momentum, creating a feedback loop that not only gets you closer to your goals but also makes you the *person* who moves toward what you want. Showing up becomes a habit.

When you pair this energy with divine timing, you cannot lose.

DON'T IMPOSE YOUR WILL ON TIMING

You've likely tried to outduel, outmatch, and out-hustle divine timing.

Maybe you were single and craving a relationship. So, you went on an astonishing number of dates (more awkwardness than any human should endure) and even created a cute vision board.

You thought about your dream partner; what the person looked like, how you laughed, but you kept winding up in the same place—alone on a Saturday night with nothing but a pint of Halo Top and watching *The Proposal* or some classically bad and oh-so-painfully-good romantic comedy. A few potentials fell through. Every time you opened up social media, there was a stark reminder: you're destined to be alone forever while your friends plan their wedding in sheer bliss.

Or are you?

Frustrated, you started to live your life more. You went deeper into your yoga practice, a hobby you'd stopped. You were less obsessive over the whole *find-your-soul-mate-tomorrow* thing. You detached from expectations and noticed the few dates you went on, while not in alignment, weren't completely dreadful. You made some connections. And *gasp*, you even started to have fun!

Most importantly, you stopped trying to impose your *will* on timing.

Instead of wasting energy on why it's not happening or why everyone's in relationship heaven except you, you channeled this energy back into yourself: self-care, fun, "you" time, and doing the things that make you feel awesome.

And then it happened.

An old friend you hadn't talked to in three years invited you to a group dinner. You reluctantly agreed—having a cancellation text ready—and chose to show up. With zero expectations, it mysteriously came together: you sat next to someone unique, interesting, attractive. The conversation flowed. You were present and connected. You agreed to hang out again, exchanged numbers.

And the rest is history.

Now, you may be rolling your eyes and I get it. But if you take a moment to think back to some of the *best* moments of your life—you'd be hard-pressed to find the seven-step blueprint that you were 100 percent in control of to bring it to life. That, if you're honest . . . there was something else at play you can't put your finger on. What we call it doesn't matter . . . chance, synchronicity, being at the right place at the right time, or even sheer "luck"—it's all the same.

Here, we'll call it the Law of Divine Timing.

THE LAW OF DIVINE TIMING

The Law of Divine Timing states that there are greater forces at play always in motion, but not always seen, that must be fully trusted in regard to your hustle.

In business, this is going out on your own, launching, and putting yourself on the line. It's getting up every day and putting in the work. The work that's supposed to, you know, pay a return.

But the clock ticks with no sign of results.

You have real bills. Your landlord doesn't care about how marketing is harder than you imagined. Time's running out, and all of a sudden you start to miss your biweekly direct deposits to your account. Why isn't this happening faster!? Are all of these online business gurus Ponzi scheme artists!? Are these people on social media photoshopping revenue numbers? You may be onto something there.

Then, you start to release a little control. You focus on what you *can* do. You invest in your business out of faith, even when the account is spiraling downward. You overcome procrastination. You make offers and follow up, each time doubling down.

And then one day, it *clicks*.

A client finally pays their invoice, three weeks late. A prior client refers two people to you. An organization wants you to come in and do training. You almost spit your coffee out during the call when the person mentions your fee. You get invited on local media. You have your biggest month since going out on your own. You're on fire. All because you let go.

This is divine timing in action.

This is the equal balance of hustle.

This is trusting there is always movement beneath the surface.

Make no mistake: divine timing requires *more* emotional grit than hustle. Not in actions, of course. But those can be cheap because at least you *feel* like you're doing something. The sense of control can be soothing.

But letting go and trusting when there's no proof?

This is the game of masters who see the unknown with wonder and a knowing that timing is not under our control. That what most people call "luck" is actually a merging of both sides—urgency and divine timing.

And it will wait patiently until we honor it fully.

PRACTICE DIVINE TIMING

Divine timing is a practice in letting the mystery of the unknown spin in your favor, to allow the space for synchronicities and being at the right place at the right time.

But there's a kicker.

You can be at the right place at the right time and miss your shot. If you're not flexible to a *different* way of achieving your goal, the investor may pass right by you at the cocktail mixer. Your future spouse may leave the coffee shop while you're glued to your phone. The door that opened for your breakthrough may slam shut because you were rigid.

This is the great paradox, the crossroads of hustle and divine timing. Sure, you're going to pursue goals with vigor but be completely open to possibilities you can't quite imagine today. When you calibrate these two worlds, you end up always being exactly where you're supposed to.

This is freedom.

Here, you let go of beating yourself up or thinking how you're in your midthirties and everyone's married and making babies and you're here reading a self-help book by your lonesome on another Saturday night. You can *be* when your ego wants you to *do*. You open yourself up to a synchronicity that connects seemingly unconnectable dots in a way that leaves you stunned.

Sure, letting go brings uncomfortable emotions—that's the point. In order to deal with this discomfort as it comes up, you'll:

- ▶ **Recognize faith is a muscle.** Your ability to stay steadfast during this process requires faith that gets stronger with use. Faith is choosing *not* to follow up with a client again or not checking the email again waiting to hear if you got accepted into the program.
- ▶ **Use resistance to let go.** When you're experiencing resistance around letting go—remember you're going against the ego's desire to control (or the illusion of it, because, hey, we're spinning on a blue rock going 1,000 mph right now). See the resistance as proof to why you *must* do it.
- ▶ **Use foresight before hindsight.** Divine timing won't always make sense today, yet think back to some of the best moments of your life: Did you have every answer ahead of time? Was it all about urgency or are there examples of divine timing? By reflecting, you'll notice where this has already worked in your favor.
- ▶ **Start small.** Divine timing can be tough during high-stakes situations of our lives if we've never practiced during low-stakes ones. Find small ways to lean into this energy, like choosing to step away from the laptop or making a spontaneous decision.

Divine timing is not some ethereal concept the guru said on a podcast.

It's being able to stay mentally sane, honor your process, and recognize sometimes *not* getting what you want is a blessing.

Surely, there are those who take this to the extreme. They're "detaching" under the guise of divine timing but lacking courage. They're waiting for the conditions to arise, but not doing anything to compel those conditions. They're not starting the business because, well, we're in Mercury retrograde all month.

In most cases, those who identified as hustlers before this book need *more* divine timing. They realize what got them *here*—the nose-to-the-grindstone drive—will *not* get them there. Those who identify as seekers need the urgency to step up to the plate now instead of "figuring themselves out" for another 18 months . . . at their third vision quest this year.

Good luck with that.

WHAT TO LEAVE BEHIND WITH CONVENTIONAL URGENCY

The right urgency compels action with a calming effect. The wrong urgency compels the same action but feels stressful. Specifically, here's what to let go of:

- ▶ **Manic urgency that creates overwhelm.** Remember: urgency is a thoughtful and grounded reason on why today today matters. Living in a frenzied panic is not doing it right.
- ▶ **Setting deadlines that are fantasy.** While deadlines are powerful, you're not running the Badwater 100-miler if you've never even done a 5K. Everyone has a point where deadlines feel so impossible, our minds turn them into fantasies.

WHAT TO LEAVE BEHIND WITH CONVENTIONAL DIVINE TIMING

Too much divine timing is the person who lives in delusion around his or her goals and is literally doing *nothing*, all under the guise of "waiting for it to come together." So, what are we not keeping with this principle?

1. **Divine timing does not mean you do nothing.** This is not an excuse to be lazy and not do anything. In fact, it's the opposite: divine timing means you keep planting seeds even when there are no results yet.
2. **Divine timing is not giving up**. There's a stark difference between giving up and divine timing. When you give up, you play victim. When you practice divine timing, you release control. You surrender.

NO ONE "MAKES IT"
AT 60 . . . RIGHT?

In actor Jeff Daniels's mind, it was too late to "make it."

He'd starred in supporting roles from *Terms of Endearment* to *Dumb and Dumber*, showcasing range—a knack to play serious roles and keep up with comedic genius Jim Carrey. But as he says: "You're not supposed to do it this way, who hits their stride in this business at 59 years old?"[2]

But that's precisely what Daniels did.

He married the worlds of urgency with what he could control—work ethic, preparation, and focus on his craft—with divine timing and detaching from *any* expectation of fame or success. To showcase this, Daniels moved back to Michigan to raise his family as his career trended up, a move agents attempted to talk him out of. Unlike today's virtual auditions, if you weren't in L.A. or New York—and didn't look like Clooney or Johansson—it *wasn't* happening.

But Daniels didn't care because he'd detached.

And so when his moment arrived—after a dry spell—it was time to deliver. He'd been written a heroic monologue by Aaron Sorkin for a new HBO series called *Newsroom*. In the scene, Daniels plays anchor Will McAvoy, who sits on a panel in front of weary-eyed journalism students. While discussing the state of America, he skims past the surface, offers jokes, and seems aloof. His fellow panelists challenge him to say more; he jokes back.

Until his moment.

Daniels had been waiting for this his entire life as he saw others get the big scene, the inspiring monologue, the dramatic moment. Ever the standby, Daniels was a solid supporting actor. But it was always someone *else's* time and now the lights were on him—could he deliver?

Hello, urgency.

During the next three minutes and 16 seconds, McAvoy embarks on an iconic rant that catapulted Daniels's career. Daniels didn't merely show up that day, he knocked it out of the park with tenacity. He revealed his state of mind knowing HBO executives, the cast and crew, and an entire room were watching a scene that would play a major role in getting the television series picked up: "I'd been waiting for this; I'd seen other people get those roles. And so, when the moment comes, you are ready because you've done the work. And if you're not interested in doing the work, then get the fuck out."[3]

The rant is now revered as one of the best opening scenes of any series, nabbing Daniels a surprising Emmy in 2013 against the likes of Jon Hamm and Bryan Cranston. In an interview, Daniels talks about his detachment, even from the Emmy:

> The Emmy, I didn't see coming. In fact, I was told, "Just go for the salmon." It took two or three years before James Gandolfini was even considered, so HBO told me to just enjoy the meal. That was a shocker.[4]

Daniels's midwestern roots mean he *literally* went for the salmon—and had married two worlds: urgency and divine timing.

You'll do the same as you manufacture urgency while letting the conditions arise. You'll stay ready at the intersection of skill and opportunity, so you don't simply open the door—you steamroll through it.

Best of all, you won't waste precious bandwidth on things that aren't under your control. Had Daniels tried to achieve success at 35 or 40, he would have given up too soon and missed out on becoming a bankable dramatic actor into his mid-60s.

You'll do the same by harnessing urgency and simultaneously being open to a completely different path.

Chapter

15

Mentorship
&
Be Your Own Guru

There is no such thing as self-made.

Examine any of the world's greats, those on the peak of their mountains, and you'll find an infinite stream of support, encouragement, and feedback from those who have their back. The mentality of the lone wolf is dangerous. It leaves us empty, scattered, and lost on the Hero's journey of our lives because it's simply not realistic.

In other words, you cannot do this alone.

And even if you could, *why* would you?

Without a backbone of support to navigate the abyss, valleys of growth, and emotional questioning—the chances of persisting are next to zero. And because intimate relationships are a vital source of fulfillment, we *need* people along for the ride.[1]

Say hello to mentorship—seeking support and wisdom from those further along. Those who have carved their own path and stepped into the unknown. Been there, done that. And, ultimately, those who see your blind spots from a mile away and give you real-world feedback that may sting the ego, but comes from a place of respect.

On the hustler's side, you're going to enroll mentors, models, coaches, and peers—to blaze your path with the much-needed perspective from those who aren't in the trenches of your life. You'll collapse the time it takes to achieve your goals, develop unbreakable relationships, and turn blind spots into cheat codes.

On the seeker's side, you're going to take the wisdom and guidance you've gathered and filter it through your own lens . . . as you become your own guru. To do so is to develop the self-trust, intuition, and skills to practice personal agency—things one would usually go to a spiritual guide to cultivate.[2]

The best mentorship relationships are never about dependence, they are about bringing your gifts to life in a synergistic exchange with someone who has your back. And when the lights are on, the stakes are high, and your coach or guru isn't available—you step up. Because you don't *need* them, which is entirely why the relationship is cherished. It's a cocreation of the best kind.

Because what holds us back in life are the obstacles we can't see—but the right mentor can spot them from miles away.

THOSE DAMN BLIND SPOTS

We all have blind spots.

These are ways of thinking, acting, and responding that make us get in our own way. They show up regardless of success and accomplishments. It is part of life, Plato's allegory of the cave, things we simply cannot see in the trenches of our lives.

We've all been a version of the friend who's been in and out of a toxic relationship for four years who continues to come to us for advice with the answers being so blatantly clear we wonder WTF is happening that our friend can't see it.

Yeah, we have that too.

Growth, then, is about identifying blind spots and reducing their negative effects. When you add in mentorship, you turn what was your blind spot into a competitive advantage.

However, a blind spot left unchecked runs rampant.

It's lurking in the background yet impossible to notice. We learn to live with it. We adapt, and become comfortable with it. These blind spots vary in size, form, and consequence, but we all have them.

The consequences of blind spots include:

▶ Making us get in our own way
▶ Self-sabotaging after a big success
▶ Creating unnecessary stress and chaos
▶ Quitting right before a big opportunity
▶ Leaving the next level of income on the table
▶ Making us feel like we're going nowhere fast
▶ Having us live in comparison and not enough

As you create results you'll naturally reduce your blind spots—right?

Well, kind of.

While your blind spots do become smaller, there's a catch: a smaller blind spot is harder to see *and* more costly. Add in the tempting vices of the ego to believe its hype as it creates success and it's no wonder why most of us get stuck on a barren plateau with no end in sight.

Think about this in sport. The raw basketball player has obvious blind spots: they can't shoot a jumper and rely on blinding athleticism. Lebron James doesn't have obvious blind spots; his are in the situational nuances as someone who is at mastery level. But these can come up when they matter most: the game is on the line and there are 39 seconds left.

The same applies in business. On one hand, you have someone who runs the entire show as a freelancer who brings in $34,000 a year. On the other hand, you have a CEO of an 89-person organization with revenues of $4.9 million.

Whose blind spots are more costly?

If you've connected the dots, then it may have hit you—we need *more* support, perspective, and mentorship as we tackle the rungs of success, not less. Higher stakes bring higher consequences. Enter the five rules of blind spots:

> **Rule 1: Everyone has them.** It doesn't matter how much business success, accolades, or Super Bowls you've won, *everyone* has a blind spot.
>
> **Rule 2: The smaller the blind spot, the more costly.** Spotting the blind spot of someone drifting is easy. As you succeed, it becomes harder as you buy your own hype, people stop telling you the truth, and you become the great white shark in a bathtub.
>
> **Rule 3: Finding a mentor is the fastest way to leverage a blind spot.** Enrolling others is the fastest way to turn a weakness into a hidden opportunity, and yet, that same act requires us to admit we don't have *all* the answers.
>
> **Rule 4: Overcoming blind spots creates fulfillment.** Overcoming blind spots is an incredible success amplifier, but also a direct path to fulfillment like none other. You overcome challenges, build self-awareness, and turn weaknesses into strengths.
>
> **Rule 5: What makes you great is also a weakness.** Our biggest strengths are a double-edged sword. Without recognizing the law of diminishing returns, what makes us great can kill us. Focus can become rigidness. Intensity can lead to burnout. Audacity can lead to delusion.

THE SUCCESS PARADOX

The more you succeed, elevate skills, and accumulate wins, trophies, awards, and respect in your field—the less coaching, guidance, and support you'll need, right?

Not quite.

Enter the success paradox: the more you grow, the *more* you must invest in models, mentors, coaches, and peers. It sounds counterintuitive but examine those on the world's stages who weren't only flashes in the pan, but iconic, and you'll notice a theme—they increased help as they grew.

Why?

For starters—handling success is harder than dealing with failure. There is limitless advice on how to bounce back from letdowns, but little focus on dealing with the challenges of success, including that people are less likely to tell you the truth, one's ego tends to inflate, and it is harder to stay motivated.

Second, success opens the door for complacency. It's why those who succeed stop doing the little things. The details matter less, and what got them *there* starts to fade away. Distracted by the glitz of results, they start to slide back to where they came from.

Last, as we noted earlier, success reduces the *size* of blind spots, and yet—they are more costly. The nuances now contain all the gold for future growth but require attention. The Hollywood actor has more to lose than the local improv star, the executive more than the entry-level employee.

And that's precisely why mentors, models, coaches, and peers are needed to help you turn blind spots into fertile opportunities.

MODELS, MENTORS, COACHES, PEERS

Blind spots are masters of disguise and, hence, must be addressed from all angles. They can be relentless and conniving, hiding in the dark shadows of our psyche and ruling our behaviors from an unseen control room tucked deep in our subconscious.

As you experience results, you must match your growth with perspective, support, and much-needed real talk from those who have your best interests in mind, rooted in respect.

In the world of mentorship—we break it up into four distinct worlds:

▶ **Models.** These are the people in your niche you aspire to be like—you literally use them as a model. They are doing what you want to do *while* being who you want to be (as much as you can tell). The relationship is usually one-sided, i.e., there's no direct exchange—you learn from afar. Models can be found everywhere, in books, videos, speeches, podcasts, events, or the throngs of culture.

▶ **Mentors.** These are people often, but not necessarily, in your craft, niche, or marketplace who have paved the path before you and are now there to provide guidance. They are wise, have been through the battles, and are in a place where they desire to give back to those who are hungry. Typically, there is a real relationship here, although not always an exchange of money. Mentors are lighthouses, allowing you to stay grounded through the fog of failure, plateaus, and resounding successes.

▶ **Coaches.** These are people who are digging into the trenches with you and who are designed to elevate your performance. They are with you on the ride, and there are clear outcomes you've mapped out. A coach holds you to the fire, and there is a formal relationship, usually with an exchange of time and money. The best ones will be able to address both inner work (seeking, fulfillment) with external performance (success, results, tangible growth).

▶ **Peers.** These are those who are on a similar track either inside or outside of your industry, with whom you've chosen to cultivate a relationship. There is a dose of competition here, but it comes from a place of mutual respect as discussed in Chapter 13. The interactions are informal, but you feel supported. You can dial one another up as needed, and there is a real sense of camaraderie and reciprocity. You celebrate one another's wins.

Consider this four-pronged approach a way to obliterate blind spots on the regular. Each serve a unique purpose and provide a dose of much-needed perspective.

It may seem like overkill, but it's not.

A high-growth, purpose-filled life comes with high vulnerability and emotional trials. While these relationships are invaluable, be careful not to trade your inner agency, authority, and power away.

In other words, use this outer perspective and advice to become your own guru. You'll be able to make your own decisions, find clarity on your own accord, and trust yourself like never before.

BE YOUR OWN GURU

While immersing yourself with A players, mentors, and those that demand excellence from you is nonnegotiable—you will simultaneously become your own guru.

This means you learn to listen to the inner voice, sharpen your inner dialogue, and cultivate your own answers. You don't desperately rely on someone else; instead, you come to each relationship clear on who you are and what matters.

The worst use of mentorship is when you become solely reliant on someone else, giving your power and agency away. When the relationship ends, you feel stuck and lost—which belittles its purpose. This is the person who feels unable to make a decision without input from the mentor, coach, or speed dialing their favorite psychic.

To become your own guru is to:

- **Sharpen your internal signal.** Create pockets of silence, solitude, and *seeking* to understand what is happening under the surface—allowing answers to arise. Think back to what we learned about honing intuition in the previous chapter—those skills come in handy here.
- **Learn to listen and trust yourself.** As you sharpen your signal, you hear answers with more clarity *and* move toward them, building your own self-trust.
- **Ask better questions.** Through this process, you learn to ask better questions and learn that knowing the *right* questions

at the right time can solve any problem or obstacle. The better the questions, the grander the answers.

▶ **Use the raw materials to create.** Mentors and other support systems are designed to give you the raw materials to create your vision from an empowered place.

▶ **Develop a healthy relationship with your ego.** By detaching and recognizing how the ego flares up, you develop a relationship with it. You use it when it is needed but have a toolbox to disarm it when it acts up, to lower its roar to a faint whisper. We'll dive into this in Chapter 20.

▶ **Acquire skills.** Becoming your own guru means pursuing skills to amplify every part of your life, vision, and growth. It's being willing to get uncomfortable and look like a rookie.

All of these coalesce with our inner belief system so we can move forward as we become our best coach. As a Harvard Business study on coaching said, "Like good parents who encourage their children to leave the nest, good coaches help their students learn how to rely on an inner coach."[3]

By merging these, you drop the me-against-the-world mentality that hustlers tend to love—wrapped up in their egoic success— believing they know better. You avoid the perils of the seeker who has become dependent on a throng of conflicting opinions from psychics, shamans, and life coaches galore. As the quote from Zen Kōan goes: "If you meet the buddha on the road, kill him."[4]

In other words, have an unquenchable fervor to seek wisdom, guidance, and advice. Drop the façade that you have all the answers. Ask for help. Invite feedback that stings like tequila to the back of the throat as you swallow your pride. Then, curate this wisdom through your own prism of self-knowledge, trust, values, and principles. Parse out the essential—that one sentence that made your heart flutter, what you needed to hear.

And then tattoo it into your mind, body, and spirit as you become a master integrator—while becoming the best coach you could ever have—with a level of self-trust that makes others' knees buckle.

Here, it's game over.

WHAT TO LEAVE BEHIND WITH MENTORSHIP

Models, mentors, coaches, and peers in your life will appear at the right places and right seasons of your career and life. Here's what you *won't* be bringing with you:

▶ **Always seeking validation.** Mentorship is crucial but being in a constant state of seeking external validation for all your choices and decisions will leave you unable to access inner wisdom. The point is not to rely but to amplify.

▶ **Choosing coaches who do the work for you.** A second-rate coach or mentor tries to "save" their clients by doing the work for them, leaving them powerless. An excellent coach provides a compass and is willing to sit back and watch you through it, so you are equipped with the self-reliance you'll need.

▶ **Getting stuck in a constant feedback loop.** Gathering information, advice, and feedback without integration creates more confusion, not less. These are the people who reach out to five mentors and yet do nothing. There is no tangible growth here, only overwhelm, leading to inaction.

WHAT TO LEAVE BEHIND WITH BEING YOUR OWN GURU

Becoming your own guru means filtering information you've received and taking aligned action from it. While doing so is essential, skip the following:

▶ **Ignoring external advice.** Like all opposites in this book, this is a tightrope. As you make progress, you must stay open to feedback and seek it actively. The ego can quickly become uber-confident and avoid what it needs to hear.

▶ **Letting the ego run rampant.** Becoming your own guru is not an egoistic mechanism where you think you have all the key codes. Rather, it is a humble way of asking deeper questions, not out of lack, but out of self-awareness.

COACHABILITY IS A SUPERPOWER

Russell Wilson wasn't supposed to be a star.

In a league where the mold of a quarterback has become near exactitude—height, weight, pedigree—Wilson was seen as too small, too short, and too ill-equipped to perform at the next level. As a result, he was passed on for the first two rounds of the NFL draft while scouts expected a middling career as a backup, noting "he would struggle to see the field."[5]

What they missed with Wilson was invisible to the naked eye—his obsession with preparation, an unquenched thirst for learning, and a devotion to being the most coachable person in any room. Ever the student, Wilson sought out sports psychologists and mindset professionals who could give him even a decimal increase in performance.

Wilson has an uncanny level of coachability—the ability to drop one's pride and ask for help—rare even in the world of professional sport. One of those coaches is Trever Moawad, who trains Wilson to seek "neutral" thinking in everything he does to avoid the emotional roller coaster of playing football and to stay grounded, focused, and present.[6]

And it has paid off.

Wilson has become one of the league's elite quarterbacks and destined to do the unthinkable when he was scouted a decade ago: adorn a gold jacket from the Hall of Fame in Canton, Ohio, one day. Had he not been the most coachable person in any room, this would be nigh impossible.

No matter who you are, coaches, mentors, models, and peers are *crucial* to your success. This is the support system that celebrates you like hell when you win instead of sulking in the corner. They'll support you, but they won't stop there. They'll also see when you're not living up to your standard and call you out. They'll challenge your beliefs, excuses, and ego-inflated narratives.

In other words, they respect you.

In this place, you become the student willing to face the truth and look nakedly at blind spots without defensiveness.

You avoid the all-too-common symptoms of self-sabotage, drama, and mental gaffes that come with success or failure.

Here, blind spots are transformed into opportunities, results, growth, and cash in the bank. What was a weakness, like Wilson's height, becomes an opportunity to develop a skill set that overrides it. Along the way, you build your inner guru, sage, and mentor. The end result is a lethal combination to move forward on your path with a rousing level of self-trust plus the knowledge you can handle the hard seasons of life.

Heed the call. Be open. Choose wisely.

Chapter

16

Leave Comfort Zone
&
Recover Wisely

Adaptation is the endgame.

Our ability to adapt is why you're reading this book. Humans are hardwired as the most adaptable species on the planet—which is why we're winning. We're not the fastest[1] (hey, cheetah), the strongest[2] (damn you, elephants), or the most elusive[3] (snow leopards).

But goddamn, we can adapt like no one's business.

Our lives are the same: what stands between where you are today and the gripping life you want isn't about talent. It's not about luck. It's not about being "discovered" by a stranger who hands you the keys to the castle nor pinning your career hopes on a tweet from Oprah.

It's about adaptation.

Say hello to leaving your comfort zone on the hustler's side and pushing the limits of your capacity often—to improve skills, increase your bandwidth, and level up your resilience in pursuit of what you want.

And then to balance the intensity required to leave your comfort zone with physical, mental, emotional, and spiritual recovery—to induce the key elements of adaptation—from the seeker's side.

By doing so, you reliably find the sweet spot between stimulus and recovery to prompt the most useful form of adaptation. You'll adapt to a higher baseline in your day-to-day—both how you perform *and* how you feel—as well as raising your "comeback" rate after a challenge.

In other words, you'll raise your lows and your highs.

Which means today's stellar output becomes a *meh* day six months from now. As a result, your performance blossoms. Recovery increases. Your new normal blows other people away while your emotional set point rises.[4] But before we get to the good stuff, let's be real: adaptation has a dark side that we've all experienced.

We can adapt to a life we know isn't working.

THE DARK SIDE OF ADAPTATION

Adaptation can work against us.

Think back to a time when you knew something wasn't right for you, maybe a new gig, a relationship, or a business collaboration. At the time, your urgency to change it was high: this *isn't* working. You couldn't get out fast enough.

You told yourself you'd only stay a few weeks.

But time passed and the adaptation process kicked in—the pain of change became *greater* than staying the same. Since adaptation all but kills urgency, you had less desire and motivation. And you started to look at the bright side, seeing those cute Instagram platitudes about being grateful for what you have.

In other words, you talked yourself into an awful circumstance.

We've all been there: justifying, rationalizing, and talking ourselves into a situation we never wanted in the first place. Maybe
we even used "fake" gratitude and let ourselves off the hook with
feel-good clichés that masked what we really felt, including:

▶ **You knew the job wasn't right**—but you've got killer health,
dental, and biweekly bank deposits.

▶ **You knew the relationship wasn't right**—but it's the holidays
and you don't want to be alone . . . plus your partner cares.

▶ **You knew the collaboration wasn't right**—but there's
potential to make serious dough.

Notice a pattern here?

The word *but* is present in each of these—an obvious sign
that we're justifying an experience for external reasons. On a
long enough timeline, a couple months turns into a year, and
that year turns into a decade as you wake up and wonder how
the hell it all went wrong.

No, thanks.

Make no mistake: while adaptation can be the catalyst for
transformation, it's also responsible for wasted careers, halfhearted dreams, and graveyards full of shadow lives and missed
callings.

Here's why:

▶ **Adaptation creates comfort.** Yesterday's pain becomes what
we tolerate today as we talk ourselves out of changing. We
become comfortable with mediocrity. Due to sunk cost, we
talk ourselves into staying put.

▶ **Adaptation diminishes urgency.** Because of comfort, we're
in no rush to change: we can do it tomorrow, next month,
next January. Without urgency, we'd rather sit on the couch
spread-eagle than confront the challenge.

▶ **Adaptation lowers the baseline.** Adaptation lowers our
"average" level of performance and fulfillment. As nothing
changes, our baseline decreases until we arrive at what my
friend Jay Nixon calls "suddenly" syndrome: *suddenly* I felt
off track, *suddenly* I was 45 pounds overweight, *suddenly* I
hated my career.

Adaptation is a powerful force.

Consider a study by researchers who examined amputees—people who lost a limb—and tracked their fulfillment based on that life-shifting event. What researchers found was stunning: the amputees were back to their original *baseline* within six months of the incident.[5]

Let that sink in.

This is the incredibly useful part of adaptation: ensuring we don't stay emotionally wrecked for the rest of our lives after a tough break-up, a disability, or the death of our beloved golden retriever. But adaptation can be a silent killer—especially if it's working against us.

In the case of the job you can't stand, it's debilitating.

Being aware of adaptation's dark side is step one—consider step two an active process of swimming upstream against this mechanism. But first, let's dive into two invisible, yet potent, markers of success: your baseline and comeback rate.

RAISE YOUR BASELINE

You have a baseline for both how you perform on a daily basis, which I'll call your performance baseline, and how you feel, which is your fulfillment baseline. While these ebb and flow, if enough data is accumulated, it is possible to find your "average."

It's how you show up on any given day.

And here's the fun part: when you're committed to growth, you're constantly raising your baseline. Using the right hustle, you're increasing your performance baseline. With the right seeking, you're expanding your fulfillment baseline.

By merging both, you're raising all tides.

Enter adaptation done the right way. A steady, consistent raising of your baseline across time, resulting in:

▶ **Your performance increases.** Your performance output from six months ago becomes a standard day today as you are constantly elevating your ability to perform.

- **Your fulfillment expands.** By doing the inner work of the principles I've covered, you're raising your ability to feel emotional states of peace, joy, and freedom.
- **You raise your "highs."** By harnessing adaptation, you constantly raise your highs and train yourself to elevate the bar regularly. Your best moments happen more often and to a greater degree.
- **You raise your "lows."** You'll raise the times when you feel off and recognize your worst performances are still pretty damn good. Your worst moments happen less often and are *still* higher than they used to be.

By raising your baseline, you increase your belief, confidence, and skill set as you chase goals. Yesterday's star-studded performance becomes a normal day while you tap into the emotional state of success on the regular.

In doing so, you tap into the most potent marker of personal growth: increasing your comeback rate.

INCREASE YOUR COMEBACK RATE

The best NFL quarterbacks are not the ones who make zero mistakes.

Let's be real: when you've got a 298-pound behemoth who runs a 4.7 forty-yard dash zeroing in on your kneecaps, blunders happen. Those who avoid mistakes don't take the necessary risks to win at the highest level. Instead, they use a safe approach designed to pad their statistics, but they don't go for the kill.

In other words, they play *not* to lose.

The best, instead, are willing to let 'er rip when the game is on the line, and they'll be the only ones answering questions from the throngs of media about their split-second decision-making.

So, what separates good from great?

It's what happens after a mistake—the greats are able to immediately *come back* to a clear, levelheaded state as fast as possible. They don't dwell on what happened or let emotions take over. Professional scouts call this poise, the ability to stay grounded despite the chaos, adapt to high-stakes situations, and learn quickly.[6]

This is what we're calling your comeback rate—what psychologists call cognitive flexibility[7]—the speed at which you're able to quickly pivot back into a state of clarity toward the mission at hand. And the same goes for your growth even if you're not launching footballs.

For example, your comeback rate looks like these:

- ▶ Being triggered from a message by your boss and *coming back* to a state of clarity
- ▶ Launching a new brand, service, or product to minimal results and *coming back* to a state of focus
- ▶ Putting yourself out there for a new gig and being rejected and *coming back* to a state of confidence
- ▶ Giving everything you've got to a creative project and seeing minimal response and *coming back* to your craft
- ▶ Having that emotionally tinged argument in your relationship and *coming back* to peace

Ultimately, your comeback rate gets faster as you improve.

A challenge that used to make you emotionally disoriented for two days now takes a couple hours. The uncertainty after being rejected lasts 40 minutes instead of the whole day. The scathing reply on Twitter that used to knock you off-kilter fades away in seconds. Your comeback rate is the invisible factor of success most people rarely talk about.

And it's using the adaptation effect for you, not against you.

HOW TO HARNESS THE POWER OF ADAPTATION

There's good and bad news and I don't have the luxury of asking you which you want, so I'll start with bad: if you don't proactively use adaptation to work for you, it will work against you.

You'll adapt to what you don't want.

And then there's great news—using adaptation to work for you doesn't require colossal efforts of earth-shattering performance: it requires daily doses that reward consistency over intensity, the long game versus the short one.

In other words, it doesn't take much.

To harness the power of adaptation, you're going to:

- ► **Seek the challenge before it seeks you.** Instead of waiting around for a challenge to induce adaptation, take command. Challenge yourself in small ways—physically, mentally, emotionally, and spiritually. Do a few more reps during your workout when you think you're toast. Have the awkward conversation *now* before it becomes a full-blown crisis tomorrow. Consider this a daily practice.

- ► **Leave your comfort zone by at least 4 percent.** Steven Kotler, the bestselling author on flow states, talks about the challenge and skills balance. He's determined the sweet spot is about 4 percent out of our comfort zone.[8] If you've never given a public talk, it's probably not the best idea to sign up for a TEDx talk, but you could volunteer to present at the staff meeting. If you go past this, you can get overwhelmed—and if you don't nail this—you can get bored. It's about finding your sweet spot and going *just* past it regularly.

- ► **Create bigger challenges.** While 4 percent is great as a daily practice, we also need event-based challenges to test ourselves. Both monthly and quarterly can work here. Some examples include signing up for a 10K, spiritual retreat, or big marketing launch.

- ► **Enter thriving environments.** One of the fastest ways to harness the adaptation effect for good is to enter thriving environments with people who either have or are working toward your same goals or are further along. Join the writing program with those who have MFAs, enter the training facility of endurance athletes, or go to the mastermind with six-figure business owners.

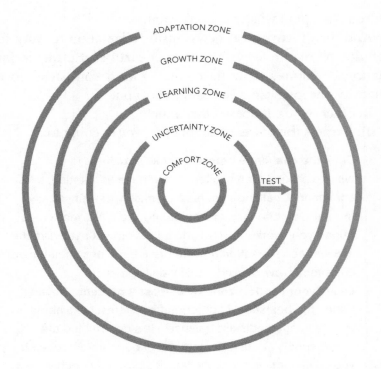

Comfort Zone Stages

To ensure you adapt wisely, you must also understand the four levels of leaving your comfort zone—the uncertainty zone, the learning zone, the growth zone, and the adaptation zone. Here's what each is about:

▶ **The uncertainty zone.** Right outside your comfort zone, this is when you feel doubt, fear, overwhelm—and want to sprint back to your comfort zone. It's a place of emotional vulnerability and erratic decisions, and where you're most likely to quit. It's where dreams go to die.

▶ **The learning zone.** You've done enough to leave uncertainty but are still overwhelmed and challenged *while* learning as much as you can. You've activated the spark of curiosity and have overcome initial resistance—the unknown has turned from intimidating to engaging, but you're not off the hook yet; there's another zone coming.

▶ **The growth zone.** Here, you're equipped with the resilience of overcoming fear and doubt plus acquiring skills. This is a state of palpable growth, results, momentum. However, this is also the place where a test can either hurl you back into you comfort zone or push you to the event horizon known as the adaptation zone . . . so don't stop here. Keep going.

▶ **The adaptation zone.** This is where the magic happens. The buildup of the prior zones turns into your new baseline as your mind, body, and spirit integrate this "new" normal. Your baseline, capacity, and confidence all go through the roof.

This cycle repeats itself.

When these zones work in tandem, you'll harness the power of adaptation. But much like our physicality, we don't actually grow when we're performing on stage, blitzing through a marketing project, or in our creative cave.

Rather, we grow when we recover, rest, and recharge.

RECOVERY ISN'T SEXY

Say it with me: recovery isn't sexy.

It won't sell out packed arenas and books on the topic aren't going to top bestseller lists—yet recovery is the missing link between adaptation, a higher baseline, and increasing your comeback rate.

With all things being equal, what separates two athletes, creatives, or business owners?

It's those who recover and adapt *faster,* so as to harness the positive effects of adaptation that allow them to get back to the field of play to improve their skills, pattern recognition, and creative output.

Recovery is where the magic of growth happens, where you're able to do more work in less time. Where you can focus for two hours instead of 45 minutes. Where you can do better work as a business owner, employee, or creative professional. Where you integrate skills, learning, and lessons.

Enter recovery, your ability to accelerate, optimize, and adapt from pushing the needle of your growth on a daily basis. To understand recovery, I'll first break it down into two versions: passive and active.

Recovery Type 1: Passive Recovery

When most people think of recovery, they daydream about staying in bed with the curtains drawn, ordering tacos, and binging their favorite show. And sure, passive recovery has a part to play. We all need to relax. We all need rest. We all need nothingness. We need to allow ourselves to be lazy sans guilt.

But think about that one time you were brutally sore.

You did an ungodly number of squats or lunges and walking upstairs was impossible as parts of your body ached that you didn't even know you had. Let me ask you: in this state, is it better to do absolutely nothing—or would it be better to do some light activity? In nearly every case, blood flow *speeds up* the recovery process.

Something is better than nothing.

Consider passive recovery to be sheer nothingness: lounging, hanging out, naps, reading, resting, shutting the world off, and taking time to slumber. While important at times in a nonstop, cult-of-busy world, there's a much more potent way to recover. That's what I'll call active recovery.

Recovery Type 2: Active Recovery

Active recovery, as it sounds, is an engaged and deliberate process.

It means you don't go from 100 mph to standing still—otherwise you end up stagnant, hurt, or disoriented. Rather, you use movement, activity, and tools to speed up the process at a low threshold to propel adaptation and get you back into a state of homeostasis, after you have dosed intensity.

Active recovery isn't simply about physicality.

It can be used for every area of life—and is often underutilized in different domains. By actively recovering, you will lower the negative impact of intensity and instead reap the rewards of coming back refreshed, engaged, and ready to integrate your breakthrough.

Active recovery includes:

- ▶ Walking
- ▶ Work at low threshold
- ▶ Reading and learning
- ▶ Engaged meditation
- ▶ Cold and hot therapies
- ▶ Ice bath or contrast shower
- ▶ Journaling and debrief
- ▶ Yoga and stretching
- ▶ Massage and bodywork
- ▶ Studying and learning
- ▶ Hobbies

The list goes on, but the litmus test is simple: low-intensity action that induces the adaptation effect. Enough to keep the recovery process flowing, but far from taxing you. This is activity designed to keep you physically, mentally, and emotionally in movement.

When there is movement, the recovery process is active.

THE BETTER YOU ARE, THE MORE RECOVERY

If you're more skilled, better at your craft, and perform at higher levels—you'll need more recovery, not less. As you reach the upper echelons of skill, the separator is found in the margins of recovery.

Take, for example, someone who finished a 5K versus someone who completed an Ironman. Both people may have hit the edges of capacity and left their comfort zones, but because the

Ironman is a grueling, multisport experience—recovery may take weeks or months. The training was long, intense, and required peaks, valleys, and tapering to even arrive at the starting line.

This athlete needs a hard reset.

Even someone who went all out for a local 5K likely won't need more than a few days or a week. Even if the person went full tilt, he or she is likely unable to tap into the same effort as the above—due to the event itself and personal skill level. And hence, the golden rule: the larger your capacity and the harder you can go—the *more* recovery matters.

This applies to every field or craft, and here's what to keep in mind as you optimize recovery:

- ▶ **Recover *before* you need it.** Don't wait until you're in dire straits clinging to your last thread of energy. Rather, prioritize recovery before you feel like you need it because once you need it . . . it's too late.
- ▶ **Recover to integrate.** Consider recovery a must-have when it comes to integrating your intensity. It's common to go through an intense experience and then do nothing, which means missing out on the actual integration piece.
- ▶ **Recover to avoid plateaus.** A plateau of growth can be frustrating and often involves a lack of systemized and consistent recovery to fuel one's adaptation. When you find yourself there, ask: Where can I deepen my recovery?
- ▶ **Increase baseline, increase recovery.** As you improve your baseline skills and capacity, recovery becomes more essential. Since you can dig deeper and go harder and longer, you must double the time spent recharging.

The elite athlete needs more recovery than the rookie. The award-winning filmmaker needs more incubation than the young buck. The CEO needs more time off than the mailroom clerk. The higher your capacity, the harder you can go . . . the more you need to recover.

WHAT TO LEAVE BEHIND WITH CONVENTIONAL COMFORT ZONE

For the type A, hard-charging ambitious folk—leaving their comfort zones is the status quo and they often push too hard. Here's what to leave behind:

- ▶ **Living in intensity.** Intensity is about strategic dosing. Otherwise, you burn yourself to the ground and often don't end up improving as fast as those who prioritize recovery.
- ▶ **Going too hard, too early.** Early on in your endeavor, it's easy to go too hard since you're new and intensity isn't as taxing. This quickly works against you. Instead, leave some gas in the tank for tomorrow; otherwise, you'll fizzle out.
- ▶ **Comparing yourself.** Intensity is relative. What is intense for you may be recovery for someone else and vice versa. There is no need to compare; otherwise, you may hurl yourself into oblivion to match someone else or pursue something you don't even desire.

WHAT TO LEAVE BEHIND WITH CONVENTIONAL RECOVERY

While recovery is no doubt useful and a key to ongoing growth, here's what you'll be leaving behind:

- ▶ **Only passive recovery.** We need both passive and active recovery. However, people tend to ignore active recovery and spend too much time in passive, wondering why they're not motivated. Active recovery engages the mind, body, and spirit and keeps things in motion.
- ▶ **Not taking it seriously.** Recovery is usually an afterthought, a "have to do" once the tank is running on empty. Understand recovery is a competitive advantage and the more you progress, the more it better be a priority . . . or else.
- ▶ **Staying in the recovery comfort zone.** We can become stagnant in our own recovery routines even if they're

working. Change it up. Engage in mental recovery if you're physically wiped and vice versa. Integrate a new modality or technology. Do 30 days of ice baths if you've never done them. Keep it fresh, fun, and exciting.

WORK HARD, RECOVER HARDER

Lindsey Vonn is intense.

Known for hurling herself at a brisk 85 mph on the world's steepest climbs—she redefined the sport of downhill skiing with a tenacious knack to put it all on the line.

She's also crashed more than anyone else.

With a catalog of injuries that would make an orthopedic surgeon's career, she's endured 10 major surgeries, broken bones, shredded ligaments, ruptured joints, snapped elbows, twisted ankles . . . and a few concussions for good measure.

As she says, "What separates me from other competitors is just my willingness to always throw my body down the mountain. That's probably why I've been injured so many times. But it's also why I've won a lot."[9] In 2016, she was even helicoptered off a mountain in Turin after a vicious crash with onlookers fearing the worst . . . but 48 hours later was back on her skis.

So, what gives?

Vonn harnessed adaptation to become the best in the world. She expanded her capacity and mastered her craft while overcoming injuries that would leave most of us comatose. She raised her baseline to astonishing levels.

She made leaving her comfort zone as routine as brushing her teeth and thrived in both the growth and recovery zones. According to designer and friend Cynthia Rowley, "She was the most self-possessed, fearless, brilliant, focused, glamorous yet down-to-earth, hard-core, badass woman I have ever met."[10]

And you can do the same, even if your craft isn't going tips down.

Adaptation is the most powerful force on the planet, but most of us fall prey to its dark side. But we can use it to create a level of growth, results, and performance that stun others. And ourselves.

What Vonn gets is what we miss—we don't grow when we're doing *the work*, we grow when we recover. We adapt when we recharge. And surely, this is evident in athletics, but it's as important in our careers, craft, and creativity.

Leave your comfort zone. *Feel* that knot in your throat, the unease of self-doubt, the gnawing impostor syndrome. The questioning. Do that thing that scares you. Push toward that promotion, submit your work to the panel. Work on you craft, sharpen your skills, slam down on the accelerator when it's needed.

And then, as hard as you pushed, if not harder—put that energy back into your recovery. Take your foot off the gas. Give yourself some breathing room.

As you do, you'll adapt to a new normal you never thought was possible.

17

Priorities
&
White Space

Our lives resemble the busted white '89 Buick at our local grocery store parking lot, bursting at the seams with toys, trash, and newspapers galore—a perfect candidate for the next episode of *Hoarders* on A&E. We are stuffed to the gills, drowning in a sea of more stuff: more tasks, more noise, more people who are no longer aligned with who they are.

And it's only getting worse.

This culture of *more* acts as deadweight at best and an anchor to keep us stuck at worst. We use a lack of clarity as an excuse as to why we're not making the progress we desire.

While we may feel we're not the hoarder in the parking lot, we tend to do this with our lives. Because of the pressure to hustle, succeed, and figure out our life's purpose, we equate "more" with "better." We fill our lives with seven priorities and wonder why none of them come to life. We add tasks so we're constantly overwhelmed. We enroll in the cult of busy. Always hurrying, we take panicked exhales when people ask us how we're doing to showcase our worth.

More is always better, right?

Actually, no, it's not. Instead, more often becomes less.

Less clarity, growth, results. Less consistency, momentum, endurance. Fewer bank account deposits, clients, opportunities. And worst of all, less mental real estate, sanity, and freedom.

No, thank you.

It's time to embrace a minimalistic approach to life and business by ruthlessly identifying priorities. To delete what is consuming our space and get rid of the fourth side hustle so we can focus . . . on one. To drill down on *one* skill instead of haphazardly trying to get better at nine, which leads to mediocre results.

When we do this right, we clear a ton off our plates—to the tune of 30–50 percent. Exhaling, we practice the art of only keeping what's essential in a world bursting at the seams. With breathing room, we can harness white space: swaths of open calendar, the time for yourself you've put on the back burner, and the self-care or hobbies you *used* to do before life got crazy.

Combine these and you have a rich, meaningful life of progress plus the space to unplug, disconnect, and "be" without guilt, overwhelm, or the low-level buzz of FOMO that resembles an always-on refrigerator.

In other words, you tap into the emotional freedom that most of us desperately crave, and yet find so elusive.

DELETION AND MENTAL FREEDOM

At this moment, there are at least 30–50 percent of inputs, tasks, obligations, relationships, projects, clothes, physical possessions, clients, and more that can be deleted from your life. All of this fluff robs you of focus in addition to your ability to stay consistent and have a steady dose of clarity.

It may sound bold but take a moment to reflect.

Walk into your closet and examine how much of your clothes you *actually* wear. Go to the office and examine the clutter. Look at the calendar and ask yourself which meetings and social outings are of utmost importance. Scroll through your smartphone with the 114 unread texts or the email app with 4,011 unread emails.

You may think to yourself: what difference does it *really* make?

The problem is these take up precious mental real estate in your mind. They eat away at your willpower, they contribute to decision fatigue, and they create a low-level hum of anxiety that only *increases* with success.

Left unchecked, you make more money but have more on your plate.

While countless books, tips, tricks, and hacks tell you to add more to your plate to optimize your performance and fulfillment—they're setting you up for failure.

You can't possibly add more to your plate.

Not unless you delete, automate, delegate, and create space. By doing so, you'll realize real change starts with subtraction, not addition. To do this, you'll need to take inventory, seek a yes or a no, and start deleting what's unnecessary.

Instead of being the high-maintenance guy or gal who packs four suitcases for the weeklong getaway, you'll roll freely with a carry-on. You'll be light on your feet, nimble, and adaptable. You won't take 90 minutes to dress for the lake since you've introduced constraints from Chapter 12.

Instead, you'll be having a blast because you know what matters and have released the burden of more that our culture wears like a badge of honor.

TAKE INVENTORY

There's a reason your local department store shuts down once a year to take a count of what's on hand—or take inventory. It's hard to make decisions and get clear when you have no idea where you are. Operating out of assumptions leads to bad decisions at best and paralysis at worst.

Instead, take inventory.

Pull out a notepad or digital whiteboard and make a list of all of the pluses in your life today: what's *working*—driving you forward and fulfilling you. This includes habits, actions, rituals, people, places, media, food and drink, content you listen to, and anything else that comes to mind.

Then make a list of everything that is *not* working: the minuses that make you feel stuck and overwhelmed. These items zap your life force energy and send you into uncertainty. They sabotage your growth and make you feel worse.

Challenge yourself to write down at least 20 on each side.

Get granular, vivid, and specific. This is not about the size of the plus or minus, it's about the feeling it creates. A life of minuses likely means a life that feels out of alignment and spiraling out of control. It feels hazy, complicated, and emotionally draining.

SEEK A HELL YES OR NO

Armed with your inventory, take a step back.

You breathe, do something else for a little bit, and come back with fresh eyes. You start to ask questions:

- ▶ What has served me in the past but no longer does?
- ▶ What must I double down on in the plus category?
- ▶ What is the first thing I can delete on the minus?

As you answer these, the litmus test is being honest as to whether something is still aligned with not only who you are today, but also your *future* self. The self that is 12, 18, or 24 months down the line. To do so, you can ask:

- ▶ If I woke up in two years and created everything I wanted, would this be part of my experience?
- ▶ If I had a full bank account and didn't worry about finances, would this be part of my life?

▶ If I wasn't operating out of the ego's desire for comfort and what's known, would I keep this?

There are only two possible answers—yes or no.

There is no need to justify, rationalize, or let feelings or nostalgia talk you into doing something you know isn't allowing you to be the best version of yourself.

If you don't see your current happy hour circle as part of your thriving life in two years, make a change. If you're devoting nine hours a week to fantasy football with your college buddies and aren't where you desire to be in your career, make a shift. If someone on social media is getting you riled up, it's time to tap the unfollow button.

Be willing to practice the art of deletion.

START DELETING THE UNNECESSARY

Start small and fast with deletion.

Even the tiniest of changes creates breathing room. For some, this may be as simple as deleting the clutter in an office, car, or home. For others, this may be rebooting their technology. The key is to make deletion a habit.

We often add stuff to our plate, but rarely delete things. This is human nature; we are much more likely to fear losing something we already have than the potential for something new.[1] And therein lies the problem: your old life, the worn-out possessions, the habits that got you *here* are precisely what's stopping you from getting *there*.

And you can't possible replace something that isn't working if there's no space for something new to come in.

Make deletion a daily and weekly exercise, using:

▶ **Delegation.** Just because you *can* do everything, should you? The world is teeming with talent and people who will happily take tasks, chores, and "have to do's" from your minus list off your hands. Make a list of three things that zap your energy but need to get done and find creative ways to delegate. For example, trade services, use freelance platforms, or tap into your local college's intern program.

▶ **Automation.** Technology, apps, and tools have made automation easier and cheaper. Tired of back-and-forth emails about scheduling? Get an email scheduler. Want to know your budget? Get a real-time tracker. Leverage technology to do the heavy lifting for you.

▶ **Systemization.** Is it better to hit the grocery store daily or once a week so you are all set? In business, would you rather dedicate 90 minutes of focused time to a specific weekly endeavor, or scatter your energy daily? Systemization is chunking and batching things *once* to then create free time in the future. Whether it's groceries, laundry, or business, systems create freedom.

The purpose of a system is to create space.

Even if you barely scratch the surface, 10 percent of your life needs to *go*. And without clearing the decks of the unnecessary, you will never be able to tap into the undeniable power of priorities.

Without priorities, we never have time for white space.

We consider it a luxury for the 1 percenters, the entitled, the privileged—those who come from trust fund homes and unlimited resources.

And that couldn't be further from the truth.

THE PRIORITIZED LIFE

At any given time, you're going to have three priorities funneling your most prized resources—time, energy, attention—into *less* . . . so you can create more. After a decade helping people achieve goals, I've found what I call the "Big 3" to be the sweet spot for priorities. Three is small enough to make significant progress, while having enough novelty to stay stimulated.

Because let's face it: the cult of busy is so prevalent in the hustler's ethos that its disciples never have time for anything, choosing to run around like their hair is on fire—and getting to the end of their day with *just* enough energy to crush a cocktail or pass out on the couch with their shoes on.

It's exhausting for a life well-lived.

In contrast, the prioritized life seeks *less*, not more. It knows there is limited willpower, focus, and emotional capacity and protects these like the treasures they are. It harnesses the 80/20 rule that says, in almost any endeavor, project, or business, 20 percent of the actions lead to 80 percent of the results, as seen below.

It knows clarity is a byproduct of being aligned in priorities.

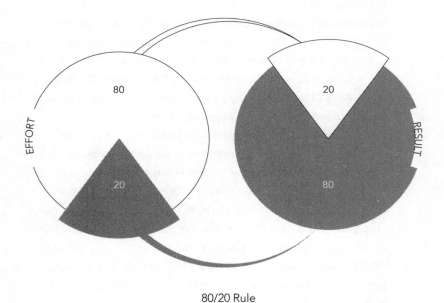

80/20 Rule

To identify what's most important to you and what your Big 3 priorities are at any given time, you're going to:

1. **Get clear on your North Star.** Your North Star is the brightest star on the horizon, the compass you're aiming at. You don't need to have it *all* figured out; a compass is not a map. A general idea is enough. If I asked you where you'd want your life to be in three years, what comes up? Write that answer down.

2. **Reverse engineer your North Star.** Keeping your answer above in mind, ask yourself: If this was the most progress-filled year toward that vision, what would happen in one year? Write down details and specifics.

3. **Compress the year to the next 90 days.** Now that you have your one-year markers written down, you need to break down the next 90 days, which I call a season. Do this by asking: What are the most important *priorities* I can get done in 90 days to make those year one goals possible? Feel free to write a few more than you need, since we'll curate your list in the next step.

4. **Write down your Big 3 priorities.** Now it's time to set those Big 3. Take a step back and reflect on your list from step 3 and cross off what doesn't stick or isn't relevant. Now, you'll set your priorities in stone by writing them down. (I'll share more about this later, but you should do this process for both your professional life and personal life.)

5. **Identify the first step.** Armed with three priorities, break each down toward the simplest first action step you can take today or tomorrow to make it real. Make sure it can be done in 15 minutes or less. Don't make this complicated; rather, make it so simple it can seem trite.

6. **Use your Big 3 as a filter.** If you get asked out to happy hour, a random meeting, or invited to volunteer—ask if it's aligned with the three priorities you've just identified. This question serves as a simple filtering mechanism and makes your yes or no easy.

7. **Be rigid *and* flexible.** While being focused on your Big 3, you also are going to leave some *slack* on the rope—priorities change, shift, and evolve in real time as you do. What does this mean? You'll use white space and seeking to make small pivots and tweaks along the way.

This seven-step process is how you get clear on your priorities.

By funneling your time, energy, and attention into only *three* priorities in a 90-day season, you'll be able to:

▶ **Make decisions.** When your priorities are clear, you can quickly make decisions by filtering everything with them in mind. You can say no to a random "collab" or email about getting your brain picked over stale coffee.

▶ **Take needle-moving action.** Without priorities, we take random actions and *hope* for a result. We take the path of least resistance. We check email all day. When you're clear, your actions go from random to deliberate.

▶ **Experience progress.** A life of few priorities means a life of *progress*. If you only have three priorities during the next 90 days, it's nearly impossible to not harness serious momentum.

▶ **Delete distractions.** Without priorities, we find ourselves spending an entire afternoon on the couch watching *Real Housewives of Orange County* with zero growth. No, thanks.

▶ **Build a tribe to support you.** It's hard to ask for support when we don't know what matters. With clear priorities, you'll attract a tribe that supports you, introduces you to new people, and helps get you there . . . faster

I've been referring to the Big 3 priorities in relation to your professional goals, but there is no doubt that life has other priorities: health, relationships, and spiritual well-being. When I work with clients in a coaching capacity, we create a professional Big 3 and a personal Big 3 that looks like this:

Professional
▶ Q4 sales target
▶ Launch side hustle
▶ Enroll in Toastmasters

Personal
▶ Complete 10K race
▶ Create eight date nights
▶ Meal prep every Sunday

Having professional and personal Big 3s fuels both parts of your life without getting out of whack. Too often, we overvalue professional priorities while our health and relationships pay the price—or we stop making progress in our careers and wonder why we're not motivated.

By addressing both, you'll raise all boats.

Setting both personal and professional goals will allow you to escape the incessant desire to do more so as to "feel" busy, and in turn, harness the power of white space in a loud, raucous world.

WHITE SPACE

Armed with the space you've created in deletion and the newfound clarity of a prioritized life—you'll engage in white space.

White space, as it sounds, is reclaiming a chunk of your life and calendar back for *you*. Time for self-care, reading, relaxation. For leisure, play, fun, unplugging. For hobbies that don't need to be monetized, for actions that don't correlate with sales, for, you know—the things you used to do before it all got so damn crazy!

White space is *yours* to bring to life and varies from person to person, but can include things like:

- ▶ Hobbies
- ▶ Unplugged time
- ▶ Time blocks with yourself
- ▶ Improvised and spontaneous activities
- ▶ Adventure, fun, and play
- ▶ Dates with significant others, family, and kids
- ▶ Novelty
- ▶ Naps, reading, and leisure

Let's be clear: contrary to the hustler's beliefs from Chapter 1, white space is *not* something you put off until you arrive at some arbitrary benchmark of success. Because if you can't shut it off during the pursuit, you'll *never* shut it off during the arrival. Rather, you infuse it into your life *before* you arrive. You don't wait for a personal crisis, a fading marriage, or your adrenals resembling burnt toast to prioritize this.

White space is not a nice to have. It is not for the 1 percent. It is not for the rich and those who fly private; it is for you. You get to define and use white space in a way that works for you, but follow these tips to maximize its effect:

▶ **Shift from a *nice to have* to a *must have*.** Delete the mindset that you have to *earn* white space, that it is a nice to have, a luxury. Instead, make it nonnegotiable and a must have for your mental sanity.

▶ **Block it out.** White space is not reserved for convenient seasons of life; otherwise, it won't happen. Make white space a priority. Block it out on your calendar—personally, mine is 3:30–5:30 every day. If Oprah called and invited me on her show at 4:00 p.m., I'd have to decline. Okay, I may make *one* exception . . . but you get the point.

▶ **Don't feel guilty.** When did we become a culture that feels guilty not *doing* and bustling around from appointment to appointment with no end in sight? White space is pointless if one feels guilty the entire time. Bask in your white space.

What you'll realize is white space accelerates growth, fulfillment, and oddly enough—performance. You'll find clarity on a problem you'd been banging your head on. You'll encounter a key insight, a creative aha, or the solution to an employee crisis while being away. You'll realize stepping away is where the best ideas come from . . . sans pressure.

And, even if they don't, you are recharged, rejuvenated, and restored. You're able to process difficult emotions, see things from a novel perspective, and release the blame we place on ourselves or others. Maybe you're even able to take a nap!

All of these make you an even better performer, artist, creative, or career professional when you step back into the game. They make you a better parent and a more patient human being at the grocery store parking lot when four cars are backing out at once and you can't hear yourself think through the shitstorm of honking.

Because of this, emotional freedom is your new normal.

WHAT TO LEAVE BEHIND WITH CONVENTIONAL PRIORITIZING

A prioritized life means taking back control of what matters and investing your precious resources into less. Here's what to be cautious of:

- ▶ **Only prioritizing what's new.** It's easy to be intoxicated with new—the *next* goal, mile marker, or promotion. But it's also important to reprioritize parts of our lives that may have slipped through the cracks, such as relationships, family, and so on.
- ▶ **Making everything a priority.** We all have a baseline to attend to—physical, mental, and emotional needs. But we also operate in seasons. For example, you may need a season (or three) where health is a personal priority.

WHAT TO LEAVE BEHIND WITH CONVENTIONAL WHITE SPACE

White space is a rarity in today's hyperconnected culture. Here's what to be careful of to ensure you don't tip the scales too much:

- ▶ **Leaving white space for last.** When white space is not prioritized, it doesn't happen. We check email for another hour. We stay late at the office to impress the boss. We work more so we can say we did on social media.
- ▶ **Thinking white space needs to be filled.** White space does not need to be filled with *more* activities, even if they're fulfilling. Play around with your white space. Be spontaneous. Some days, you may want to make it an active experience, while on others, you may need that damn nap.

WHITE SPACE IS NOT A LUXURY

White space comes in all shapes and sizes.

There is Sarah Blakely, the youngest self-made female billionaire who creates a "fake" commute to her downtown Atlanta Spanx headquarters—saying it's the best time of her day to think.[2]

There's Google's 20 percent time where employees carve out a fifth of their bandwidth toward their passion projects—responsible for the apps you use daily—including Gmail, Maps, and AdSense.[3]

There is Lin Manuel-Miranda, the creator of *Hamilton*, who protects his morning walks with his dog so as to induce new ideas. He notoriously got the spark for *Hamilton* on vacation in Mexico, saying: "The moment my brain got a moment's rest, *Hamilton* walked into it."[4]

And you may be thinking—good for these titans of industry, *of course* they have the time for white space. But the reality is white space was the *precursor* to their success, not the result of it.

Read that again.

White space is not only *needed* in a cult-of-busy, always "on" world—it leads to reflection, deeper thinking, and countless breakthroughs. This is the intersection of a prioritized life with a dose of white space.

Whether you get yours during a made-up commute, a walk in the evening, or a daily hour of "you" time—white space is how you let go of anxiety, overwhelm, and distraction.

By having space to breathe and reflect, you'll trade aimless tasks for deliberate ones. You'll focus on needle movers. You'll know that effort for the sake of effort without intentionality is a waste. You'll tap into new ideas, solutions, or breakthroughs.

Best of all, you can engage in the undeniable power of unplugging—the thrill of having some much-needed "you" time and shutting it down. You'll avoid the incessant trap of success, the cult of busy so many can't live without. You'll get your sanity back.

This, my friend, is priceless.

Chapter

18

Grit
&
Gratitude

The word *grit* conjures images of those with a nose-to-the-grindstone, whatever-it-takes attitude toward their boldest ambitions. The late Kobe Bryant's tenacious practice routines and Beyoncé's notorious eight-month Coachella rehearsals come to mind—the hard-charging, type A, no-holds-barred personalities of the world that #GetShitDone 24 hours a day.

During certain seasons of life and business, this effort is required.

However, what makes grit special lies in a nuance most miss: grit is about playing the *long* game. It is a desire that endures. It transcends seasons of life, failures, and successes. Grit is a quest, an odyssey, one that doesn't diminish with time—but rather intensifies with it.

To define grit, we turn to researcher and University of Pennsylvania psychologist Angela Duckworth who made the concept mainstream in her aptly titled book, *Grit*:

> Consider what grit isn't—it isn't talent, luck and how intensely, for the moment, you want something. Instead, grit is about having what some researchers call an "ultimate concern"—a goal you care about so much that it organizes and gives meaning to almost everything you do. And grit is holding steadfast to that goal. Even when you fall down. Even when you screw up. Even when progress toward that goal is halting or slow.[1]

And therein lies the power.

Hustlers are typically pulled by short-term fixes, a need-it-now timeline awash in the feel-good chemicals of starting, launching, and creating. But when the high fades or they enter an inevitable plateau and find themselves past the point of diminishing returns, they tend to jump ship or burn out.

People who blend hustling and seeking play the long game. They explore what matters to them intensely until it becomes what they *can't* not do . . . even if they tried. They trade short-term dopamine for long-term purpose and meaning.

Let's be real, the ambitious lifestyle has always come with a loaded question: How do people balance their desires *while* being grateful for what they have? The manifestation to pursue more can put blinders on what we *already* have. But the flipside is also true. If we spend our days soaked in gratitude, what's the point in striving? If you're fulfilled and nothing is missing, there may not be a reason to leave the couch today . . . except for a fresh refill.

Hello, dilemma.

On the hustler's side, you're going to harness grit like never before and tap into what professor Dr. Ellen Winter calls a "rage to master"[2]—to find what you would show up and do every day . . . even if you failed. By doing so, you'll be passionate, engaged, and absorbed.

All three are vital to a thriving life.

On the seeker's side, you're going to marry grit by embracing a level of gratitude that brings you to your knees. Not the fake, synthetic gratitude we see on social media—but one that moves mountains.

You'll realize gratitude becomes the elixir to push through obstacles when you're struggling and need some serious *oomph*. And by harnessing grit and overcoming what you deemed impossible, the payoffs are that much stronger—and feed right back into gratitude. It's an endless cycle of the best kind.

But first, it's time to get gritty.

CULTIVATING GRIT

To help you understand how grit and gratitude magnify one another, we must cover how to cultivate grit. Notice the word choice: *cultivate*. Grit is an active process. It's a skill to be practiced, not a genetic trait. As Duckworth has stated, this is not about talent, your hometown zip code, or demographics.[3]

To cultivate grit, you'll need to:

▶ **Actively explore your desires.** You won't create grit sitting on the couch exploring videos on life's purpose. You'll do so by getting uncomfortable and pulling on what interests you. Go deep enough to know whether your interest intensifies or wanes. Push the boundaries and test yourself. Get messy.

▶ **Immerse yourself in practice.** It's impossible to be gritty about something we're terrible at or have zero interest in. On a long enough timeline, none of us does anything we hate or that we're awful at. This is where deliberate skill acquisition and practice comes in.

▶ **Leave your comfort zone.** Grit won't be developed while you're wrapped in the soft blankets of your comfort zone; it will be found in seeking challenges that unlock a previously unavailable layer of performance. Instead of "waiting" for these, you'll manufacture them.

▶ **Deepen your why.** It's hard to be gritty for two decades if your dream is all about *you*. At some point, money, accolades, and clapping hands from peers becomes irrelevant, and instead, you focus on a *bigger* picture—a deeper purpose for your pursuit.

▶ **Surround yourself with the right people.** Being gritty as an entrepreneur can be hard if your entire circle is made up of 9–5ers who live for Thursday happy hours and long weekends. Being a gritty creative is difficult when everyone around you thinks art is for lost people. Choose your environments wisely.

Grit is an ongoing process. It's an evolution that leads to a deeply fulfilling and meaningful life. It gets you up in the morning. It shines a light on who you are. It reveals character and creates a balanced emotional life.[4] It creates raptured levels of meaning and on-your-knees moments of total absorption.

As much as what grit brings to the table, it's also what it automatically deletes that makes it as potent. When you're cultivating grit, you have *no time* for comparison, overthinking, or picking fights with social media trolls. Furthermore, you stop obsessing about the arrival moment and focus on the step in front of you.

The gritty love the pursuit more than the arrival and don't see the process as a means to an end—they see it as *the end* itself. If the process encompasses 97 precent of the time and energy along your path—doesn't it make sense to love it? Success surely isn't waiting for the 3 percent of mountaintop moments as we white knuckle our actions from a place of self-loathing.

You can tell Bryant's love for shooting 1,000 practice free throws at 4:30 a.m. matched his desire to win a championship ring. You notice Beyoncé's obsession with her craft runs deep in her veins, way beyond the external rewards she's created. You get that Taylor Swift lives for those late nights in the studio as much, if not more, than sold-out arenas. Lindsey Vonn is as liberated during her practice runs as she is hurling herself to another gold at 80 mph.

Which is why gratitude for the ride—before you get "there"—is not only an insurance policy against moments of doubt and uncertainty, but it unlocks a deeper, more aligned version of grit.

This type of grit comes without the baggage of obsessing over what others are doing and how you're not where you want to be yet, because if the process makes you feel alive—what else is there? You have everything you need . . . not in some clichéd way, but from every fiber of your being.

Which, of course, is what gratitude is all about.

WHAT IF GRIT AMPLIFIED GRATITUDE AND VICE VERSA?

Conventional wisdom shuns people away from being grateful for what they have today due to the fear of complacency. If you're blessed for your current life experience, why bother to strive, pursue, and face the adversity that comes with a high-growth lifestyle?

Yeah, I'll pass.

Hustlers download hacks and life optimization tips telling them to be grateful but miss the mark. They use it as a means to an end—the end being solely more performance, followers, cash. With one eye open, they practice gratitude hell-bent on not losing their *edge*.

It's the executive who uses gratitude as a "hack" but stops short of fully embracing it. It's the entrepreneur who practices appreciation when everything is working but stops when something goes haywire. It's the difference between using gratitude to get a reward . . . rather than seeing the potent *practice* as that reward.

This is the knockoff version of gratitude found in life-hacking lists and the social media influencer who repeats Rumi quotes ad nauseam with the backdrop being his or her oh-so-perfect life, the 13th take with just the *right* lighting.

This is synthetic gratitude; cheap and easy.

Instead, make gratitude an active, daily practice you feel on a cellular level. Researchers have found a daily gratitude practice literally rewires our brain.[5] Lower the bar instead of waiting for something good to happen. Rather than expressing gratitude for what directly benefits you, show gratitude for adversity or even for *other people's* wins. And if you want to be a true master, practice the hindsight of gratitude . . . *before* you arrive at hindsight. In other words, in real time.

To unlock this deep level of gratitude, you'll:

1. **Lower the bar.** Challenge yourself to step away from surface-area circumstances, and instead, tap into the gratitude that understands the miracle of this experience, the 400 trillion to 1 odds of being alive, having legs, hands, eyes, sight, the relentless consistency of a beating heart that pumps 1,900 gallons of blood daily.

2. **Be grateful for valleys and peaks.** Being grateful once the eye of the storm leaves is *easy*, you've got the benefit of perspective from the other side. Instead, show gratitude when you're in the middle of the challenge. Learn to appreciate contrast in the moment with foresight, knowing what's happening is an opportunity for perspective, depth, and learning.

3. **Engulf yourself in the rapture of gratitude.** You're doing it right when you get emotional. This is the data of our hearts knowing we've pulled on the *right* thread. This is the rapture of gratitude, the ecstasy of escaping the day-to-day matrix and understanding the countless miracles we take for granted.

4. **Use gratitude to deepen your grit.** When you tap into deep gratitude, not only do you *not* lose your edge, but you amplify it by creating a deeper purpose. Our why is never logical; it is found in the place gratitude comes from: deep emotional states. By owning gratitude, you sharpen the sword of your emotional commitment and you tap into your most actualized, aligned self.

Gratitude is about depth and intensity.

It is not a passive practice of sitting in the lotus position mumbling platitudes; it's visceral. It is about pushing yourself to look at the parts of your life that are "problems" and recognize others would write you a blank check to experience them for a day.

This level of gratitude amplifies grit . . . while grit amplifies gratitude as you play the long game.

WHAT TO LEAVE BEHIND WITH CONVENTIONAL GRIT

As you dose the right amount of grit into your professional life, here is what to be aware of that shouldn't come with you:

- ▶ **Being gritty around the wrong things.** In Duckworth's interviews, she states she "never encountered a gritty person who was forced into what they were doing."[6] Agency is the key here, something you have chosen.
- ▶ **Not honoring your process.** Grit is the long game, which means plenty of peaks, valleys, and plateaus. You'll have plenty of chances to quit or not honor your process. Stay focused, yet open. Be relentless, yet ask the right questions during seeking.
- ▶ **Turning passion and persistence to desperation.** The two core ingredients of grit are lauded by society and are no doubt valuable. But persistence and passion gone awry lead to desperation, *neediness,* and the pushing away of the very thing you were bringing to life.

WHAT TO LEAVE BEHIND WITH CONVENTIONAL GRATITUDE

As you couple grit with deep levels of gratitude, you harness a potent stack that feeds itself, but here's what you won't be taking with you inside of gratitude:

> ► **Skimming the surface so as not to lose your "edge."**
> Authentic gratitude never means losing your edge, but the
> ego will convince you to stay at the surface-area, kiddie-
> pool version of gratitude to get a quick hit of its benefits and
> miss out.

> ► **Turning gratitude into complacency.** Seekers do this on the
> regular: they are bursting at the seams with fulfillment, so
> what's the point in *doing* anything? They miss the mark and
> become gluttons of nothingness.

GRITTY GRATITUDE

Colin O'Brady has done the impossible as an extreme athlete
and modern explorer of human potential—culminating in
crossing Antarctica by his lonesome—setting a world record in
54 punishing straight days of subzero temperatures. All while
carrying a 300-pound sled by himself.[7]

No one had done it before; all attempts had gone awry.

There is no doubt O'Brady is as gritty as they come—you
cannot summit Everest, canoe the treacherous Drake Passage,
and set the record for climbing the seven highest peaks on each
continent without it. During interviews, he's constantly hard-
pressed to answer the question: How the hell do you keep going
when everyone else quits?

As if baiting him, the interviewers seem to expect him to say
he harnesses the dark side of his psyche—pain, trauma, hurt—
to push him over the edge to do the unthinkable. To say he
thinks about haters, critics, trolls, and the people who shunned
or mocked him.

But he doesn't.

Instead, he reveals his insatiable drive during his quest's
toughest moments to come from a different place—gratitude,
love, and a reservoir of emotions he cultivates from an intense
devotion to seeking.

As an obsessive meditator who engages in 10-day silent
Vipassana meditation retreats—O'Brady has certainly *not* lost

his edge. In fact, he credits these practices with not only elevating his performance and grit but tapping into an infinite fuel source that can't be found anywhere else, saying:

> The work between the ears, the silence, the ability to think deeply has allowed me to cultivate what I call infinite love . . . which is what I tap into when I'm at my most physically and emotionally wrecked.[8]

And there it is: grit and gratitude fuel each other as both require practice, engagement, and curiosity. They both require active exploration and showing up day in, day out.

By being grateful for today's process—in every sense of the word—we release chasing our goals with desperation like the person who sends seven texts . . . after the first date. We let go of thinking all our goals and desires must happen on *our* timeline, the incessant need to control our lives that often leads to anguish.

By doing so, we not only perform at our best, but we also keep our mental sanity in check. Which means we stay in the game longer than everyone else. We endure because grit is playing the long game, and that long game involves intense challenges.

We show up when others are bored. We persist when the high fades. We see challenges as opportunities. The sting of rejection is alchemized into a better yes around the bend. We understand if we're grateful today, we're playing with house money. But that doesn't mean we stop. Rather, we use it to create. In this state, it's only a matter of time until the conditions come to life.

And if for some reason they don't . . . we're *still* fulfilled.

At the end of the day, we're able to stand shoulder to shoulder with the grittiest out there. But unlike most, we're grateful for this moment. Nothing is missing. We're no longer running away from pain, hurt, or trauma, but chasing the present moment of liberation.

True freedom.

Chapter

19

Show Up
&
Be Unavailable

We're one connection away, right?

The right introduction, the synchronistic encounter at Starbucks, the impromptu run-in. One connection from being discovered, plastered on the next magazine cover, poached by an all-star recruiter for a C-suite gig, and finding the investor who's ready to write us a blank check.

Okay, maybe not so fast.

Sure, these are exaggerations, but we often view relationships this way: the grass is *always* greener. We must find the person who holds the keys to the castle, the gatekeeper to our potential. The one book agent, investor, or faculty member. The one reference on LinkedIn who can change it all.

Make no mistake: cultivating thriving relationships with like-minded peers is an essential lubricant for progress. It opens doors that would have otherwise been slammed shut. It provides the much-needed connection we all crave but has become unfamiliar.

However, we tend to *overvalue* new relationships. Why? Because, well, they're new, novel, and stimulating. Much like the hot rod we've dreamt of, the sheer novelty makes us salivate in anticipation of driving it off the lot even when we have a clean, cool, and highly functional vehicle right now.

Inside of hustle, you're going to show up—fostering relationships to amplify connection, expand fulfillment, and build a tribe who has your back. You'll identify the people, environments, and connections aligned with your future self. You'll engage with those who hold you to excellence, who have enough respect to notice when you're playing small . . . and call you out.

On the seeker's side—you'll be unavailable when you're deep in priorities, an intense creative season, a time of inner work. You'll set boundaries to protect your time, energy, and mental real estate. You'll be comfortable saying no without apologies or rambling explanations.

You'll show up and then be unavailable . . . often.

Connection is the result—to yourself, your work, others. You'll cultivate a flourishing tribe who has your back and celebrates when you kick ass. You'll embrace the power of solitude, retreat, and mini-sabbaticals.

But first . . .

SHOW UP FOR YOUR CURRENT (AND FUTURE) TRIBE

Crafting meaningful relationships takes work.

There are no hacks to get there—they take intention, energy, time.

In a world where we're more cheaply connected than ever and are skimming the thinnest layer of relationships, we delude ourselves into thinking a random text or direct message represents connection.

We keep tabs on hundreds of people's highlight reels and curated public feeds, but we don't really know them. We may know what they had for dinner last night (steak salad) and what movie they watched (*Interstellar*), but we don't know how they're *really* doing.

They don't know us; we don't know them.

We haphazardly reach out. We email when we need a favor. We build storylines as to why they haven't answered. We feel guilt ridden for not answering them, as they trickle down our text feeds until they're out of sight and out of mind. If you've felt overwhelmed at the scope of modern relationships, you're not alone. Two-thirds of people say the constant need to keep tabs on their daily inputs is a "major concern" in their lives.[1]

But connection is vital. The key finding in Harvard's 75-year colossal study on fulfillment was that *relationships* are responsible for infusing life with meaning, purpose, and engagement.[2]

Showing up, then, is about two core parts:

▶ **Nourishing connections.** We undervalue known connections, which means we're terrible at nurturing them. We seek numbers instead of appreciating those around us today. We have gold in front of us, but don't acknowledge it. We rarely tell people how we feel; we let relationships turn comfortable with time.

▶ **Cultivating future connections.** The second part of showing up is about future pacing and identifying people, tribes, and environments aligned with that vision. Those who support *and* challenge us. Those we want to emulate, model, and adapt their mindsets and habits. Those who will have our backs as we pursue our visions vehemently.

Here's how to nourish your current connections in a way that brings you joy and enthusiasm and leaves you *and* them better off:

- ▶ **Start deep, not wide.** We are not meant to know the inner workings of hundreds of people. Due to social media, digital Rolodexes, and a feeling we know everyone, we go wide. We value quantity over quality. Instead, shift your mindset from many to few.

- ▶ **Send a daily appreciation message.** Get used to sending messages of appreciation . . . daily. I don't mean standard fluff. Think of someone in your network or close to you. Get centered using the principles of seeking. We often don't even tell the closest people in our lives how we *really* feel. If you run out of people, get uncomfortable, and message someone you wouldn't normally.

- ▶ **Play text message, video, or phone call roulette.** Whip out your phone and scan randomly until you choose someone you haven't connected with in ages. Go above and beyond; call them. Send an audio note or a video. Get creative. Send a heartfelt message. Pen a handwritten letter in a digital age. Surprise them with a gift.

- ▶ **Set time blocks for connecting.** Unless we make connection a priority, we won't bring it to life powerfully. We won't "feel" like reaching out. We'll cancel lunch plans or say we're busy. Use time blocks in your calendar that *must* be filled with connection. This scheduling trigger reminds you to fill those slots.

- ▶ **Give, connect, share at least once a week.** Selfless giving pays off in droves. Introducing two people who can create together or who can solve each other's needs makes you an instant leader and can bring two separate groups together to make something special.

- ▶ **Step out of your comfort zone.** No one wants to drink another tepid coffee in the boisterous coffee shop. Instead, be different. Get yourself and others out of their natural element. Connect over rock climbing, yoga, or a heart-thumping spin class. You'll stand out in a world of coffee-laced brain-pickers.

We often wait for someone within our network to step up and be the one who connects others, who gives freely, who cares enough to make an introduction. But why can't it be us, why can't it be you?

With intention and a little effort, it can.

HOW TO NOURISH FUTURE CONNECTIONS

Let's turn our attention to future connections—these are people you haven't met but desire to. They should be living with the values you want to live with, often are further along than you, and nudge you to get uncomfortable and commit in a deeper way by doing the following:

▶ **Identify people, places, environments.** With your future self in mind, make a list of those you want to be connected to, where they spend their time and energy; where they work, play, unplug, and train physically; how they learn; where they gather; and so on.

▶ **Be creative.** No one wants their brain picked and high-performers loathe vague requests. Impersonally reaching out will immediately put you in the "avoid" pile. Instead, be creative, specific, and intentional. Give people an out and never ask for 60 minutes; instead, start low with 10–15 minutes.

▶ **Stand out.** If you do this right, you'll recognize a place where the person may need help. You may not hold the keys to the solution, but you may know someone who does. The fastest way to grab someone's attention is to offer help with zero expectation of return.

▶ **Invest resources.** As you grow, you'll notice some rooms are full of boundaries to protect the community's ethos. This means you'll have to invest time, money, and energy. This can involve seminars, events, mastermind experiences—even graduate programs or professional studies. The people here are often the most committed, which will rub off on you.

To ensure you do this right, let's explore some common mistakes.

DON'T BE THIS GUY OR GAL

We've all made mistakes we wish we could take back when connecting with others—being the snake-oil salesman at the local networking mixer, salivating like a dog at the *next* connection, cutting others off midsentence, and going home with 39 business cards.

Don't be that person—here's what to avoid as you nurture, develop, and find *key* relationships:

- ▶ **Valuing quantity.** Remember, this is about *depth*. In the next 90 days, if you could develop three powerful relationships or 15 random acquaintances, which would you choose? Less is more.

- ▶ **Being the "taker."** Takers show up with ulterior, covert motives. They use relationships as a means to some end. When they get what they want they are never heard from again.

- ▶ **Feeling entitled.** In a world where everyone is accessible, it's easy to feel like they *should* carve out time. You listen to someone's podcast and watch him or her on social media so you *feel* like you know the person. Ditch this energy as it can be felt from a mile away.

- ▶ **Pitching and selling.** This should be obvious, but it happens every day. Pitching and selling are *not* connecting. Business deals happen all the time in relationships, precisely because there is real trust and depth. Start there.

As you *show up*, nourish and cultivate relationships you'll need to ensure you avoid the trap of being accessible 24/7— by being unavailable. Otherwise, you'll become someone else's doormat, say yes when you *really* want to say no, and resent yourself (and your dreams) along the way.

The solution?

BE UNAVAILABLE . . . OFTEN

If you're one random text, direct message, or tweet away from anyone—can you *really* be trusted to do your best work and live an intentional life?

Think about someone you highly respect. Now imagine you want to ask that person out to lunch, so you send a message on a social media platform and get a response within three minutes.

After the thrill, are you *more* or *less* impressed with the person?

We respect those who value their time, space, and energy. We get that people have priorities. We understand we are all humans and we also never know what challenge someone is going through.

To be unavailable is an art. To set boundaries is to have self-respect. Retreat into the cave to take your craft seriously. To recharge, rest, and practice self-care is honoring yourself. To say no without a 200-word rambling explanation is to stand your ground. Ultimately, by making yourself unavailable and setting boundaries, you'll remember you're a human being who is run by the laws of nature and there's no amount of caffeine you can intravenously inject to always be "on."

Being unavailable includes:

- ► Owning "no"
- ► Choosing to unplug
- ► Setting and maintaining boundaries

OWNING YOUR NO

No.

The word alone is drenched in finality, a hint of confrontation—a two-letter declaration that does not invite explanation or justification. Most of us shudder at the thought of telling someone no. When we are on the receiving end, it can sting.

And so, we agree with a lukewarm yes.

We show up to a cocktail party we wanted nothing to do with. We force ourselves to slog through a meeting we agreed to six months ago. We agree to the couple's excursion, the Zoom meeting with a stranger, a networking mixer that can't end fast enough.

All because we don't own our nos.

We agree out of guilt, obligation, the desire to be validated. Here's why this is crucial: our choices do not happen in a vacuum. There is always an opportunity cost to saying yes to something we knew deep down was a no:

- ▶ When we say yes to an early morning coffee meeting, we say no to our morning ritual.
- ▶ When we say yes to grabbing a drink with the team, we say no to our partners at home.
- ▶ When we say yes to a random invitation with a stranger, we say no to purposeful work.

None of these are soul-crushing as one-offs, but it is their *compounding* over time where we grapple with the stark reality that when we say yes to other people's needs, desires, and agendas—we say no to *our* needs, desires, and agendas.

This can manifest in saying yes to everyone except ourselves, leaving the scraps at the end of our day for our dreams, our vision, our people. And it's no wonder why we're tapped out and have no energy except to scroll.

So, how do we end up here so often?

- ▶ **We desire to be validated**. This is hardwired as we are evolutionarily built for survival, to fit in, to be part of a collective.[3]
- ▶ **We aren't clear on our priorities.** If we aren't clear on our priorities from Chapter 17, we say yes to everything.
- ▶ **We live with the fear of missing out.** We often picture an ideal scenario where we missed a huge opportunity or lifelong connection by saying no, so we say yes too often.
- ▶ **We don't want to reject others.** We know what rejection can look and feel like and we naturally don't want others to experience this same feeling.

It's time to own your *no* with the clarity and conviction people do all the time: those who know their priorities. We don't make fun of the vegan who says no to a tomahawk steak because, well, they don't eat meat. We never mock the recovering alcoholic who's spent a decade in AA for declining a fresh scotch. We don't get upset when we tweet Elon Musk and he doesn't reply.

He is, uh, working on that whole Mars thing.

In all these cases, these people are hyperclear about who they are and what they stand for. From this place, owning your no is easy—and guilt-free. To arrive at this state, here's what to ask yourself:

▶ **What is your gut feeling or intuition saying?** Circle back to Chapter 11 where you learned to minimize the signal-to-noise ratio to make swift decisions from a place of checking in with yourself. Doing this right means you don't say yes as an egoic desire, for validation, or because you feel obligated. This becomes a practice rooted in self-trust.

▶ **Is it in alignment with your vision and priorities?** Take a step back and ask if the opportunity is in alignment with your current self, future self, *and* priorities. If you want to be a full-blown entrepreneur, does graduate school align? If you are on deadline for a client, does picking up another one for extra cash fuel your priorities? Be clear, honest, and deliberate.

▶ **Would you still say yes if it was tomorrow morning?** We are incredibly inept at looking at the consequences of an agreement in the future. To minimize this impact, shorten the time frame and ask yourself if you'd *still* say yes if it was tomorrow morning. This will get you thinking clearly about the logistics, the trade-offs, and your true desire.

▶ **Is it a hell yes or is it a tepid, mundane agreement?** Enter the yes/no matrix: make a list of what you're saying yes to—and by doing so, what you're automatically saying no to. As you do so, get honest about what you're saying no to. Think in potential and possibility, not by what has already happened to you.

Here's how that looks.

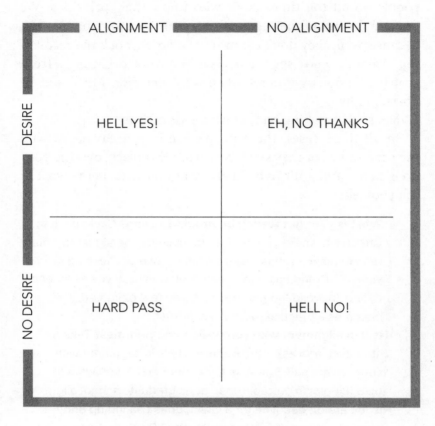

The Yes/No Matrix

BE UNAVAILABLE AND UNTOUCHABLE

Being unavailable to others' requests and demands on your time, energy, and mental real estate means being available to yourself. It means having the audacity to honor *your* dreams by stepping away.

It's having the courage to retreat from the noise.

There are times when you literally have to close the door on the world. You have to retreat to your cave and do the *work*.

You must immerse yourself creatively, obsess over a skill, or spend a chunk of time unplugged with your loved ones. You have to turn the devices off and breathe.

Being unavailable means:

- ▶ **Having "off limits" time.** Choose blocks of time where you are simply not available. Communicate this to others. Honor your reasons *why* and don't let guilt win the battle. Then, protect this time at all costs.
- ▶ **Blocking time for self-care.** We often wait for solo time until it's too late. Block time off every week and day for yourself— for the activities or practices that bring you back to center.
- ▶ **Honoring seasons of life that require immersion.** The more you grow in your life, business, and craft, the *more* periods of immersion and being unavailable you will require. Turn back to Chapter 16 if you need a refresh on recovery.
- ▶ **Having *untouchable* time—an hour, a day, or even a week.** On a microlevel, have time where you can't be reached unless it's an emergency from a small group of people. Take a complete hour or three off. Take multiple days off every quarter to recharge, incubate, recover.
- ▶ **Owning boundaries.** Boundaries are the highest form of respect for your time and energy. As a parent, you may need to carve out 90 minutes for your dream and communicate this to your family.

While the benefits of being unavailable are endless—you'll also be creating buffers and swaths of time to leave space for the magic, the mystery, and divine timing.

Because this is where the best moments of your life will arrive.

LEAVE SPACE FOR MAGIC

Think back to life's riveting moments, the on-your-knees synchronicities that were unexplainable. The random occurrences where you found yourself at the right place, at the right time.

That time you got fired unexpectedly, only to meet someone at Starbucks and land a dream gig. The time you'd given up on dating—and then the unexplained happened on a cross-country flight you had missed and you met the partner of your dreams.

These are the magical moments we're not supposed to know about in advance. Similar to divine timing in Chapter 14— these occurrences are sprinkled throughout what *seem* like ordinary moments.

But they're not.

These moments are chock-full of ingredients that take our fulfillment and appreciation for life to the next level—awe, wonder, surprise.[4] They dismantle the ego's prediction-making machine—the *been there, seen that*—and invite a curiosity that often lies dormant as we age.

They wake us up in the best of ways.

But what if there's *no space left* to experience these?

- ▶ If your calendar is always slammed—you don't have the time for the unknown, life-changing encounter.
- ▶ If your goals are meticulously planned out—you become so laser focused that you miss out on a chance to get there faster . . . and with more fun.
- ▶ If you have zero buffers in your day-to-day and are always pushing—there is no space left to receive.
- ▶ If you are online and reachable 24/7—you won't experience the spontaneity and synchronicities of life.
- ▶ If you are consumed with multitasking—the person who may change your life can pass right in front of you.

By being unavailable and not cramming another two-hour work block—you create space for the unknown. The insight in the sauna, the random book you read stumbling into the bookstore when you had 45 minutes that gave you the message you needed.

Leave space for the magic or miss out on some of life's best moments.

WHAT TO LEAVE BEHIND WITH CONVENTIONAL SHOWING UP

Showing up can be taken to the extreme and start to work against us, including:

▶ **Showing up, but not for yourself.** Showing up and cultivating nourishing relationships is no doubt a skill, but at some point, this energy needs to be used wisely. Show up for yourself *first*, then others.

▶ **Being too much of a "giver."** Giving is crucial to standing out, adding value, and being noticed in a world where everyone wants *theirs*. At the same time, there are *takers*, to use Adam Grant's language in the book *Give and Take*, who are there to use what you have to offer. Be aware of crossing the line.

WHAT TO LEAVE BEHIND WITH CONVENTIONAL BEING UNAVAILABLE

Being unavailable in an always-on world will naturally make you an outlier, and this mysteriousness can work to your advantage . . . until it doesn't. Here's what to avoid:

▶ **Not communicating.** Going into the abyss without saying a word isn't the best idea. We live in a digital communications world full of covert rules on how long is "too long" to not respond to a text or an email. Be open, and let people know. Set an autoreply on your email.

▶ **Being unavailable through challenge.** We tend to go into the cave of our lives when we're challenged. Surely, there is value in licking our wounds in solitude. But disappearing into the ether simply because of a challenge means we miss out on the best parts of relationships: vulnerability, connection, and perspective.

ADELE DOESN'T TWEET

Adele is one of the most successful recording artists of our time, already having sold an astonishing 60 million albums with only three records to date[5]—but she doesn't tweet, do live videos, or document on YouTube what she ate for lunch.

In other words, she's unavailable.

While she could provide her legion of fans an array of updates, content, and a "day in the life"—she doesn't. Because, in her own words, she'd lose her focus on what matters and what got her success in the first place, saying this after she made her seminal record 25: "I've made the realest record I can make, and it's the real part of me. How am I supposed to write a real record if I'm waiting for half a million likes on a f*cking photo? That ain't real."[6]

Sing it, sister.

By practicing the art of being unavailable in a world that demands we *all* have personal brands, side hustles, and mini media empires, Adele recognizes it'd take her away from pushing her creative edge.

And what makes her feel most alive.

Instead, she steps away to incubate her next idea. She doses white space for reinvention, clarity, insights. She focuses on the nuances of her craft that can't be accessed from the shallows. All of these, at her level, would be impossible to tap into if she was always "on."

Which leads one to ask: Do we want to be available to others at the expense of our craft, growth, and mental sanity? Do we want to be in the Hall of Fame for inbox zero, Twitter zingers, fantasy sports—or do our best work? Do we *really* want to look back at our pandemic timeline and see it full of mask politics?

No, no, and . . . pour me a triple.

Sure, at times, show up and put yourself out there. Be present, be engaged, and take the lead if the community doesn't exist. Put yourself in environments full of other high performers—seminar rooms, masterminds, gyms, studios—to connect and grow.

But then be willing to tap out.

By hitting both ends of the spectrum, you develop relationships based on trust, depth, and shared values. You are full of relationships and full of space, which means you're connected to yourself, the people around you, and the work you can't wait to do.

And then, you experience the power of being offline guilt-free as you turn the fear of missing out . . . into the *joy* of missing out.

JOMO has a better ring to it, right?

Chapter

20

Build Identity
&
Slay Ego

The ego wants you to play small, seek comfort, and buy your excuses. It'd rather see you in searing physical, mental, and emotional pain than watch you expand. It creates false narratives leading to erratic behavior, baffling decision-making, and self-sabotage.

Sounds great, huh?

But of course, we *need* ego. If you want to fully own your desires, chase your ambitions with zest, and boldly take steps into the unknown with confidence, you need, well . . . ego.

Looks like we've got ourselves a dilemma.

Enter building healthy identity from the hustler's side— expanding your self-esteem, confidence, and values. To know yourself as the Greeks stated, to amplify strengths, and develop the grit to pursue your calling. To curate a philosophy, a set of principles. To know what you stand for.

Without a powerful identity, nothing comes to life.

A shaky identity plays small. It doesn't take risks and it sure as hell doesn't withstand the volatility of growth. Under tension, it folds like a house of cards. It lives in a seesaw of doubt and desire, a flurry of action followed by disappearing into the void of discouragement.

Not quite a formula for success.

On the seeker's side, you'll merge healthy identity with slaying the ego—the indispensable practices designed to release its chokehold from the part of ourselves that craves validation like a teenager on prom night. The part that stays stubborn, dismisses feedback, and avoids the people who want to help.

The part of you that wants to *be* right, not *get it* right.

By doing so, you'll tap into a previously inaccessible level of performance while avoiding the traps of an ego gone haywire as we've already explored.

You'll develop a new sweet spot.

The end result is what we call mastery—found when we're living up to our potential—while simultaneously dissolving our need to feel worthy from strangers on the internet.

Instead of becoming the success story that has to show it off on social media—you experience success, yet are humble. You don't "talk" a big game; instead, you walk into a room and turn heads . . . because of *who* you are.

IDENTITY VERSUS EGO

The distinction between identity and ego can be confusing, so we'll keep it simple to make it as useful as possible:

► Your **identity** is your beliefs, principles, thoughts, words, and actions. It is what you stand for. It is who you believe yourself to be, and who others perceive you to be.

► Your **ego** is the part of yourself that wants to feel special through the lens of the external world. It's not *all* bad, but in this context we'll focus on the part of the ego that craves validation, can be laughably insecure, and isn't above using cheap shots to bring you or others down.

To build a healthy identity while slaying ego creates the ultimate sweet spot: a functional, developed identity that lives in alignment, coupled with an ego that is wiped clean regularly to diminish blind spots and bizarre obsessions.

Make no mistake, this is a potent duo.

Hustlers tend to slam the accelerator of ambition full throttle—often operating from egoic needs: the need to prove others wrong; running away from past hurt, trauma, or rejection, or a me-against-the-world mentality full of made-up critics.

Although useful for short-term performance, this model is exhausting.

On the flipside, seekers tend to fixate on slaying the ego through endless practices, rituals, and retreats focused on "inner work"—but can wind up getting lost in a never-ending rabbit hole where the ego takes on a new form or talks them *out* of bringing a desire to life.

As researcher Wendy Smith, who explores how identity and ego can be both useful and destructive, says: "The self can be our greatest resource, but it can also be our darkest enemy."[1] In order to solve this puzzle, you'll start by building a healthy identity that even *allows* for the minimizing of the ego.

Without this, we're never willing to drop our guard.

HOW TO BUILD IDENTITY

Your identity, said simply, is your sense of self.[2]

Without a stable, clear, and functional identity developed with intention, nothing sustains. Performance is a pipe dream if you have a shaky identity that is always half-hearted, timid, and unsure. If you don't know who you are, how can you step into the best version of that self on the field of play, at the concert hall, in your career?

You can't.

Consider building identity akin to the work of building a skyscraper. Picking the right lot, structures, and scaffoldings—these are the components under the surface that tend to be undervalued and overlooked. Yet they are precisely what will withstand the pressure, weight, and storms of the world.

Building your identity involves:

▶ **Developing a philosophy.** We all stand for something even if we do not express it. Actions tell a story. To develop a philosophy, identify a phrase, mantra, or a couple sentences acting as your identity's guiding light. Ask yourself: What do you stand for? What do you believe in? What do you want to lean on during tough times? An example helps—mine is "the purpose of life is growth." This filters my world and allows me to see both opportunity and challenge through an equal lens, knowing if growth is the endgame . . . it doesn't matter how I get there. Identify yours. Keep it simple.

▶ **Building guiding principles.** Consider your philosophy the compass and your principles the mile markers that help ensure you're living up to it. According to the philosophy you identified, what principles and rules act as guardrails to keep you in check? Here are some examples of principles:

> *Vulnerability is strength.*
> *I take full responsibility for my actions.*
> *Integrity is who you are when no one is watching.*
> *I will listen to my intuition, even when it doesn't make sense.*
> *I show up for my vision, self, and others regardless of how I feel.*

▶ **Growing your self-belief, efficacy, and confidence.** Your philosophy and principles aren't cute phrases, they're actionable. They're designed to be integrated on a daily basis, especially when it's hard. They matter most when you've gotten your ass kicked, as vulnerability researcher Dr. Brené Brown says, and rising back up.[3]

▶ **Acquiring skills.** Your identity involves the pursuit of real-world skills that amplify who you are. These include tangible skills, such as sales, speaking, negotiation, content creation, learning, etc., as well as soft skills like emotional intelligence, empathy, and resilience.

Consider building your identity to be an ongoing process.

It is an evolution rooted in two places: the parts of yourself that are in alignment with who you are today *and* who you're becoming.

To build your identity long term, you'll have to:

▶ **Spend time alone.** You can't do this work surrounded by ravers and thumping bass music. Solitude is where this reflection thrives, and it must be prioritized. If you don't build a powerful identity, others will build a weak (and fake) identity for you.

▶ **Do the inner work.** The inner work is unavoidable for a meaningful life. Harvard's 75-year study said as much—part of life is having a willingness to wrestle with life's questions and build the self-awareness to seek answers.[4] What does this look like? Spend time journaling. Develop a mindfulness practice. Examine your past. Ask bigger questions . . . seek out mentors and guides. Reflect.

▶ **Be willing to be challenged.** Building a solid identity won't happen watching YouTube videos and philosophizing about life on the couch. Challenge is where the magic happens, where one is tested, where identities are pushed to the brink, and where we find out the capital-T Truth.

Now, with as much vigor as you built your identity—you'll need to harness this energy to slay the ego on the regular, too.

THE EGO IS RESPONSIBLE

Your ego hates your future self.

It loathes the person you could become.

It will do anything to stop you from growing.

It's your ego and wants you to lose, play small, and stay exactly where you are. If this sounds baffling, this is the core mechanism of the ego—protect the status quo like its life depends on it.

Even when it sucks.

Because the ego registers your desire to change and evolve as an existential threat to its existence. It associates this with a part of itself dying and would rather keep you in pain than allow for future possibility . . . no matter how riveting that future may be.

It will go to any extreme necessary to avoid the bigger bank accounts, the aligned career, the city you so desperately want to move to, the relationship that feels whole, or even finishing this book you're holding now.

Even if the consequences are dire, including existential questioning, divorce, or simply waking up to a life that doesn't feel like yours anymore, it's indifferent. It wins even when you lose. Especially when you lose.

WTF!?

You may have not thought of your ego in this manner. You may have handled it with kid gloves. You may have understood it is a part of all of us, and that we need the ego to build a strong identity and have the confidence to move through life.

And therein lies the problem—what fuels our identity to a healthy place is precisely the *same* mechanism that keeps us stuck and overreacting to a random message by sending a scathing response.

The ego is responsible for:

▶ **Keeping you stuck.** The ego would rather experience the predictability of discomfort than the unknown of future possibility.

▶ **Justifying excuses.** Since it knows you better than anyone else, it's a master excuse-maker, knowing precisely what makes you tick and what stops you cold.

▶ **Compelling self-sabotage.** It loves seeing you fail, on the verge of outgrowing the old you and pulling you right back down into the pit.

> ▸ **Creating random resistance.** The ego creates random emotional outbursts before a breakthrough, such as sending a nasty email on the verge of a promotion.
> ▸ **Avoiding the direct path.** It can lead you down paths with clear dead ends, even shadow careers, or worse, a shadow life that isn't yours.
> ▸ **Killing your life force.** The end result of an untamed ego is a barren wasteland where your inner fulfillment and outer potential are unexpressed.

Enter slaying the ego: a nonnegotiable daily practice designed to give you your power back.

BRUSH YOUR TEETH, SLAY THE EGO

Slaying the ego is like the final level in that old *Mortal Combat* video game when you've chopped the opponent's head off, but they come back countless times until it's a lethal, final kill. Just when you think you've won, it comes back stronger.

This is a problem.

Most people believe the ego can be dealt with casually. Others believe that it takes a rock-bottom moment or embarking on a mystical expedition to the forests of Peru, sipping plant medicine with Shamans where it will vanish for all eternity.

Unfortunately, neither is true.

Because of its chameleon ability to shapeshift at will, this must be a *daily* practice. As important as brushing your teeth, taking a shower, and you know, being a good, normal, clean human.

The first rule is there are no *zero* days.

By slaying the ego daily, its chokehold on your psyche gets loosened just enough to create some much-needed breathing room. While it never fully goes away, it'll stop being your auto-pilot mechanism. Eventually, it becomes your servant—not your master. It will be at your disposal; not treat you like one. It will be under your command instead of the dictatorship it thrives off.

It will go from an amps blaring volume to white noise.

This nonnegotiable practice gives you your agency back. Agency is your ability to choose and exercise your will, instead of being run by the ego and having the illusion of agency but being entirely run on it.

Let's dive into how to slay the ego.

HOW TO SLAY THE EGO

Diminishing, squandering, and slaying the ego must evoke your creative powers and consistency. You'll need to come at it from all angles, and, as you grow, find new ways to overcome it.

Enter the matrix below, a by no means comprehensive list of some of the ways to practice slaying the ego. They include the seemingly obvious to the possibly once-in-a-lifetime experiences.

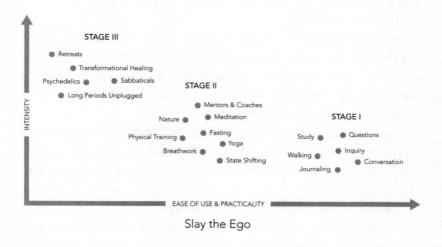

Slay the Ego

Make no mistake; this is a proactive process—because unfortunately way too many people wait for a rock-bottom crisis moment to finally stare at the ego nakedly and see it for what it really is.

And that's not a strategy for success.

WAITING FOR ROCK BOTTOM IS NOT A STRATEGY

Most people wait for rock bottom, a watershed season of existential crisis, to get serious about finally releasing the grasp of the ego. These moments of awakening come in all shapes, forms, and sizes, but the end result is the same.

Here, the ego has been stripped naked.

The perceptive reality it has used for years has now vanished; the rug pulled underneath only to reveal an *Inception*-like dissolving of the ground below us.

In this place, we finally see the light.

We learn the lesson that we stubbornly avoided for years. We stop bullshitting ourselves. We step away from halfhearted, convenient narratives and cheap justifications. We finally allow ourselves to be real, vulnerable, and open.

As author and commentator David Brooks says, "Seasons of suffering kick us in the ass. They are the foghorns that blast us out of our complacency and warn us we are headed for the wrong life."[5]

This valley is no doubt a powerful place.

The wounds are fresh; one is knocked sideways, disoriented in the haze of whiplash. Done right, the ego is dissolved, and we can finally get a clear look at ourselves. We can stare nakedly at ourselves, flaws galore.

This self-awareness is the starting point to a new reality.

But let's be real—this can be excruciating and an energetic hog to our psyche. We all know or have been people who wait for a crisis to get honest, then tread water . . . and wait for the next downfall.

On one of those valleys, you may simply give up on yourself for good.

CONSCIOUS OR UNCONSCIOUS

We know waiting for rock bottom is not only a terrible strategy but leads to the darkest corners of human existence. This is unconscious growth. Waiting on the beach with our backs toward the ocean during a hurricane—until the riptide sucks us dry.

We may never make it back to shore, let alone in one piece.

Instead, we must choose conscious growth—knowing the ego must be questioned and challenged daily. Knowing that overcoming today's challenge equips us with the tools we need going forward: strength, grit, and resilience.

Here's what conscious growth looks and feels like:

- ▶ **Developing awareness.** Awareness is the meta-skill we covered in Chapter 10 of becoming the observer of our thoughts, beliefs, and actions rather than being run by them.
- ▶ **Dropping the ego constantly.** Humbling ourselves is the path to conscious growth. Having an openness to realize we don't have all the answers and seeking them.
- ▶ **Choosing real friends over enablers.** The ego loves to surround itself with enablers—of its excuses, justifications, and defensiveness. Instead, choose real friends, people who respect you enough to challenge the small part of you.
- ▶ **Seeking challenge before it seeks you.** Choosing to push past the comfort zone of your physical, mental, and emotional self to seek perspective on a daily basis, as we covered in Chapter 16.
- ▶ **Delaying gratification.** The ego seeks instant validation. Your higher self is patient and abiding, and plays the long game. Delaying gratification is a nonnegotiable factor in long-term growth and mastery.

Conscious growth is facing the challenge today for a better tomorrow.

It's seeing resistance in real time, and facing it head on. It's having the willingness to drop our self-defense armor of needing to be right and have all the answers.

It's being goddamn willing to ask for help.

It's the leader who doesn't have all the answers. It's the parent who is real about personal struggles. It's having the hard conversation with a team member. It's listening to a critic while being open.

Which means our identity is whole, integrated, and . . . complete.

WHAT TO LEAVE BEHIND WITH CONVENTIONAL IDENTITY

Building your identity from the ground up is a worthy pursuit—but here's what you're leaving behind:

▶ **Making your identity fixed.** A healthy identity is one that is not overly rigid; rather, it is flexible, open, and malleable to change. It leaves doors open to adjust opinions, worldviews, and beliefs.

▶ **Getting attached.** Attachment to identity is common with roles in life. As a parent, as an employee or business owner, as a person in public. It is no surprise that when this shifts unexpectedly, one is left in the dust asking oneself who he or she is. Practice healthy boundaries and detachment.

WHAT TO LEAVE BEHIND WITH CONVENTIONAL EGO

While reducing the ego and its conniving ways is a pillar of self-transformation, here's what to be aware of:

▶ **Believing in the ego-less oasis.** Say goodbye to your dreams of permanent enlightenment. Rather, see slaying the ego as a daily process. What you did yesterday doesn't quite matter, today is a new day to dissolve the ego.

▶ **Not using the ego wisely.** There are times and places the ego needs to be on display. There are times when you have to own the room, pitch the sale, make the move. There are times when you do have to lean on the ego, in a healthy way, to achieve a result.

FROM SERVANT TO MASTER

I sat at lunch, fork in hand, listening to my guest rattle off a highlight reel of his latest triumphs—exponential profits, building a world-class team—even a sizzling relationship.

All completely out of context.

I'd agreed to meet as we had mutual friends and I showed up ready to connect . . . but I could barely get a word in. It became a one-way monologue, the physical equivalent of scrolling a stranger's social media feed full of trophies and filtered sunsets. I had that odd feeling when people talk to you—*but are looking right through you*—a glassy-eyed gaze that something isn't quite right.

I wanted him to drop the façade, share vulnerabilities, and, you know, connect. I attempted to lure him in with some of my own struggles, but it didn't work. Months later, the truth was revealed: he was in full-blown crisis mode, hanging on by a thread, the business imploding.

This is the ego in action. Instead of dropping its guard, it clings to what it *thinks* others will be impressed by. It puts on a show. A performance. Theatrics. By doing so, it bypasses the direct path to personal and professional growth.

None of us is immune to its tricks, erratic behaviors, and weird plots. None of us can avoid the part of ourselves that needs applause. The part that sets goals not from desire, but to impress . . . and needs to "talk" a big game.

So, build your identity with vigor. Do the inner work. Have a set of concrete principles. Have "strong opinions, loosely held," as Stanford professor Paul Saffo says.[6] And because you've built the very foundation that allows you to rise above egoic needs—you'll develop awareness, insights, real connection, and a confident, yet humble attitude others find irresistible.

Which, in turn, allows you to regularly drop the ego.

When you do, you'll elevate both fulfillment and performance—without the sticky residue that comes with an ego hell-bent on looking its best. As psychologist Scott Barry Kaufman writes, "A noisy ego spends so much time defending the self as if it were a real thing, and then doing whatever it takes to assert itself, that it often inhibits the very goals it is most striving for."[7]

Build identity. Slay the ego.

Rinse, repeat, and watch the magic unfold.

Chapter
21

Hustle
&
Seek

Steve Jobs built the biggest company on the planet while studying Zen Buddhism and noting an LSD trip as one of the "most
important things" in his life.[1] His audacity disrupted our lives.

David Lynch became a Hollywood icon and swears by a
40-year practice of twice-a-day Transcendental Meditation[2]
while having the maniacal focus and imagination to create
masterpieces.

Ariana Huffington disrupted the media world through
the *HuffPost*, an innovative journalism platform acquired for
$315 million in 2011—and is now a leading voice for self-care,
unplugging, and meditation.

Phil Jackson brought mindfulness to the NBA and gifted
the book *Siddhartha*, a fictionalized account of Buddha, to

players in the cutthroat world of sport to the tune of 11 world championships.[3]

Danica Patrick disrupted the racing world and credits her lifelong seeking and spiritual exploration for her rousing success[4] while harnessing an intensity and competitive spirit unlike any other.

Michelle Yeoh is considered the greatest action heroine of all time and thanks her Buddhist upbringing and practices[5] for keeping her grounded amid her success.

Stephen Curry turned basketball into an art form and gave kids all over the world permission to dream about greatness while being unplugged in float tanks[6] and winning back-to-back championships.

Rick Rubin, who has won eight Grammys and produced number one albums for an outrageous number of iconic artists across genres, swears by the state-shifting tools of ice cold baths and piping hot saunas.[7]

Jack Dorsey runs not one, but two Silicon Valley behemoths in Twitter and Square, and regularly unplugs for 10-day Vipassana retreats and spends copious amounts of time in solitude.

The secret is officially out.

The mavericks, rebels, disruptors, and creatives we admire most are not only creating, achieving, and performing like never before—they're seeking, *being,* and shifting their consciousness on the regular. But instead of staying stuck in one world, they're using both to fuel one another.

They've officially cracked the code.

By doing so, they've escaped the messy middle—where results and fulfillment die—to unearth a heart-thumping sweet spot. They are both *doing* and *being,* equally gripped by the future and present, merging the West's living boldly ethos with the East's be-here-now way. They chase a compelling horizon that wakes them from their slumber every morning yet are able to torch it and allow something new toward their path.

They've solved the timeless E. B. White riddle,[8] where he posed his morning dilemma of either saving or savoring the world, only to recognize both need each other: the desire to save the world means it must be *worth* savoring, and to savor the world . . . well, it must be saved.

In other words, the truth is found in the paradox.

While the above are public-facing figures, those merging hustling and seeking are among us all. They are full of meaning, results, and growth. They operate with a sense of aliveness sorely missing in today's world. They are not defined by one side. They have unraveled the riddle of knowing when it's time to light themselves on fire and when it's time to detach into the void.

And now you've done the same.

By finishing this book, you are now equipped with the mindsets, concepts, and tools to arrive at the same intersection of a life well lived—with unabashed performance and deep fulfillment—by becoming a hustler *and* a seeker. You will no longer be confined to the boardroom or the ashram, the stage or the altar, the podcast studio or the seminar room.

You'll thrive in both.

And as you continue to develop this skill of hustling and seeking, you'll find new ways of doing and being.

You'll experience peak emotional states . . . that become hardwired traits. You'll supercharge your pattern-recognizing machine and intuitive knowing. You'll rewire the brain through neuroplasticity to be more resilient so you can handle gut checks. You'll control what you can and discard the rest. As you experience results, which you no doubt will, you'll avoid its traps and pitfalls . . . and reap its insatiable rewards. Because you're doing *both* the inner and outer work, success will amplify more of what and who you are.

You'll raise your baseline *and* comeback rate.

Best of all, you'll release the relentless pressure, haste, and anxiety most operate by because you don't look at hustling and seeking as some far-off destination to arrive at as fast as possible, but rather, a process. A practice. Because of this, the daily practice doesn't become a means to some distant end.

It becomes *the end* itself.

Which means you rush less, have way more fun, and create results with more ease as you arrive at what the Buddhists call effortless effort—where the outside world believes you're moving a mile a minute, but you may as well be standing still.

This is mastery.

THE PROCESS IS NOT A MEANS TO AN END

What if your process was not some means to an end—but the very *end* itself?

Let that sink in.

Think about your ambitions, dreams, and vision—and the person capable of bringing those to life. Instead of seeing the process as some irritating chore to slog through—what if you were playing with house money? What if you could *not* lose? What is the process brought you to your knees?

If you do this right, it will.

Hustling and seeking represent emotional states: the confidence of your dream salary, the freedom of retiring your parents with one check, the peace of making your meditation a habit—and the insatiable harmony of reconciling your past.

By merging both sides, you tap into those feelings today, which means you're able to:

- ▶ **Collapse your vision.** You don't need to wait for the six-figure gig or the fourth meditation retreat to feel freedom—you can tap into those states today—and collapse tomorrow's vision to this moment.
- ▶ **Experience "success" now.** By collapsing your vision, you learn how to experience emotional states of success. You raise your baseline, you become equipped, and when success does arrive, it feels like *you*. You feel worthy.
- ▶ **Stop waiting for some future.** By making the process the end, you dispel the myth of getting *there*. You're inspired to chase the horizon, but for the right reasons—understanding growth is the currency that gives you life.
- ▶ **Avoid striving from lack.** Your striving is not based on proving others wrong or making your high school sweetheart

realize they made the biggest mistake of their life. Rather, you're able to strive from a place of abundance *and* love the present moment.

▶ **Play the long game.** If the process is the end, where's the fire? You release the hurry and rush of wanting to get there tomorrow and save yourself eons of mental bandwidth.

Curiously enough, another paradox emerges when you make the process the end: you arrive at bigger, more expansive ends. Why? Precisely because you're *not* rigidly focused on the outcome. It's the old can't-find-the-car-keys paradox: by *not* focusing on finding the item we desperately need . . . we remember it rained last night and put it in a jacket we haven't worn in years.

Much like the happiness paradox[9] psychologists refer to that explains the happiest people are the ones who don't have the bandwidth to overanalyze their happiness, because, well, they're doing incredible things—you'll do the same.

If the process is the end itself, you're happier because you're *not* focused on how to be happy. You're purposeful because you're *not* obsessed with finding one life purpose. You're fulfilled because you're *not* scrutinizing how fulfilled you are.

You're creating it every day.

And you're on fire because you're not scrolling to vicariously live through someone else's highlight reel.

As psychologist Abraham Maslow noted, the self-actualized don't have time to be anxious about whether they're happy—because the process consumes their bandwidth—and thus, makes them happy:

> The actualizing person is busy with the concerns to which he has chosen to commit his living and seldom stops to assess his happiness. It seems only the neurotic and the unhappy that expend their concern explicitly and directly on their happiness. . . . Happiness is a state that is pushed away by the hand that would grasp it but that tends to accompany the person who is alive to his own being.[10]

Straight facts.

When the process is the endgame, you show up and hustle so as to make a dent on your vision while leveling up your consciousness game and unplugging from the void.

No drama, no noise, no look-at-me gloating.

Ultimately, you'll tap into a state of self-actualization.

SELF-ACTUALIZATION IS WHAT YOU'RE HERE FOR

A self-actualized life is what we're here for.

It is the apex of the ingredients, tools, and principles we've covered in this book. It is your life's work, turning the blank canvas into a living masterpiece. While *self* may precede the word—actualization is altruistic. When you're actualizing, you take attention *off* yourself. You develop perspective, hone empathy, and find gratitude in what others deem mundane. You are more likely to find the silver lining when you're cut off in traffic or receive a comment that irks you. You recognize your purpose may start with you, but it's not *about* you.

Best of all, you thrive in the paradoxes most people find uncomfortable.

You're able to transcend the binary, black-or-white thinking that has become the status quo. You'll be able to:

▶ Craft a vivid vision that brings you to your knees and then be open to something completely different.

▶ Relentlessly chase the compelling horizon with vigor, but find absolute freedom right here, right now.

▶ Dose high levels of structure, routine, and habits, but also shatter them through radical novelty.

▶ Harness the power of self-discipline and following through on your word, but then surrendering.

▶ Push the throttle of your skills and pursue mastery of your craft, while staying open and having a beginner's mind.

▶ Have a desire that borders on obsessive, and lights your life on fire while being able to enjoy life's small, yet precious moments.

This is where the magic happens.

Before Maslow's death, he worked tirelessly on a new framework, and he updated his model of self-actualization in the book *The Farther Reaches of Human Nature.*

Naming it Theory Z, he detailed the commonalities of people who transcend in an integrated manner.[11] Once we remove the jargon, you'll notice it's nearly identical to what we've presented in this book—the merging of hustling and seeking to find a new way.

Your way.

Here's a quick summary of how Maslow described how we know we're in this state:[12]

▶ Spend time in *being* and understand the language of mystics and artists as well as paradoxes.

▶ Recognize the miracles in life while staying rooted in practicality.

▶ See the beauty in all, constantly experiencing moments of awe, wonder, and surprise.

▶ Transcend and lessen the grip on their ego.

▶ Experience deep clarity and visions for the future and *act* on these.

▶ Think in the clouds but live in the dirt.

▶ Experience breakthroughs but do not *escape* or avoid the reality in front of them and they integrate.

▶ Recognize the pursuit of knowledge only leads to more mystery, awe, humility, and reverence for the unknown. In fact, there is a *love* of the unknown.

▶ Appreciate the contrasts of life (war and peace, good and evil, love and fear) and how they are not to be understood.

▶ Are childlike in their wonder and curiosity and are the first to stop to appreciate a sunset, a sunrise, or the small moments of life.

> ▶ Merge work and play; they tend to get paid and create value
> in what they would do for *free* and find careers that *feed* their
> peak experiences and meaning.

Sound familiar?

This state is *the* endgame.

It is uncanny how this describes hustling and seeking. In interviews for the book, I would have gripping dialogue with those who experienced the above. Each used different words to describe the state, but they felt exactly the same.

Whole. Integrated. Actualized. Thriving. Aliveness. A rage to exist. To be here now.

And the best part about this state is it's a daily practice—one you get to show up for every day.

THIS IS A PRACTICE

To take hustling and seeking from something you know, to something you do, and who you become . . . requires practice. This matters because a "practice" means you will develop this skill. It is trainable.

And you'll give yourself grace when you mess up because you are learning as you go.

Some days, you'll attempt to merge both worlds and fall on your face as you take hustle too far and arrive at exhaustion. On others, you'll lose yourself seeking . . . but discover it stopped you from *one* action you needed to take.

Then, you'll hit the sweet spot and feel on top of the world.

In order to practice, you'll need to:

> ▶ **Show up.** The ethos of practice is we show up whether or not
> we feel like it. Even on days where it takes all our energy to
> do so. We trade expectations for immersion and entitlement
> for absorption.
> ▶ **Start small.** Lasting change is laughably unsexy. Start small
> and become the person who shows he or she can change.
> Use these principles in the micro moments of your day.

► **Execute and deconstruct.** Through action and reflection,
   you will learn individual lessons not found in this book
   that will help you merge both worlds as you carve your
   unique path. You will notice patterns.
► **Find your sweet spot.** As you practice, recognize
   patterns, and notice what makes you feel your best, you'll
   curate and refine until you've tapped into your unique
   sweet spot.

By definition, practice is messy.

As former NBA star Allen Iverson once said in his iconic
rant, "We talkin' 'bout practice, man."[13] In other words, release
the expectation of "perfect," the illusion of getting it right
on day one. When you mess up, you don't feel like a failure.
Instead, you stay curious and learn the lesson.

You adapt.

Some of the most common questions I hear from people are:

► How do I know if I'm pushing too hard, or not enough?
► How do I stay grateful while allowing myself to want more?
► How do I know when it's time to put my foot on the gas, or
   time to let go?

Your practice is how you answer these questions.

I could attempt to define it for you, but that would be inau-
thentic and rob you of your process.

HUNTING FOR WISDOM

As I obsessively hunted wisdom, truth, performance, and seeking during my decade-long quest, the walls of separation came
crashing down.

I'd sit on the cold ashram floor and receive a principle that
translated flawlessly into business. I'd be at the seminar and
realize an insight made *more* sense at the meditation altar. I'd
use seeking insights to hustle and hustling insights to seek.

Both sides were merging together in real time.

There was no need to separate these worlds any longer; the human experience is all-encompassing. We are not meant to be *one* or the *other*. We are not meant to be put in one box, a convenient label: introverts or extroverts, left brained or right, visionaries or detail-oriented, ambitious or detached, hustlers or seekers.

And each side had what the other side oh-so-desperately needed.

I realized hustlers needed to seek to break through the plateau that inevitably comes with ambitious achievement alone—while seekers could pick themselves up by their boot-straps and infuse some much-needed hustle—to make a dent on their vision.

So, what now?

You plug back into your world with a new framework.

You understand the perils of too much of either. You'll see the Law of Diminishing Return before it strikes. You'll use the tools from each world to arrive at your sweet spot.

This is never about "balance." Rather, you'll operate in cyclical seasons—some demand you light a fire in life, business, and craft. You'll make the bravest moves of your life on a level that blows your mind. You'll seek rejection and have doors slammed in your face . . . as the right ones open.

You'll pass tests like a Rhodes Scholar.

During other seasons, this ambition softens as you take your foot off the gas. You'll recognize it's time to release the reins . . . and be less available. You'll limit inputs and experience the winter of hibernation. You'll allow ideas and incubation for your next fire season with divine timing. You'll double down on self-care, break patterns, and reflect.

There is not a one-size-fits-all approach.

As you sharpen your intuitive sword, you'll know *exactly* when it's time to put your foot on the gas and when it's time to take a step back. Not only on a grand scale, but in your day-to-day and from moment to moment.

Hello, self-trust.

You will recognize this game—your game—is a process. It's an evolution that has no end. You'll understand that, sure, at each mile marker you will hang, deconstruct, and celebrate . . . but a new horizon will reveal itself, all of which will not come from a place of lack, but the thrill that comes with your personal evolution.

You'll take the next step.

As you do, you'll recognize you don't want it to end because you've never felt so alive. But when it does, you'll be ready for that too. You'll know you left it all out on the field of play, and that's what matters. I can't wait to see you out there.

Congratulations, you are now a Hustler *and* a Seeker.

Want more? Download free bonus chapters at
www.ResistAverageAcademy.com/HustlersSeekers

ACKNOWLEDGMENTS

That was . . . wild.

This idea has been burning deep inside for years. I couldn't have brought it to life without over-the-top passionate conversations, riveting podcast interviews, and amazing people who moved the idea along. Thank you to those who reviewed messy versions early on. I'm appreciative to Ann Maynard from Command + Z for the first conversation with another human being around the concept (always vulnerable AF) and for both massive help and laughs. Thank you to Vivian Syroyezhkina for clean, succinct edits. Thank you to my agent, Steve Harris, who showed instant enthusiasm for the idea and bucked the trend that it takes agents four months to answer email. Thank you to dear friends who help keep my head on straight—Jay Nixon (honored to be in the circle of success, man!), Howard Falco, Mike Zeller, Seth Mattison, Jarred Smith, Naveen Chathapuram, Anahata Ananda, and many more . . . you know who you are!

Thank you to the people at McGraw Hill who were as enthused as I was about the idea and brought on a star-studded team, including Cheryl Segura as editor, Donya Dickinson as publisher, Matchbook Creative, Inc. as the cover artist, and the behind-the-scenes team, including Peter Mccurdy, Maureen Harper, Joseph Kurtz, Steve Straus, Jeff Weeks, Scott Sewell, Jonathan Sperling, and the rest of the McGraw Hill team. Thank you to Hanna Parshyna for your illustrations. Thank you to Nick Tantillo for producing the audiobook, as well as every single episode of the Academy podcast for the last 6 years.

Thank you to the listeners of the Academy podcast and those who have read any of my nearly 4,000 public posts over the years. My readers are my lifeline. People in my space get hopped up on ego with messages saying, "You changed my life" . . . but remember, no, *you* changed your life. You did the work. You asked questions. You are the guru.

This book is influenced by mentors from near and afar, from whom I've learned so much—Dr. John Demartini, Steven Kotler, Robin Sharma, Scott Barry Kaufman, Abraham Maslow, Martha Beck, Dr. Michael Gervais, Tal Ben-Shahar, Rich Roll, Jonathan Fields, Lisa Nichols, Cal Newport, Tara Brach, Dr. Joe Dispenza, Ryan Holiday, Charlie Gilkey, and countless others.

Thank you to epic ambient artists who fueled caffeine-laced, fist-bumping mornings before sunrise, including U137, Lights & Motion, Explosions in the Sky, Sigur Rós, Moby, Good Weather For An Airstrike, Keith Jarrett's *The Koln Concert*, and soul-thumping punk rock when I needed a pick-me-up.

Thank you to my wife (whoa, I can say that now), Taylor, who was exposed to the thrill and challenge of bringing an idea to life during a season of being locked indoors and ordering way too much True Food.

I love you.

NOTES

INTRODUCTION

1. https://www.gallup.com/workplace/313313/historic-drop-employee
   -engagement-follows-record-rise.aspx
2. https://www.hrexchangenetwork.com/employee-engagement/news
   /employee-burnout-statistics-you-need-to-know#:~:text=Gallup
   %20recently%20surveyed%20more%20than,out%20more%20often
   %20than%20not.&text=To%20put%20that%20into%20context,some
   %20point%20while%20at%20work.
3. https://www.nimh.nih.gov/health/statistics/mental-illness.shtml
4. https://www.webwire.com/ViewPressRel.asp?aId=248507#:~:text=
   Marketdata%20estimates%20that%20the%20self,audiobooks%2C
   %20and%20weight%20loss%20programs.
5. https://adaa.org/understanding-anxiety
6. https://www.psychologytoday.com/us/blog/the-peak-experience
   /201109/what-was-maslows-view-peak-experiences
7. https://positivepsychology.com/what-is-flow/
8. https://journals.sagepub.com/doi/pdf/10.1177/002216787401400312

CHAPTER 1

1. https://www.relativelyinteresting.com/what-are-the-odds-of-making
   -it-into-the-nfl/?utm_source=org
2. http://www.espn.com/espn/feature/story/_/page/enterpriseRodgers
   /green-bay-packers-qb-aaron-rodgers-unmasked-searching
3. http://www.espn.com/espn/feature/story/_/page/enterpriseRodgers
   /green-bay-packers-qb-aaron-rodgers-unmasked-searching
4. https://www.espn.com/espn/feature/story/_/page/enterpriseRodgers
   /green-bay-packers-qb-aaron-rodgers-unmasked-searching
5. https://www.brainpickings.org/2013/05/09/daniel-pink-drive-rsa
   -motivation/
6. https://hbr.org/2011/05/the-power-of-small-wins
7. https://journals.sagepub.com/doi/10.1177/0963721414547414

8. https://www.psychologytoday.com/us/blog/your-emotional-meter /201807/how-let-go-the-need-approval
9. https://www.frontiersin.org/articles/10.3389/fpsyg.2019.00137/full
10. https://www.amazon.com/Practice-Shipping-Creative-Work/dp /0593328973
11. https://www.americanbar.org/news/abanews/aba-news-archives/2019 /12/aba-reports-law-school-enrollment/
12. https://www.reddit.com/r/LawSchool/comments/31oiri/i_dont _remember_why_i_went_to_law_school_do_you/
13. http://www.lawyerswithdepression.com/articles/in-the-beginning -depression-in-law-school/
14 https://www.abajournal.com/news/article/average_age_of_biglaw _partner_is_about_52_which_firms_are_outliers#:~:text=The %20average%20age%20of%20equity,according%20to%20the %20article%20(sub.
15. https://www.talkspace.com/blog/validation-opinions-stop-seeking/
16. https://www.vice.com/en/article/nza8yq/that-photo-of-the-fyre -festival-sandwich-is-fake
17. https://positivepsychology.com/delayed-gratification/
18. https://www.today.com/money/why-you-shouldnt-work-more-50 -hours-week-2D80449508
19. https://alifeofproductivity.com/10-productivity-lessons-working-90 -hour-weeks/

CHAPTER 2

1. https://www.richroll.com/podcast/moby/
2. https://www.rollingstone.com/music/music-news/play-10-years-later -mobys-track-by-track-guide-to-1999s-global-smash-80650/
3. https://moby.com/book/
4. https://moby.com/book/
5. https://www.dailymail.co.uk/news/article-6964877/Moby-reveals-hit -rock-bottom-attempted-suicide.html
6. https://dictionary.apa.org/social-comparison-theory
7. https://positivepsychology.com/social-comparison/
8. https://www.psychologytoday.com/us/blog/meditation-modern-life /201709/your-set-point-happiness
9. https://www.psychologytoday.com/us/blog/meditation-modern-life /201709/your-set-point-happiness
10. https://www.princeton.edu/~deaton/downloads/deaton_kahneman _high_income_improves_evaluation_August2010.pdf
11. https://www.hbs.edu/faculty/Pages/item.aspx?num=53781

12. https://www.nytimes.com/2013/03/10/opinion/sunday/is-there-life-after-work.html
13. https://www.nytimes.com/2013/03/10/opinion/sunday/is-there-life-after-work.html
14. https://hbr.org/2011/05/the-hidden-demons-of-high-achi
15. http://www.espn.com/espn/feature/story/_/page/enterpriseRodgers/green-bay-packers-qb-aaron-rodgers-unmasked-searching
16. http://www.espn.com/espn/feature/story/_/page/enterpriseRodgers/green-bay-packers-qb-aaron-rodgers-unmasked-searching
17. https://moby.com/book/

CHAPTER 3

1. https://thework.com/instruction-the-work-byron-katie/
2.
3. https://www.verywellmind.com/what-are-peak-experiences-2795268
4. https://www.psychologytoday.com/us/blog/the-peak-experience/201109/what-was-maslows-view-peak-experiences
5. https://www.psychologytoday.com/us/blog/the-peak-experience/201109/what-was-maslows-view-peak-experiences
6. https://www.brainpickings.org/2013/03/26/viktor-frankl-mans-search-for-meaning/
7. https://plato.stanford.edu/entries/aristotle-metaphysics/
8. https://www.sciencedirect.com/topics/neuroscience/self-transcendence
9. https://www.nature.com/articles/ng1204-1241
10. https://www.ncbi.nlm.nih.gov/pmc/articles/PMC5002400/
11. https://www.theguardian.com/world/2020/jan/09/strange-hypnotic-world-millennial-guru-bentinho-massaro-youtube

CHAPTER 4

1. https://www.oprah.com/spirit/the-secret-is-out/all
2. https://www.theverge.com/2013/12/4/5038930/the-death-dealer-james-arthur-sweat-lodge-deaths-in-sedona
3. https://abcnews.go.com/Primetime/james-arthur-ray-arizona-sweat-lodge/story?id=11016900
4. https://www.theverge.com/2013/12/4/5038930/the-death-dealer-james-arthur-sweat-lodge-deaths-in-sedona
5. https://www.thenation.com/article/archive/secrets-success/
6. https://www.forbes.com/2009/01/15/self-help-industry-ent-sales-cx_ml_0115selfhelp.html?sh=52f813996758

7. https://www.nytimes.com/books/best-sellers/2020/12/13/advice-how
   -to-and-miscellaneous/
8. https://en.wikipedia.org/wiki/The_Secret_(book)
9. http://www.johnwelwood.com/articles/TRIC_interview_uncut.doc
10. https://www.ncbi.nlm.nih.gov/pmc/articles/PMC5854216/
11. https://www.psychology.hku.hk/ftbcstudies/refbase/docs/emmons
    /2003/53_Emmons2003.pdf
12. https://www.penguinrandomhouse.com/books/552566/transcend-by
    -scott-barry-kaufman-phd/
13. https://www.goodreads.com/quotes/8937320-the-optimal-state-of
    -inner-experience-is-one-in-which
14. https://www.sloww.co/enlightenment-chop-wood-carry-water/
15. https://www.ncbi.nlm.nih.gov/pmc/articles/PMC3312901/

CHAPTER 5

1. https://www.verywellmind.com/what-is-self-concept-2795865
2. https://news.harvard.edu/gazette/story/2017/04/over-nearly-80-years
   -harvard-study-has-been-showing-how-to-live-a-healthy-and-happy
   -life/
3. http://springer.nl.go.kr/referenceworkentry/10.1007%2F978-94-007
   -0753-5_2109
4. https://www.frontiersin.org/articles/10.3389/fpsyg.2020.00322/full
5. https://www.ncbi.nlm.nih.gov/pmc/articles/PMC3312901/
6. https://www.researchgate.net/publication/313290094_On_Being
   _Found_How_Habitual_Patterns_of_Thought_Influence_Creative
   _Interest_Behavior_and_Ability
7. https://www.apa.org/pubs/books/4317153
8. https://www.ncbi.nlm.nih.gov/pmc/articles/PMC2998793/
9. https://www.psychologytoday.com/us/basics/openness

CHAPTER 6

1. https://www.darkdaily.com/previously-high-flying-theranos-provides
   -clinical-laboratories-and-pathology-groups-with-valuable-lesson-on
   -how-quickly-consumer-trust-can-be-lost/
2. https://www.darkdaily.com/previously-high-flying-theranos-provides
   -clinical-laboratories-and-pathology-groups-with-valuable-lesson-on
   -how-quickly-consumer-trust-can-be-lost/
3. https://www.hbo.com/documentaries/the-inventor-out-for-blood-in
   -silicon-valley
4. https://www.psychologytoday.com/us/basics/cognitive-dissonance

5. https://www.hbo.com/documentaries/the-inventor-out-for-blood-in
   -silicon-valley
6. https://www.jstor.org/stable/4166132
7. https://www.12minuteathlete.com/get-better-at-goal-setting/
8. https://positivepsychology.com/benefits-goal-setting/

CHAPTER 7
1. https://blackirishbooks.com/product/turning-pro/
2. https://www.garyvaynerchuk.com/entrepreneurial-dna-do-you-have
   -it/
3. https://www.sciencedirect.com/science/article/abs/pii
   /0749597885900494
4. https://lewishowes.com/podcast/matthew-mcconaughey-keys-to
   -success-making-it-in-hollywood-mastering-yourself/

CHAPTER 8
1. https://www.cnbc.com/2019/12/30/richard-branson-started-virgin
   -atlantic-with-a-board-and-39-flights.html
2. https://en.wikipedia.org/wiki/Virgin_Group
3. https://podcasts.apple.com/us/podcast/resist-average-academy-tommy
   -baker/id1073462154
4. https://www.sciencedirect.com/topics/psychology/hedonic-adaptation
5. https://www.mentalfloss.com/article/27590/who-reads-books

CHAPTER 9
1. https://www.ncbi.nlm.nih.gov/pmc/articles/PMC5854216/
2. https://www.ncbi.nlm.nih.gov/pmc/articles/PMC5854216/
3. https://www.gq.com/story/mark-manson-airplane-mode
4. https://michaelpollan.com/books/how-to-change-your-mind/
5. https://www.udiscovermusic.com/stories/koln-concert-keith-jarrett/
6. https://www.udiscovermusic.com/stories/koln-concert-keith-jarrett/

CHAPTER 10
1. https://resistaverageacademy.com/94/
2. https://www.inc.com/melanie-curtin/in-an-8-hour-day-the-average
   -worker-is-productive-for-this-many-hours.html
3. https://www.forbes.com/sites/stevenkotler/2014/01/08/the-research-is
   -in-a-four-letter-word-that-starts-with-f-is-the-real-secret-to-ultimate
   -human-performance/?sh=41267302227f
4. https://jamesaltucher.com/blog/

5. https://www.stevenkotler.com/rabbit-hole/frequently-asked-questions-on-flow

6. https://www.brainpickings.org/2012/12/18/the-overview-effect-and-the-psychology-of-cosmic-awe/

7. https://www.youtube.com/watch?v=z2UHLMVr4vg

8. https://www.theverge.com/2016/9/30/13119924/blackberry-failure-success

9. https://www.theverge.com/2016/9/30/13119924/blackberry-failure-success

CHAPTER 11

1. https://www.ted.com/talks/barry_schwartz_the_paradox_of_choice?language=en#t-1161052

2. https://hbr.org/2006/06/more-isnt-always-better

3. https://www.psychologicalscience.org/news/minds-business/intuition-its-more-than-a-feeling.html

4. https://www.apa.org/monitor/mar05/knowing

5. https://fs.blog/2012/03/daniel-kahneman-on-intuition/

6. https://time.com/3968092/bob-dylan-electric-newport/

7. https://www.brainpickings.org/2012/01/11/intuition-vs-rationality/

CHAPTER 12

1. https://www.harpercollins.com/products/make-good-art-neil-gaiman

2. https://www.creativelive.com/blog/finding-your-creative-calling-with-chase-jarvis/

3. https://www.theguardian.com/books/2012/apr/13/toni-morrison-home-son-love

4. https://www.huffpost.com/entry/the-psychology-of-awe_n_5799850

5. https://www.ncbi.nlm.nih.gov/pmc/articles/PMC3990058/

6. https://www.nytimes.com/2012/04/08/magazine/jack-white-is-the-savviest-rock-star-of-our-time.html

CHAPTER 13

1. https://link.springer.com/chapter/10.1007/978-3-642-74474-7_13

2. https://www.theatlantic.com/magazine/archive/2015/10/why-we-compete/403201/

3. https://www.theatlantic.com/magazine/archive/2015/10/why-we-compete/403201/

4. https://findingmastery.net/ashley-merryman/

5. https://www.fastcompany.com/3060475/disney-andpixar-fight-to-be-the-mouse-house-animation-alpha-pluto

6. https://www.ncbi.nlm.nih.gov/pmc/articles/PMC4554955/
7. https://www.olympicchannel.com/en/stories/news/detail/venus-and
-serena-tennis-rivalry-5-things-to-know/
8. https://olympics.com/en/news/venus-and-serena-tennis-rivalry
-5-things-to-know

CHAPTER 14

1. https://www.psychologytoday.com/us/blog/the-athletes-way/202001
/the-neuroscience-seeking-pleasure-and-avoiding-pain
2. https://offcamera.vhx.tv/videos/125-oc-jeff-daniels-web
3. https://offcamera.vhx.tv/videos/125-oc-jeff-daniels-web
4. https://collider.com/jeff-daniels-interview-the-looming-tower-the
-newsroom/

CHAPTER 15

1. https://www.inc.com/melanie-curtin/want-a-life-of-fulfillment-a-75
-year-harvard-study-says-to-prioritize-this-one-t.html
2. https://www.ncbi.nlm.nih.gov/pmc/articles/PMC5002400/
3. https://hbr.org/2007/07/the-making-of-an-expert
4. https://www.dailybuddhism.com/archives/670
5. https://www.nbcsports.com/northwest/seattle-seahawks/russell
-wilson-remembers-pre-draft-doubters-and-proved-them-wrong
6. https://m13.co/the-power-of-neutral-thinking-with-trevor-moawad/

CHAPTER 16

1. https://blog.nationalgeographic.org/2017/12/11/cheetahs-fast-facts
-about-worlds-fastest-cat/
2. http://www.bbc.com/earth/story/20161121-the-worlds-strongest
-animal-can-lift-staggering-weights
3. https://www.treehugger.com/demystifying-facts-snow-leopard
-4869627
4. https://energypsychologyjournal.org/set-points-unconscious-triggers
-governing-behavior/
5. https://pubmed.ncbi.nlm.nih.gov/690806/
6. https://247sports.com/nfl/arizona-cardinals/Article/What-Is-Poise
-104365238/
7. https://www.sciencedirect.com/topics/neuroscience/cognitive
-flexibility
8. https://www.stevenkotler.com/rabbit-hole/frequently-asked-questions
-on-flow

9. https://nypost.com/2018/02/07/inside-lindsey-vonns-badass-grit-on
-and-off-the-slopes/
10. https://nypost.com/2018/02/07/inside-lindsey-vonns-badass-grit-on
-and-off-the-slopes/

CHAPTER 17

1. https://www.psychologytoday.com/us/blog/theory-and-praxis/201804
/the-uncanny-fear-loss-part-1
2. https://www.businessinsider.com/spanx-ceo-sara-blakely-fake
-commute-2018-11
3. https://9to5google.com/2013/08/16/googles-20-percent-time
-birthplace-of-gmail-google-maps-adsense-now-effectively-dead/
4. https://www.huffpost.com/entry/lin-manuel-miranda-says
-its-no-accident-hamilton-inspiration-struck-on-vacation
_n_576c136ee4b0b489bb0ca7c2

CHAPTER 18

1. https://angeladuckworth.com/qa/
2. https://howardgardner.com/2018/12/10/a-rage-to-master-a-blog-on
-gifted-children-by-dr-ellen-winner/
3. https://angeladuckworth.com/qa/
4. https://www.alliedacademies.org/articles/grit-happiness-and-life
-satisfaction-among-professionals-a-correlational-study.pdf
5. https://www.ncbi.nlm.nih.gov/pmc/articles/PMC4588123/
6. https://angeladuckworth.com/qa/
7. https://www.nationalgeographic.com/adventure/2018/12/explorer
-completes-historic-antarctic-trek/
8. https://www.richroll.com/podcast/colin-obrady-519/

CHAPTER 19

1. https://www.forbes.com/sites/bernardmarr/2015/11/25/why-too-much
-data-is-stressing-us-out/?sh=3f4af81af763
2. https://www.inc.com/melanie-curtin/want-a-life-of-fulfillment-a-75
-year-harvard-study-says-to-prioritize-this-one-t.html
3. https://www.psychologytoday.com/us/blog/the-objective-leader
/201506/do-you-have-external-validation-mental-model
4. https://ggsc.berkeley.edu/images/uploads/GGSC-JTF_White_Paper
-Awe_FINAL.pdf
5. https://chartmasters.org/2019/06/adele-albums-and-songs-sales/
6. https://time.com/4155795/adele-time-cover-story-interview
-motherhood-25/

CHAPTER 20

1. https://blogs.scientificamerican.com/beautiful-minds/the-pressing
   -need-for-everyone-to-quiet-their-egos/
2. https://dictionary.apa.org/identity
3. https://fs.blog/2014/03/brene-brown-critics/
4. https://news.harvard.edu/gazette/story/2017/04/over-nearly-80-years
   -harvard-study-has-been-showing-how-to-live-a-healthy-and-happy
   -life/
5. https://www.penguinrandomhouse.com/books/217649/the-second
   -mountain-by-david-brooks/
6. https://www.saffo.com/02008/07/26/strong-opinions-weakly-held/
7. https://nau.edu/psychological-sciences/heidi-wayment/

CHAPTER 21

1. https://www.goodreads.com/quotes/542554-taking-lsd-was
   -a-profound-experience-one-of-the-most
2. https://www.nytimes.com/2013/02/24/magazine/david-lynch
   -transcendental-meditation.html
3. https://www.theplayerstribune.com/articles/phil-jackson-shaquille
   -oneal-lakers-nba-hall-of-fame-2016
4. https://lewishowes.com/podcast/i-danica-patrick-mindset-spirituality
   -living-fully/
5. https://www.buddhistdoor.net/news/actor-and-buddhist-michelle
   -yeoh-visits-flood-stricken-ladakh
6. https://www.businessinsider.com/steph-curry-is-obsessed-with
   -sensory-deprivation-tanks-2016-2
7. https://www.transcripts.io/pdfs/tim_ferriss_show/2015-05-15-rick
   -rubin.pdf
8. https://www.goodreads.com/quotes/542655-i-arise-in-the-morning
   -torn-between-a-desire-to
9. https://www.successpodcast.com/show-notes/2017/2/15/the-paradox
   -of-happiness-why-pursuing-it-makes-you-less-happy-what-you-can
   -do-about-it-with-dr-tal-ben-shahar
10. https://www.audible.com/pd/The-Farther-Reaches-of-Human-Nature
    -Audiobook/1684570778
11. https://agile-od.com/reflective-leadership/maslows-final-theory-z
12. https://www.audible.com/pd/The-Farther-Reaches-of-Human-Nature
    -Audiobook/1684570778
13. https://www.inquirer.com/philly/blogs/sports/sixers/Allen-Iverson
    -practice-rant-video-Philadelphia-76ers-press-conference.html

INDEX

ABOUT THE AUTHOR

Tommy Baker is a writer, action philosopher, and self-proclaimed taco enthusiast who some have called "annoyingly" positive. He's coached, trained, and taught thousands of clients within his Resist Average Academy programs and popular iTunes podcast.

He's the author of several books, including *The Leap of Your Life: How to Redefine Risk, Quit Waiting for 'Someday,' and Live Boldly and The 1% Rule: How to Fall in Love with the Process and Achieve Your Wildest Dreams.*

His work has been featured on Entrepreneur, Influencive, Forbes, Tiny Buddha, Project Life Mastery, and more. In his downtime, you can find him on top of Camelback Mountain in Scottsdale, Arizona.